GCSE Chemistry

QuickCheck Study Guides

Graham Hill MA *(Cantab)*
Deputy Headmaster,
Dr Challoner's Grammar School, Amersham

John Holman MA *(Cantab)*
Head of Science,
Watford Grammar School

Nelson

Thomas Nelson and Sons Ltd
Nelson House   Mayfield Road
Walton-on-Thames   Surrey
KT12 5PL   UK

51 York Place
Edinburgh
EH1 3JD   UK

Thomas Nelson (Hong Kong) Ltd
Toppan Building 10/F
22A Westlands Road
Quarry Bay   Hong Kong

Distributed in Australia by

Thomas Nelson Australia
480 La Trobe Street
Melbourne   Victoria 3000
and in Sydney, Brisbane, Adelaide and Perth

© Graham Hill and John Holman, 1988

First published by Thomas Nelson and Sons Ltd 1988

ISBN 0-17-448152-7

NPN 987654321

Printed in Great Britain by Butler & Tanner Ltd,
Frome and London

All Rights Reserved. This publication is protected in the United Kingdom by the Copyright Act 1956 and in other countries by comparable legislation. No part of it may be reproduced or recorded by any means without the permission of the publisher. This prohibition extends (with certain very limited exceptions) to photocopying and similar processes, and written permission to make a copy or copies must therefore be obtained from the publisher in advance. It is advisable to consult the publisher if there is any doubt regarding the legality of any proposed copying.

Contents

Introduction
QuickCheck Syllabus Grid
Examination boards
Acknowledgements

1	Elements, compounds and mixtures	1
2	Air	7
3	Water	13
4	Particles, formulas and equations	19
5	Chemical calculations	24
6	Electrical currents and electrolysis	31
7	The periodic table	39
8	Metals and hydrogen	45
9	Acids, bases and salts	52
10	The structure of elements and compounds	59
11	Energy and fuels	66
12	Simple carbon compounds	73
13	Chemicals from crude oil	78
14	Reaction rates and reversible reactions	85
15	Nitrogen and fertilisers	95
16	Atomic structure	101
17	Radioactivity	107

Sample GCSE questions 112
Suggested answers to sample GCSE questions 125
Answers to self-test questions 136
Index 140

Introduction

How to use this book

This book will help you to revise and prepare for your GCSE Chemistry Examination. It is best to use the book when you are revising.

The book provides all the key ideas needed for your exam, and helps in revising and preparing for the exam. It also includes specimen questions to give you practice in answering exam questions. In addition, a list of the topics included in the different GCSE syllabuses is included in the form of a QuickCheck Syllabus Grid.

Using the QuickCheck Syllabus Grid

The book covers all GCSE Chemistry syllabuses, so there will be some topics which are not needed for your particular exam. Check which topics are in your GCSE syllabus by using the QuickCheck Syllabus Grid:

- ● means the whole topic is included
- ○ means part of the topic is included

If neither of these symbols appears, it means that the topic is not in your syllabus.

The addresses of the examination boards are given after this Introduction. You can write to them for copies of past examination papers and the full syllabus for your course.

Studying the topics

Work your way through the book, studying the topics one at a time.

Answer the self test at the end of each chapter before you go on to the next chapter. The questions will test your knowledge and understanding of each topic.

Don't write the answers in the book. That way, you can use the questions again for revision. When you have finished the self test, check your answers with the correct answers on pages 136 to 137.

The book also contains longer GCSE questions. Most of these questions are taken from specimen GCSE papers. Answering these questions will give you practice in exam technique. After answering these questions, check your answers against the model answers on pages 125 to 135.

How to prepare and revise for the GCSE examination

The GCSE examination aims to test what you know, understand and can do. These notes are intended to help you prepare for the written examination.

Understanding and using facts and knowledge

In GCSE, it is important that you **understand** what you have studied. When you revise, try to **understand** the topics. **Don't** just try to memorise them. If you understand a topic, you will automatically remember the key points. Trying to remember facts that you don't understand is a waste of time.

In order to **understand** a subject, you must do more than just read your notes or read a section of this book. The following activities will help you to understand the topic you are revising.

(1) **Underline or highlight** important words or sections and make a list of key words and definitions.

(2) **Make a summary of the topic**. Here are some useful methods that you can use:
  (a) **Lists**. A list of key facts and key words is a useful way of remembering things.
  (b) **Flow Charts**. A flow chart is a series of short statements connected by arrows. It is used for summarising a sequence of events.
  (c) **Diagrams**. Draw diagrams to summarize important topics. Diagrams are helpful because most people find it easier to remember things in pictures. Make your diagrams simple and easy to remember. Write the labels well clear of the diagram so that you can cover them up later and test yourself.

Keep your lists, flowcharts, diagrams and summaries so that you can look at them again.

How can I learn and understand?

Whether it's a list, a flow chart or a diagram, the method is the same. There are some facts that you will need to memorise. Here are some suggestions to help you.

Suppose you need to memorise a list of key points.

(1) Copy out the key facts in the list. The very act of writing (or drawing in the case of diagrams) helps to fix the facts in your memory. This is where many people go wrong; they just stare at their notes in the hope that they will sink in. They won't!

DON'T JUST SIT THERE, DO SOMETHING!

(2) Put your copy to one side, take another sheet of paper and copy out the list again, but this time try to do as much of it as you can without looking at the original.

(3) Repeat the process, but this time look at the original even less than before.

Next day . . .

(4) Try writing out the list again, without looking. Unless you're a genius you'll probably have to look at parts of it now and again to refresh your memory. Don't be discouraged! You can't expect it all to go into your long-term memory straight away. Just repeat the procedure outlined above every day until the information sticks.

Planning and carrying out your revision

Revising for an examination requires good organisation and self-discipline. Here are some hints about how to go about it.

(1) Plan a revision timetable well before the exam. Make sure that each of your GCSE subjects gets a share of revision time.

(2) Plan how you're going to spend the time; be sure to spend part of the time testing yourself on work covered in previous sessions.

(3) During your revision, study for about 30 minutes and then take a 10 minute break. Then, do another 30 minutes revision, followed by another 10 minute break and so on. During your breaks, try to take your mind off study completely — have a cup of coffee, talk to your family or listen to some music. Forget about GCSE.

(4) While you are working do what you can to avoid distractions. Don't have the radio or television on.

(5) Make sure you get enough sleep.

(6) Keep fit and get some exercise each day.

QuickCheck Syllabus Grid

CHAPTER	TOPIC	WJEC	NI	SEG	SEG (Alt)	NEA (A)	NEA (B)	LEAG (A)	LEAG (B)	MEG	MEG (Nuff)
1	Elements, compounds and mixtures	●	●	●	○	●	●	●	●	●	●
1	Separating mixtures	●	●	●	●	●	●	●	●	●	●
1	Testing purity	●				●			●	●	
2	Composition of air	●	○	●	●	●	●	●	●	●	●
2	Oxygen and oxides	●	●	●	●	●	○	●	○	●	●
2	Burning, breathing, rusting and redox	●	●	●	●	●	●	●	●	●	●
2	Air pollution	●	●	○	●	●	●	●	●	●	●
3	Water — properties	○	●		○		○	○	○		●
3	Solubility	●	●	●	○	●	●	○	○	●	●
3	Water supplies and water pollution	●		●	●	●	●	●	○	●	●
4	States of matter and the kinetic theory	●	●	●	●	●	●	●	●	●	●
4	Formulas	●	●	●	●	●	●	●	●	●	●
4	Equations	●	●	●	●	●	●	●	●	●	●
5	The mole, measuring moles	●	●	●	●	●	●	●	●	●	●
5	Finding formulas using moles	●	●	●	○	●	●	●	●	●	●
5	Chemical calculations	○	●	●	○	●	●	●	●	○	●
6	Electric currents and conductivity	○	○	●	○	●	●	●	○	●	●
6	Electrolysis and its uses	●	●	●	○	●	●	●	●	●	●
6	Ionic and molecular compounds	●	●	●	○	●	●	●	○	●	●
6	Cells and batteries	●	●	●	○	●	○	○	○	●	●
6	Redox and electron transfer	●	●	●	○	●	●	●	○	●	●
7	The Periodic Table	●	●	●	●	●	●	●	●	●	●
7	Group 1 — The Alkali Metals	●	●	●	●	●	●	●	●	●	●
7	Transition Metals	●	●	●	○	●	●	○	○	●	●
7	The Noble Gases	●	●	●	○		●	○	●	●	●
7	The Halogens	●	●	●	●	●	●	●	●	●	●
8	Properties of metals and the reactivity series	●	●	●	●	●	●	●	●	●	●
8	Extracting and recycling metals	●	○	●	●	●	●	○	○	●	●
8	Hydrogen	○	●	●	○	●	●	●	●	●	●

Exam board (syllabus)

	Topic
9	Acids, bases, alkalis, indicators and pH
9	Sulphuric acid
9	Neutralization and salts
9	Tests for anions and cations
10	Structure and properties of metals
10	Sulphur
10	Carbon
10	Structure of elements and compounds
11	Exothermic and endothermic reactions
11	ΔH and its measurement
11	Bond making and bond breaking
11	Fuels and alternative energy sources
11	Respiration, photosynthesis and the carbon cycle
12	Carbon monoxide and carbon dioxide
12	Carbonates and calcium carbonate
12	Hardness of water
13	Crude oil and alkanes
13	Alkenes, polymers and plastics
13	Ethanol
14	Factors affecting reaction rates
14	Explaining reaction rates using collision theory
14	Reversible reactions
14	Haber process for making ammonia
14	Contact process for making sulphuric acid
15	Fertilizers and nitrogen cycle
15	Ammonia and fertilizer manufacture
15	Environmental problems caused by fertilizers and pesticides
16	Atomic structure (protons, neutrons and electrons)
16	Isotopes and relative atomic mass
16	Electronic structures and bonding
17	Radioactivity and half-life
17	Using radioactive isotopes
17	Nuclear energy

Examination Boards

Welsh Joint Education Committee (WJEC)
245 Western Avenue
Cardiff CF5 2YX

Northern Ireland Schools Examination Council (NI)
Beechill House
42 Beechill Road
Belfast BT8 4RS

Southern Examining Group (SEG)
c/o University of Oxford Delegacy of Local Examinations
Ewert Place
Summertown
Oxford OX2 7BZ

Northern Examining Association (NEA)
c/o Joint Matriculation Board
Manchester M15 6EU

London and East Anglian Group (LEAG)
c/o University of London Schools Examination Board
Stewart House
London WC1B 5DN

Midland Examining Group (MEG)
c/o Oxford and Cambridge Schools Examination Board
Elsfield Way
Oxford OX2 8EP

Scottish Examinations Board
Ironmills Road
Dalkeith
Midlothian EH22 1BR

Acknowledgements

We are grateful to the following examining bodies for permission to reproduce questions from sample GCSE papers: The London and East Anglian Group (LEAG); The Southern Examining Group (SEG); The Welsh Joint Education Committee (WJEC); and the Northern Examining Association (NEA), which is made up of the Associated Lancashire Schools Examining Board, Joint Matriculation Board, North Regional Examinations Board, North West Regional Examinations Board, Yorkshire and Humberside Regional Examinations Board.

1 Elements, compounds and mixtures

Chemistry is the study of substances and the way they can be changed. All substances can be sorted into three groups – elements, compounds and mixtures.

Elements

An element is a substance which cannot be broken down into simpler substances by chemical reactions.

Elements are the building blocks for other substances. There are 92 naturally occurring elements. By joining these building blocks together, millions of different compounds can be made. For example, water is a compound made from the elements hydrogen and oxygen. Salt is a compound made from the elements sodium and chlorine. Table 1.1 lists some of the more important elements. Each element has its own symbol, consisting of one or two letters, and these are also shown in the table.

Metals and non-metals

Elements can be sorted into groups with similar properties. The simplest way of sorting them is into metals and non-metals. Table 1.2 summarises the main differences between metals and non-metals.

Compounds

Compounds are made when elements combine together. 'Combining' means the elements have taken part in a chemical reaction. They have formed a new substance. The compound has different properties from the elements it is formed from. Whenever a chemical change takes place, new substances are formed.

For example, sodium and chlorine are elements. They combine together to form a compound, sodium chloride (salt). Sodium, chlorine and sodium chloride have very different properties (table 1.3)

Synthesis and decomposition

When elements combine together to form compounds, the reaction is called **synthesis**. Synthesis is the building up of substances by combining simpler substances.

Unlike elements, compounds *can* be split up into simpler substances. For example, sodium chloride can be split up into the elements sodium and chlorine. This is done by passing electricity through molten sodium chloride.

Table 1.1 *Some of the more important elements.*

Name	Symbol
Aluminium	Al
Argon	Ar
Bromine	Br
Calcium	Ca
Carbon	C
Chlorine	Cl
Copper	Cu
Helium	He
Hydrogen	H
Iodine	I
Iron	Fe
Magnesium	Mg
Neon	Ne
Nitrogen	N
Oxygen	O
Potassium	K
Sodium	Na
Sulphur	S
Zinc	Zn

Table 1.3 *Sodium, chlorine and sodium chloride.*

Elements		Compound
Sodium	**Chlorine**	**Sodium chloride (salt)**
Soft, grey metal	Green, poisonous gas	White crystalline solid – safe and not very reactive
Very reactive	Very reactive	

Table 1.2 *Metals and non-metals.*

Metals	Non-metals
Examples: iron, aluminium, sodium, magnesium	Examples: oxygen, sulphur, chlorine, bromine
Usually solids at room temperature	Gases, liquids or solids at room temperature
Usually have high melting and boiling points	Usually have low melting and boiling points
Have shiny surfaces	Have dull surfaces when solid
Malleable – can be hammered into shapes	Non-malleable (brittle) when solid
Good conductors of heat and electricity	Poor conductors of heat and electricity
Density usually high	Density usually low

2 Elements, compounds and mixtures

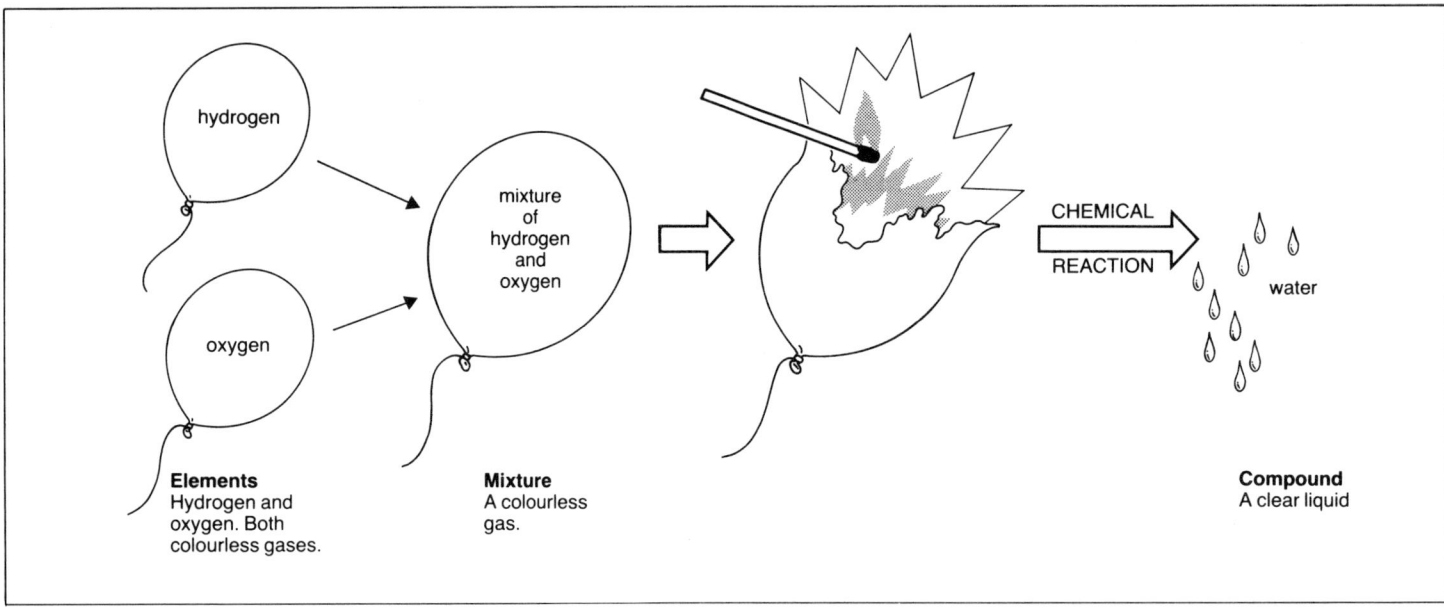

Figure 1.1 *Elements, compounds and mixtures.* (**Warning** You must never attempt to explode hydrogen–oxygen mixtures)

When compounds are split up to give simpler substances, the process is called **decomposition**. The commonest ways of decomposing compounds are either by heating them **or** by passing electricity through them (electrolysis).

Formulas of compounds

Every compound has its own formula, just as every element has its own symbol. The formula shows which elements are present in the compound, and in what proportions. For example, the formula of sodium chloride is NaCl. There is more about formulas on page 20.

Mixtures

When two elements are put together, they do not always combine to form a compound. Sometimes they just mix together.

Mixtures and compounds have important differences. A compound is a single substance, but a mixture contains two or more substances. The properties of a mixture are similar to the properties of the substances in it. But the properties of a compound are usually quite different from the properties of the elements in it. Figure 1.1 shows an example.

The difference between compounds and mixtures are summed up in Table 1.4.

Pure substances

When people use the word 'pure' they usually mean 'not mixed with anything else'. 'Pure orange juice' contains only the juice of oranges, with no additives.

In chemistry the word 'pure' means more than this. **A pure substance is a single substance on its own.** Elements and compounds are pure substances, but mixtures are not. To a chemist, orange juice is not really pure because it is a mixture of many different substances like water, sugars, vitamins and acids.

Separating mixtures

The different substances, or **components** of a mixture are not combined together. This makes them fairly easy to separate.

Table 1.4 *Compounds and mixtures.*

Compounds	Mixtures
Consist of a single substance	Consist of two or more substances
Properties are very different from the elements in them	Properties are similar to the substances making up the mixture
Can only be separated into its elements by a chemical reaction	Often quite easily separated
The amounts of the elements in the compound are fixed	The amounts of the different substances in the mixture can vary

Separating mixtures of solids and liquids

When a solid and a liquid are mixed the solid may dissolve in the liquid. In this case the solid is soluble. The resulting mixture is called a **solution**. But sometimes the solid does not dissolve in the liquid. In this case, the solid is insoluble. Table 1.5 explains some important words relating to solutions.

Table 1.5 *Some important words relating to solutions.*

Solvent	– the liquid in which the solution is made
Solute	– the substance dissolved in the solvent, usually a solid, but may be a liquid or a gas
Soluble	– if a solute dissolves in a solvent, it is soluble in that solvent
Solution	– the mixture of solute and solvent
Dilute solution	– a solution containing only a little solute in a given amount of solvent
Concentrated solution	– a solution containing a lot of solute in a given amount of solvent
Saturated solution	– a solution that contains as much solute as can be dissolved at a particular temperature

Separating an insoluble solid from a liquid

Decanting. Potatoes do not dissolve in water. When you have boiled some potatoes, it is easy to separate them from the water. You just pour the water off the potatoes. This is called **decanting**.

Filtration. Often the solid particles in a mixture are so small they float in the liquid. They make a cloudy **suspension**. A suspension cannot be separated by decanting.

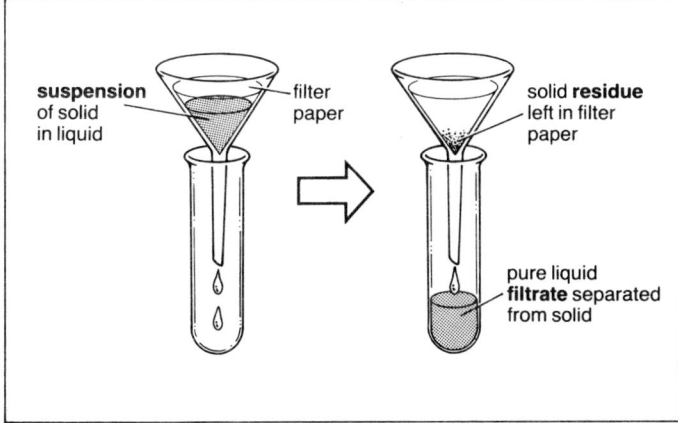

Figure 1.2 *Filtration.*

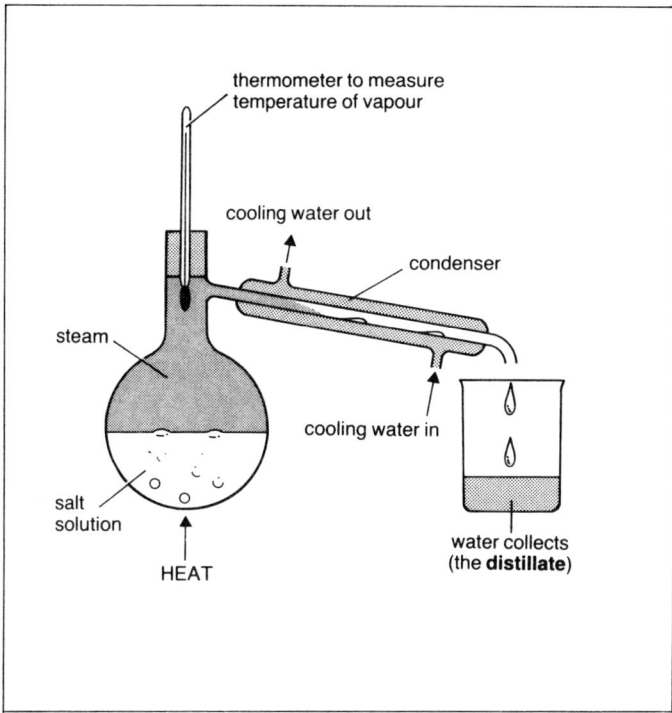

Figure 1.3 *Distillation.*

Filtration has to be used (figure 1.2). The filter paper has tiny holes that let the liquid through, but are too small for the solid particles. Filtration is sometimes used to separate the grains from coffee.

Centrifugation. This is sometimes used instead of filtration. The suspension is put in a tube, then spun round very fast in a centrifuge. This forces the solid to the bottom of the tube. After the solid has been forced to the bottom of the tube, the pure liquid can easily be decanted off. Centrifugation is used to separate milk from cream. This is possible because milk is denser than cream.

Separating a solution

Distillation. Suppose you are marooned on a desert island. You need fresh water to drink. How will you get it?

To separate pure water from a salty solution, you need to use **distillation**. If you boil the solution, water will come off as steam. The steam can then be cooled in a condenser, to give liquid water again. The liquid water is collected as the **distillate**. Figure 1.3 shows the equipment that is used in the laboratory. What sort of equipment might you use on a desert island?

Distillation can be used whenever you want to separate the solvent from a solution and collect it. For example, you could use distillation to get pure water from ink.

Evaporation. Sometimes the part of the solution you need is the solute, not the solvent. For example, suppose your desert island had a supply of fresh water. Then you would need only the salt from the sea water, not the water itself.

4 Elements, compounds and mixtures

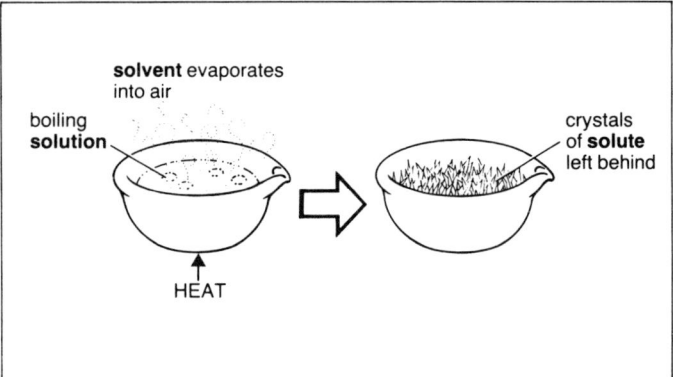

Figure 1.4 *Evaporation.*

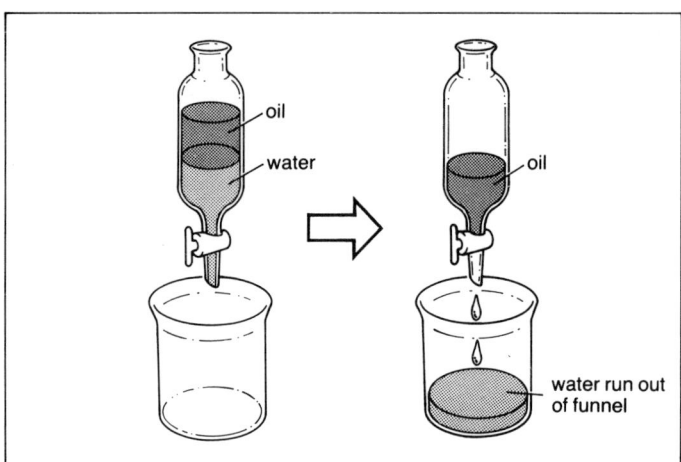

Figure 1.5 *Using a separating funnel to separate oil and water.*

To get the salt, you could use evaporation (figure 1.4). During evaporation, you boil the solution and let the solvent vapour escape into the air. The solute is left behind, usually in the form of small crystals. It is said to have **crystallised**. If you want larger crystals, you need to let the solvent evaporate slowly rather than boiling it off.

Separating liquids

When you put oil in water, the two liquids do not mix. The oil floats on the water (figure 1.5). The liquids are said to be **immiscible**. But if you put oil in petrol, the two liquids *do* mix. They are **miscible**. In fact, a mixture of oil and petrol is used as a fuel in two-stroke petrol engines. The oil lubricates the engine, and the petrol is the fuel.

Separating miscible liquids. Miscible liquids can be separated by a kind of distillation called **fractional distillation**. The different liquids have different boiling points. When the mixture is boiled, the vapours of the two substances boil off at different temperatures, and can be condensed separately.

Fractional distillation is used to separate the different substances in crude oil. Details of the process are given on page 78.

Chromatography

Suppose you have bought a green food colouring to make coloured icing for a cake. The green colouring might be made of a single green dye, or a mixture of a blue dye and a yellow dye. You could use **chromatography** to find out which it was.

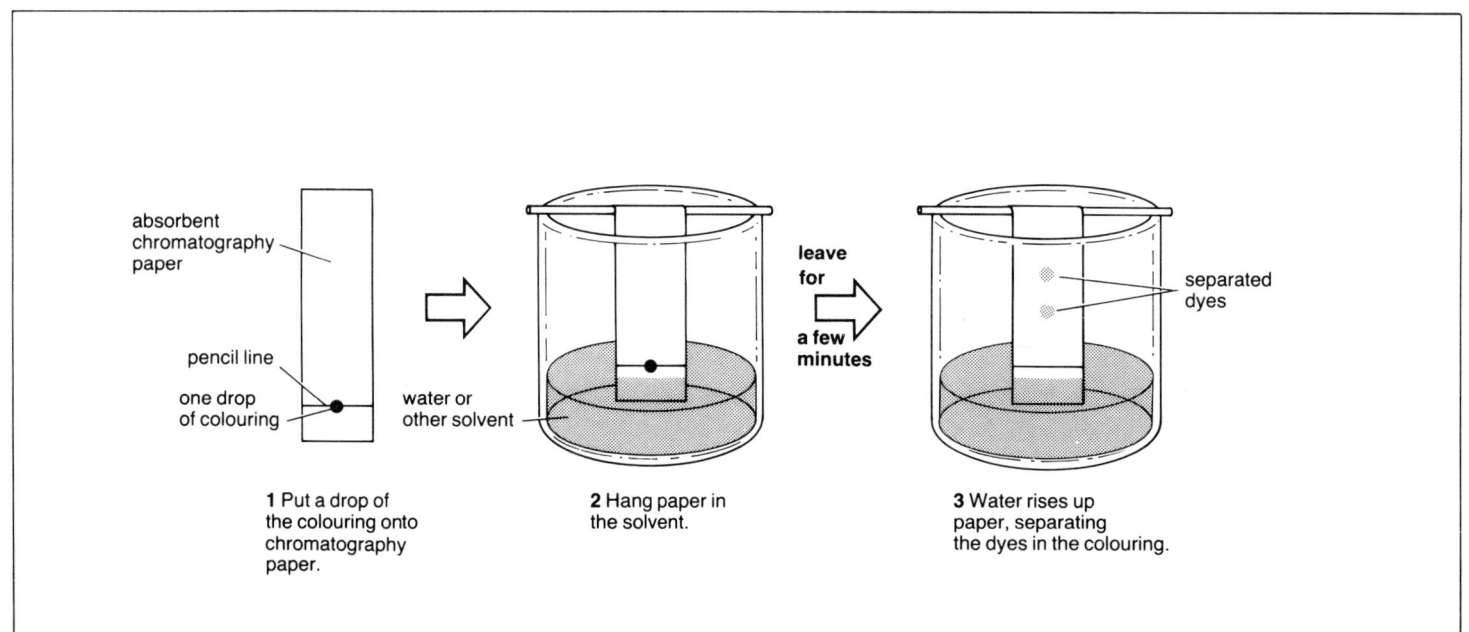

Figure 1.6 *Paper chromatography.*

Figure 1.6 shows the simplest kind of chromatography – **paper chromatography**. The dyes separate because some dyes prefer to stick to the paper, but others prefer to dissolve in the solvent. The dyes that prefer the solvent travel further up the paper.

Chromatography is very useful for separating small amounts of substances in a mixture. Chemists use it to investigate the substances in a mixture. Chromatography is often used in hospitals. For example, it might be used to find out whether sugar is present in a person's urine. This would help the doctor to know if the person had diabetes.

The substances being separated by chomatography do not have to be coloured. Colourless substances can be made to show up by spraying the paper with a locating agent. The locating agent reacts with the colourless substance to form coloured substances.

Testing the purity of a substance

Chemists often need to know if a substance is pure. For example, medicines must be tested for purity before they are sold. Impurities might harm the patient.

Chromatography can be used to see if a substance is pure. Another way of testing purity is to measure the substance's **melting point** or **boiling point**. The melting points and boiling points of most elements and compounds are known accurately. They can be found in reference books. If a substance is not pure, its melting point or boiling point will be different from the known, accurate value. For example, pure water boils at 100°C under normal atmospheric pressure. But if the water contains impurities, such as salt, its boiling point is higher.

● Self test

Questions 1–3

The colouring in five different sweets V, W, X, Y and Z were analysed using chromatography. The final chromatogram is shown below.

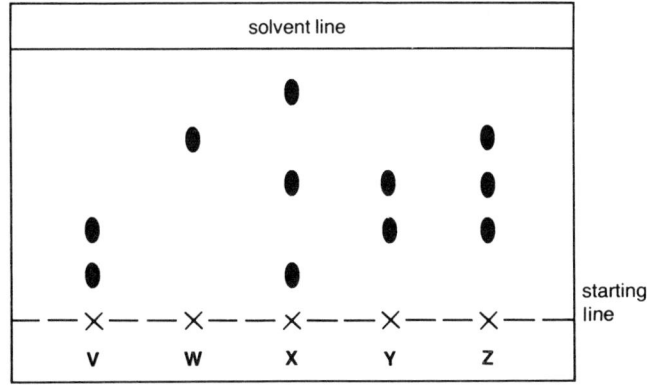

1. Which colouring might contain a single dye?
   A V   B W   C X   D Y

2. How many different dyes were used to colour the five sweets?
   A 3   B 5   C 6   D 11

3. Which two colourings could be mixed together to make Z?
   A V + X   B V + Y   C W + Y   D X + Y

Questions 4–8

  A a pure element
  B a pure compound
  C a mixture of elements
  D a mixture of compounds
  E a mixture of elements and compounds

Choose from **A** to **E** the best description for
4. the alloy brass
5. sugar
6. air
7. vinegar
8. diamond

Questions 9–12

Element	Melting point /°C	Boiling point /°C	Electrical conductivity
A	−7	58	poor
B	−101	−35	poor
C	−38	357	good
D	114	183	poor
E	1083	2600	good

Choose from **A** to **E** the element which
9. could be used for electrical wiring.
10. is a gas at room temperature.
11. is a liquid metal at room temperature.
12. is a solid non-metal at room temperature.

6 Elements, compounds and mixtures

Questions 13–17
- **A** centrifugation
- **B** decantation
- **C** distillation
- **D** evaporation
- **E** filtration

Choose from **A** to **E** the process that is used
13 to separate fat from gravy.
14 to separate grains from coffee.
15 to produce fat-free milk.
16 to obtain alcohol from fermented liquid.
17 to manufacture dried milk.

18 A substance has the formula $CaNi_2(CO)_6$. What elements are present in it?
- **A** calcium, nickel, carbon, oxygen
- **B** calcium, nickel, cobalt
- **C** calcium, nitrogen, cobalt
- **D** carbon, nickel, cobalt

19 Which *one* of the following provides evidence that air is a mixture?
- **A** Living things breathe oxygen, *not* nitrogen.
- **B** Air helps substances to burn.
- **C** Liquid air can be separated by fractional distillation.
- **D** Nitrogen and oxygen are both gases.

20 A chemical reaction occurs when
- **A** electricity passes through a light bulb filament.
- **B** petrol is distilled from crude oil.
- **C** steam is condensed to water.
- **D** chlorine is obtained from salt.

2 Air

What's in the air?

Air is a vital resource. It contains elements and compounds that are needed by all living things. Many of industry's raw materials come from the air – and some of our waste ends up polluting the air.

Figure 2.1 shows an experiment to investigate the percentage of oxygen in air, and some results. Air is passed backwards and forwards over heated copper. The copper reacts with oxygen, forming solid copper oxide. This removes oxygen and decreases the volume of the air. From the decrease in volume, the percentage of oxygen in the air can be worked out.

In fact, the percentage of oxygen in air is a little higher than the result from our experiment, as you can see from table 2.1.

The major gases in air are nitrogen and oxygen, but there are also noble gases, a little carbon dioxide and a tiny amount of hydrogen. Air also contains water vapour, but the amount varies according to the weather.

Industrial gases from air

The gases in air have some important uses. Fractional distillation is used to separate the pure gases from one another. Air is liquefied by compression, then the liquid air is allowed to boil. The different components have different boiling points, so they can be collected in turn as they boil off (figure 2.2).

Table 2.2 shows the major uses of the three most important gases that are manufactured from air.

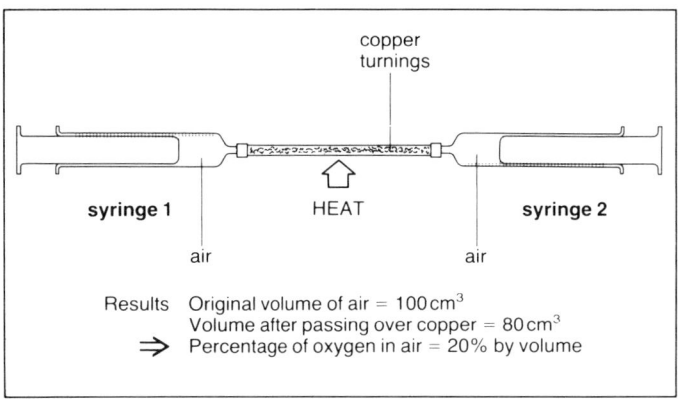

Figure 2.1 *Finding the percentage of oxygen in air.*

Oxygen – the reactive part of air

Oxygen makes up about 50 per cent of the Earth's crust. This means it is the most abundant element in the Earth's

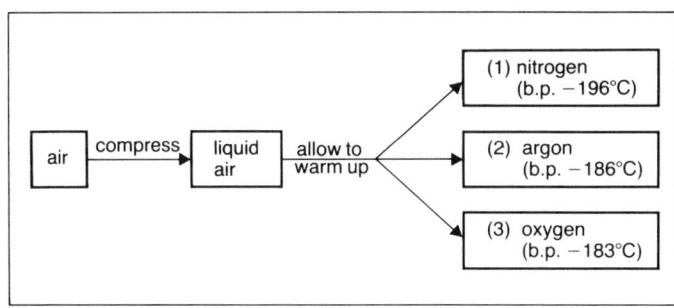

Figure 2.2 *Separating air.*

Table 2.1 *Composition of air.*

Gas	Percentage by volume
Nitrogen	78.03
Oxygen	20.99
Noble gases: argon	0.93
others (neon, helium, krypton, xenon)	0.002
Carbon dioxide	0.03
Hydrogen	0.001

Table 2.2 *Major uses of nitrogen, oxygen and argon.*

Gas	Uses
Nitrogen	For freezing – liquid nitrogen is so cold it can be used to freeze food, biological material, etc. As an unreactive gas – used as a cheap, unreactive gas 'blanket' to stop things reacting with air e.g. in petrol storage tanks, food packaging For making ammonia
Oxygen	In steelmaking – to remove impurities from iron To help breathing – in hospitals, and for divers, firefighters and climbers For welding – an 'oxy-acetylene' flame is hot enough to melt metal For treating sewage
Argon	As an unreactive gas, to stop things reacting with air – e.g. filling light-bulbs, as a 'blanket' in welding

8 Air

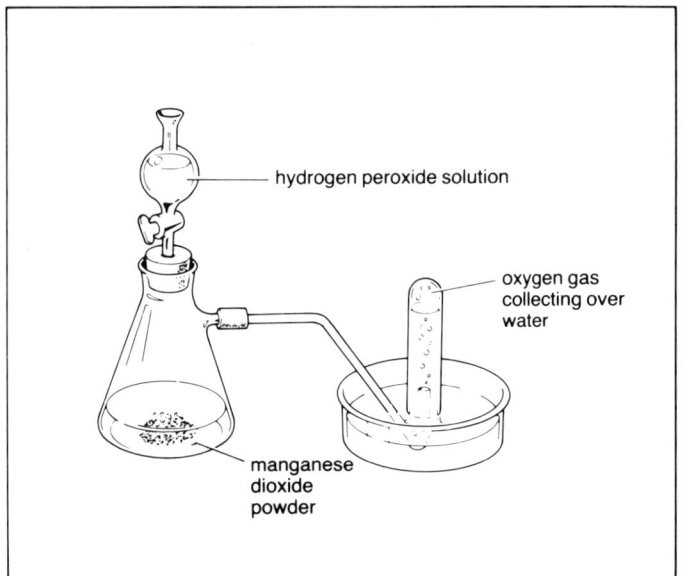

Figure 2.3 *Preparing and collecting oxygen in the laboratory.*

crust, although it is only the second most abundant in the atmosphere.

Oxygen is a reactive element. It combines with many elements and compounds. When something combines with oxygen, it is **oxidised**. Burning, breathing and rusting are three important oxidation processes (see below).

In industry, oxygen is manufactured from liquid air. But in the laboratory it is usually prepared from hydrogen peroxide, H_2O_2. In the presence of a catalyst, hydrogen peroxide decomposes to form water and oxygen. Figure 2.3 shows the apparatus that is used.

We can test for oxygen using a glowing splint. The splint will burst into flame in oxygen, whereas it only smoulders in air.

Burning

Burning is the oxidation of fuels to produce heat and light. It is also called **combustion**.

Most fuels are hydrocarbons – they contain carbon and hydrogen. When they burn in air or oxygen, carbon dioxide and water are formed. Figure 2.4 illustrates an experiment to show that these gases are formed when methane (natural gas) burns. The gases from the burning fuel are drawn through the apparatus. The white anhydrous copper sulphate turns blue, showing water is present. The lime water turns milky, indicating the presence of carbon dioxide.

The equation for the burning of methane is:

$$\text{methane} + \text{oxygen} \rightarrow \text{carbon dioxide} + \text{water}$$
$$CH_4(g) + 2O_2(g) \rightarrow CO_2(g) + 2H_2O(l)$$

Methane is a simple fuel, but other fuels behave in much the same way. For example, petrol is a mixture of hydrocarbons. Octane (C_8H_{18}) is a typical hydrocarbon found in petrol. When octane burns, carbon dioxide and water are formed, as with methane:

$$\text{octane} + \text{oxygen} \rightarrow \text{carbon dioxide} + \text{water}$$
$$2C_8H_{18}(l) + 25O_2(g) \rightarrow 16CO_2(g) + 18H_2O(l)$$

If a fuel burns in a limited air supply, carbon monoxide is formed instead of carbon dioxide. This is dangerous, because carbon monoxide is very poisonous (see page 73).

Firefighting

All fires need the three things shown in the 'fire triangle' in figure 2.5. By removing any one of them, the fire can be put out. For example, a fire blanket puts out a fire by removing oxygen. Water puts it out by removing both oxygen and heat.

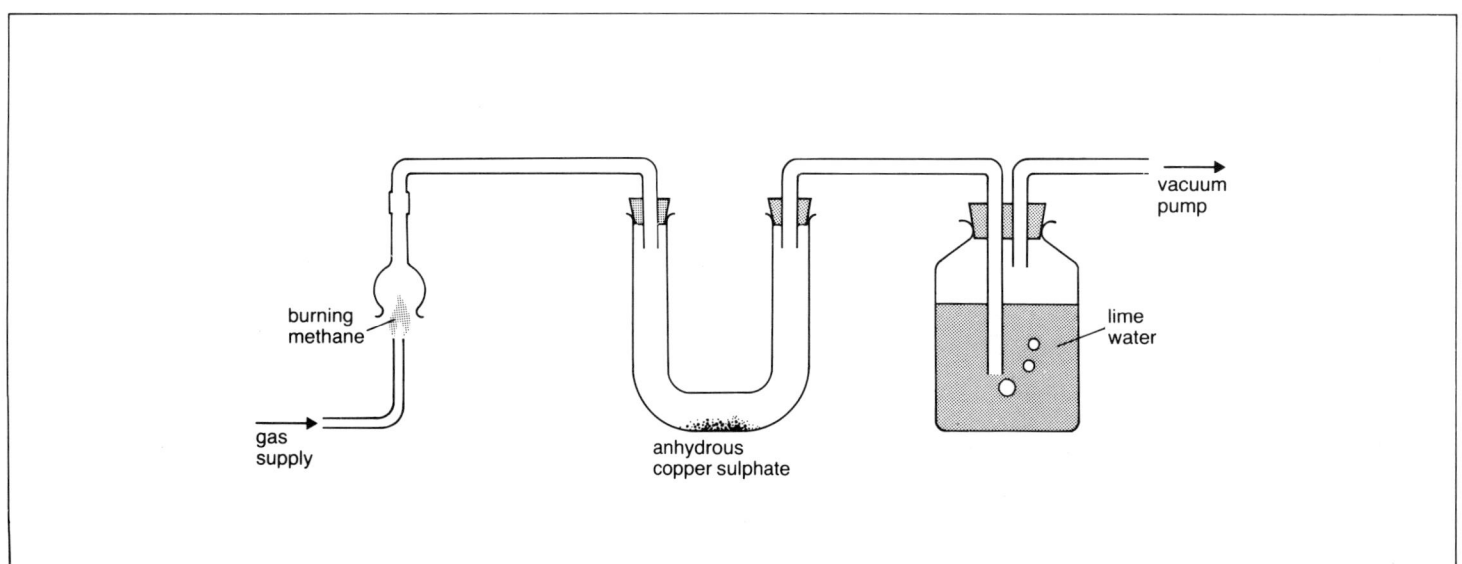

Figure 2.4 *An experiment to show that carbon dioxide and water are formed when methane burns.*

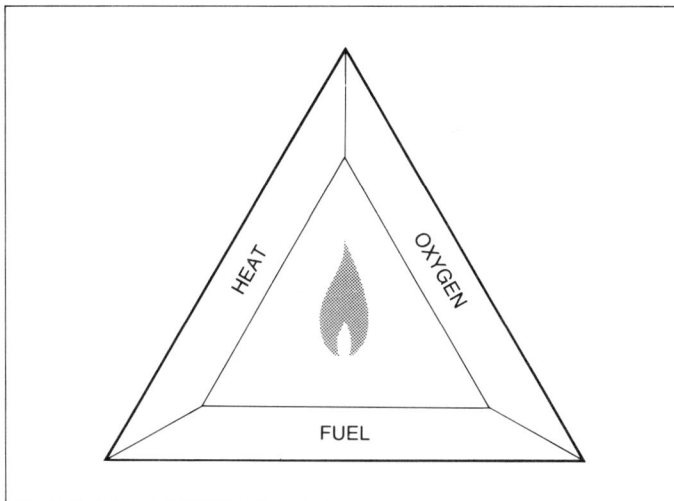

Figure 2.5 *The fire triangle*

Breathing

Humans use food as a kind of fuel. Energy foods like fats and carbohydrates are oxidised in the body to produce energy. The process is called **respiration**.

Respiration is much slower than the burning of fuels, but the overall result is very similar. For example, when a carbohydrate such as glucose is oxidised during respiration, carbon dioxide and water are formed. Oxygen from the air is used up.

$$\text{glucose} + \text{oxygen} \rightarrow \text{carbon dioxide} + \text{water}$$

$$C_6H_{12}O_6(s) + 6O_2(g) \rightarrow 6CO_2(g) + 6H_2O(l)$$

Table 2.3 compares the composition of normal air (the air we breathe in) and exhaled air (the air we breathe out). Notice that exhaled air contains more carbon dioxide and less oxygen than normal air.

Table 2.3 *A comparison of normal air and exhaled air.*

Gas	Percentage in normal air	Percentage in exhaled air
Nitrogen	79.02	79.5
Oxygen	20.95	16.4
Carbon dioxide	0.03	4.1

Rusting

Rusting is the slow oxidation of iron to form hydrated iron(III) oxide. This is the chemical name for rust.

Rusting costs millions of pounds every year because of:
- the need to protect iron and steel objects;
- the need to replace rusted articles.

The steel pipes on a car's exhaust system normally rust through in less than 2 years.

Iron and steel rust more easily than other metals. Even so, steel is used for ships, cars, bridges and other structures because it is cheaper and stronger than other building materials.

Figure 2.6 illustrates an experiment to investigate the conditions needed for rusting. The results below the test tubes in figure 2.6 show that both air *and* water are needed for rusting to occur. Rusting occurs particularly quickly in water containing dissolved ionic impurities – such as sea water. The water left after icy roads have been treated with salt often speeds up the rusting of cars.

The word equation for the rusting reaction is:

$$\text{iron} + \text{oxygen} + \text{water} \rightarrow \text{hydrated iron (III) oxide (rust)}$$

The rust is very brittle and swells up as it is formed. This causes the rusted surface of the metal to flake off. The next layer of metal is then exposed. It will soon rust and flake off as well, and so it goes on.

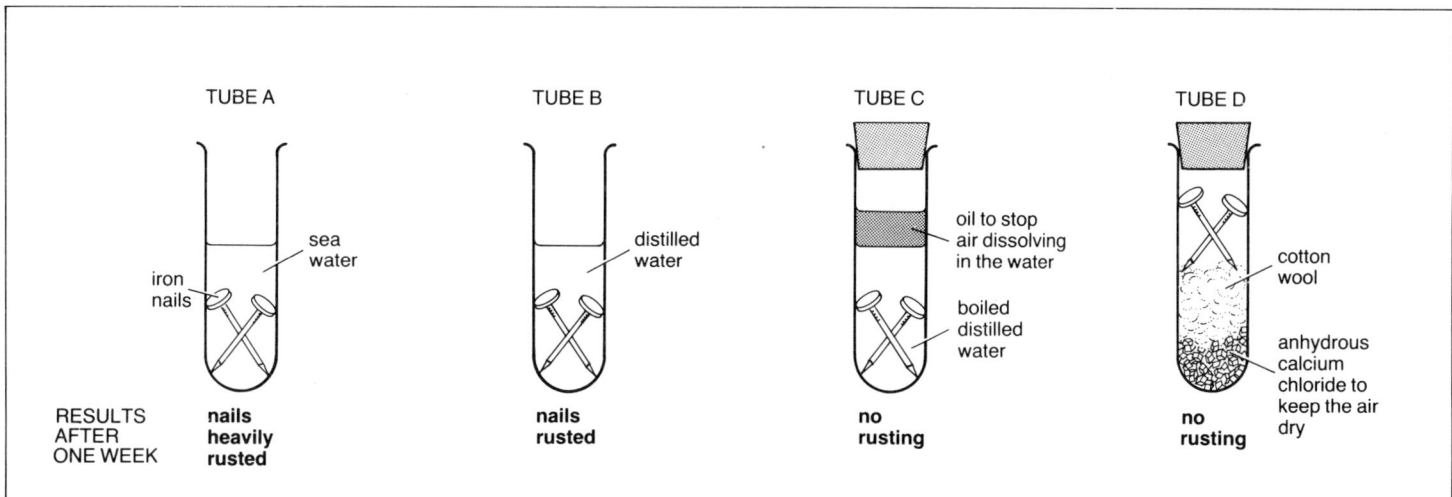

Figure 2.6 *An experiment to investigate the conditions needed for rusting.*

Table 2.4 *Methods of preventing rusting.*

Method	How it works	Example
Painting	Stops air and water reaching the metal	Ships, cars, bridges
Oiling	Stops air and water reaching the metal	Moving machine parts, engines, gear boxes, etc.
Tin plating	Stops air and water reaching the metal	Cans (tins) for food
Chromium plating	Stops air and water reaching the metal	Taps, kettles, car bumpers
Alloying	Iron is mixed with metals (e.g. chromium, nickel) which do not rust	Stainless steel cutlery, tools, etc.
Galvanising (zinc plating)	Oxygen reacts with the zinc in preference to iron	Buckets, dustbins

How is rusting prevented?

In order to stop iron and steel rusting, we must protect them from water and oxygen. The most important ways of doing this are shown in table 2.4.

Burning, breathing, rusting and redox

Many reactions that occur in everyday life involve substances reacting with oxygen to form oxides. Burning, breathing and rusting are important examples.

During burning and breathing, fuels containing carbon and hydrogen react with oxygen to form carbon dioxide and water (hydrogen oxide).

fuel + oxygen → carbon dioxide + water

During rusting, iron reacts with oxygen and water to form hydrated iron (III) oxide.

iron + oxygen + water → hydrated iron (III) oxide

Reactions in which a substance combines with oxygen are called **oxidation** and the substance is said to be **oxidised**. But if one substance gains oxygen, another substance (maybe oxygen itself) must lose oxygen. Substances that lose oxygen are said to be **reduced** and we call the process **reduction**.

So, oxidation and reduction always happen together. If one substance gains oxygen and gets oxidised, another substance must lose oxygen and be reduced. The combined process of **reduction + oxidation** is called **redox**.

Classification of the oxides of elements

Practically every element will combine with oxygen to form an oxide. (The main exception is the noble gases.) Reactive elements like sodium, magnesium and phosphorus will burn in air to form oxides. Less reactive elements may react only slowly with oxygen. Elements always react faster with pure oxygen than with air. Why do you think this is?

Oxides can be classified into different types, as shown in table 2.5.

Figure 2.7 shows the type of oxides formed by different elements in the periodic table.

Table 2.5 *Types of oxides.*

Oxide type	Formed by	Characteristics
Acidic oxides	Non-metals	Neutralise alkalis, and form acidic solutions if they dissolve in water. Usually gases or liquids.
Basic oxides	Metals	Neutralise acids, and some form alkaline solutions (**if** they dissolve in water). Always solids.
Amphoteric oxides	'Poor' metals (see page 46)	Neutralise both acids and alkalis. Always solids.

Pollution of the air

Pollution of the air is caused by **pollutant** gases. A pollutant is a substance produced as a result of human activities and released into the environment, where it causes harm to living things. Sometimes pollutants may also harm non-living things.

Because gases diffuse (spread out) quickly, air pollution can affect wide areas. For example, sulphur dioxide produced by power stations in Britain can cause acid rain as far away as Sweden.

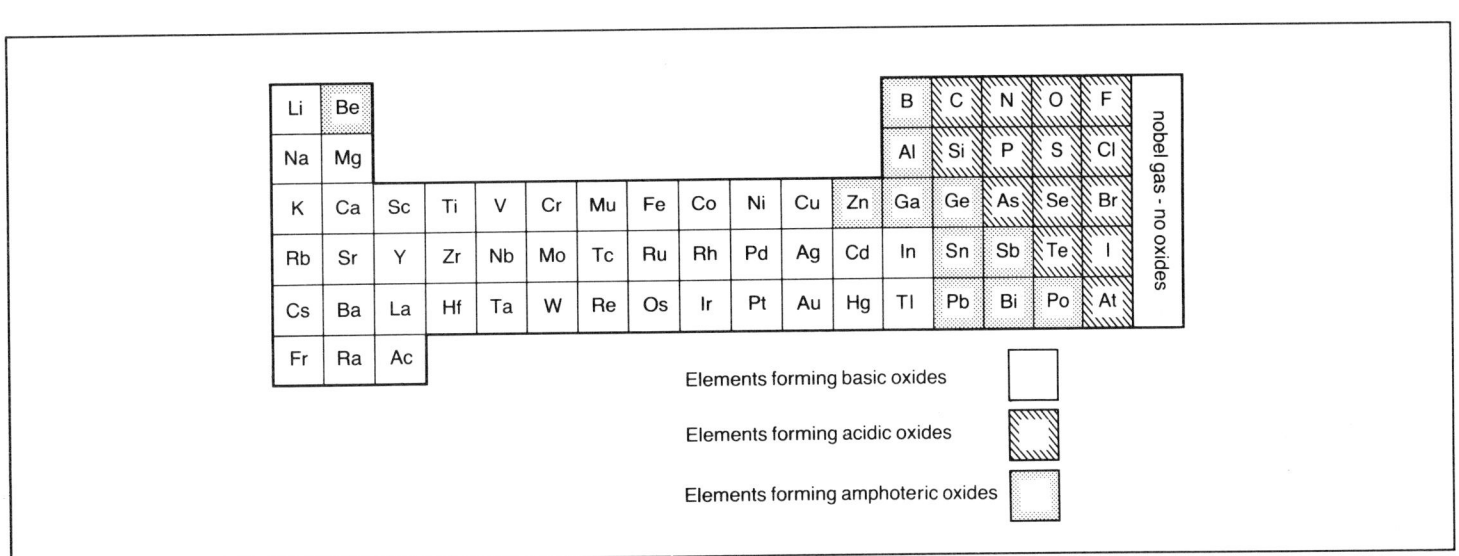

Figure 2.7 *Types of oxide formed by different elements in the periodic table.*

Table 2.6 gives some of the major pollutant gases, their sources and their effects, and some of the ways they can be controlled.

Acid rain

Some air pollutants are acidic gases, particularly sulphur dioxide and nitrogen dioxide. After they have been released into the air, these gases may react with rain water and with other gases in the air. As a result the rain water becomes acidic, forming acid rain. In some extreme cases, the water is as acidic as vinegar.

Scientists believe that acid rain is killing trees and fish, particularly in Germany and Scandinavia. It also wears away the stonework on buildings.

It is not easy to control acid rain. Sulphur dioxide is certainly involved. A great deal of sulphur dioxide is produced by coal-burning power stations. The sulphur dioxide could be removed from the chimney gases by special equipment, but this would be expensive. Another cause is the nitrogen oxides produced in car exhausts, and this can be controlled by careful engine design.

Table 2.6 *Major air pollutants.*

Air pollutant	Source	Effects	Possible methods of control
Sulphur dioxide (SO_2)	Burning fossil fuels	Causes acid rain	Remove sulphur from fuels before burning. Remove sulphur dioxide from chimney gases of power stations.
Nitrogen oxides (NO, NO_2, N_2O)	Vehicle exhausts, burning of fuels	Help cause acid rain and photochemical smog	Fit catalytic converters to vehicle exhausts. Modify engines to run on a weaker mixture of fuel and air.
Carbon dioxide (CO_2)	Burning fuels	May cause 'greenhouse effect', affecting Earth's climate	Can be controlled only by burning less fossil fuels.
Carbon monoxide (CO)	Burning fuels, vehicle exhausts, cigarette smoke	Poisonous to animals, including humans	Ensure vehicle engines are well maintained. Prevent cigarette smoking.
Hydrocarbons	Vehicle exhausts, burning fuels	Help cause acid rain and photochemical smog	Fit catalytic converters to vehicle exhausts. Modify engines to run on a weaker mixture of fuel and air.
Smoke	Burning fuels	Damages lungs; reduces photosynthesis of plants	Use smokeless fuels. Make sure engines and burners have plenty of air to burn fuel efficiently.

Self test

Questions 1–4
- A alloying
- B galvanizing
- C oiling
- D painting
- E tin plating

Choose from **A** to **E** the method of rust prevention that is most likely to be used for
1. moving machine parts
2. cutlery
3. steel bridges
4. buckets

Questions 5–9
- A carbon dioxide
- B carbon monoxide
- C nitrogen
- D nitrogen dioxide
- E smoke

Choose from **A** to **E** the substance that
5. causes discoloration of stone and brick buildings.
6. helps to cause acid rain.
7. is present in greater concentration in exhaled air than in normal air.
8. is not an air pollutant.
9. reacts with haemoglobin in the blood.

Questions 10–13
- A aluminium oxide
- B hydrogen oxide
- C iron oxide
- D sodium oxide
- E sulphur dioxide

Choose from **A** to **E** the substance that is
10. an acidic oxide.
11. an amphoteric oxide.
12. an insoluble basic oxide.
13. both a basic and an alkaline oxide.

14. Iron rusts faster in heavily industrialised areas than in country areas. This is due to
    - A higher temperatures.
    - B soot in the air.
    - C acid fumes in the air.
    - D water vapour in the air.

15. Burning, respiration and rusting all involve
    - A endothermic reactions.
    - B the formation of oxides.
    - C the production of carbon dioxide.
    - D water as a reactant.

16. Magnesium burns brightly in air, but more brightly in oxygen. From this, we can conclude that
    - A nitrogen does *not* allow burning.
    - B oxygen burns brighter than nitrogen.
    - C oxygen supports combustion.
    - D magnesium does not react with nitrogen.

17. Some phosphorus was allowed to react with air inside a closed flask. The closed flask and its contents were weighed before and after the reaction. After the reaction, the flask will have
    - A decreased in mass.
    - B increased in mass.
    - C increased or decreased in mass, depending on the mass of phosphorus taken.
    - D stayed the same mass.

Questions 18–20

The diagram below shows a flow chart of an experiment to remove different gases from normal air.

What constituent in normal air is removed by
18. heated copper?
19. sodium hydroxide solution?
20. anhydrous calcium chloride?

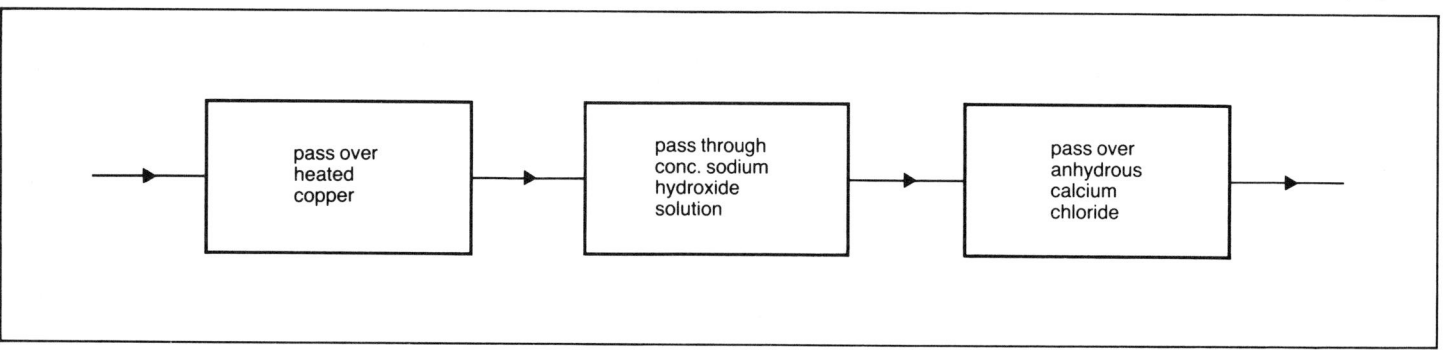

3 Water

Water is the commonest liquid in the world. There are about one million million million (10^{18}) tonnes of water on the Earth. Water determines where we can live, which crops we can grow and the weather. All living things need water – people, animals and plants. About two-thirds of your body is water. Every day you need about 2 litres (3 pints) of water to replace the water you lose in urine, in sweat and when you breathe. Water is even more important than food. Most people can live for 2 months without food but only a week without water.

What are the properties of water that make it so important?

- **Water is usually a liquid on Earth.** It melts at 0°C and boils at 100°C. Water covers about two-thirds of the Earth's surface as oceans, lakes and rivers.
- **Water expands as it freezes.** This means that ice is less dense than water and ice floats on water. For the same reason, water freezes from the top downwards. This allows living things to survive in water even in Arctic conditions. The ice on the surface of the water acts as an insulator and prevents the water below from freezing.
- **Water is transparent.** Sunlight can pass deep into clear water and help water plants and plankton to photosynthesise. The oxygen produced dissolves in the water. This allows fish and other water animals to survive.
- **Water is a very good solvent.** It will dissolve substances as different as salt, sugar, alcohol and oxygen.

When you mix instant coffee with *hot* water, it dissolves very quickly. If you tried to make a cup of coffee with *cold* water, the coffee would not dissolve. Sugar also dissolves better in hot coffee than in cold coffee. These examples show that solids dissolve better in hot water than in cold water. When sugar is stirred into coffee, it dissolves until a certain amount has been added. If more sugar is then added it remains undissolved. The coffee is **saturated** with sugar. The extent to which a solute like sugar can saturate a solvent like coffee is called its **solubility**.

Table 3.1 *The solubility of some substances in water at 25°C.*

Substance	Mass that can dissolve in 100 g of water at 25°C/g
Alcohol	infinite
Sugar	211.0
Salt	36.0
Carbon dioxide	0.144
Oxygen	0.004
Sand	0

Table 3.1 gives the solubility of a few substances in water at 25°C. Notice that solubility is given in grams of solute dissolving in 100 grams of water. The temperature must also be given because the solubility of most substances changes a lot with temperature. Notice also in table 3.1 that some substances are more soluble than others.

How does solubility change with temperature?

The graph in figure 3.1 shows the solubility of sugar at different temperatures. This kind of graph is called a **solubility curve**. You can use the graph to predict the properties given below.

① The amount of sugar that will dissolve at a particular temperature. For example, 219 g of sugar will dissolve in 100 g of hot water at 30°C.
② The temperature at which a particular solution will start to crystallise. For example, if 250 g of sugar are dissolved in 100 g of hot water and the solution is cooled, sugar crystals will come out of solution at 46°C.

Most solids become more soluble in water as the temperature rises but gases become *less* soluble as the temperature rises.

Fish and other water creatures depend on dissolved oxygen in their water. If the temperature of their water is too high, there may not be enough oxygen for them to live. This is why fish caught in rivers and lakes often die in tanks indoors.

Carbon dioxide also becomes less soluble in water at higher temperatures. This is why fizzy drinks become 'flat' when they are warm.

How does water react with metals?

Table 3.2 summarises the reactions of five metals with water. From these reactions we can write a reactivity series for the five metals as in figure 3.2.

This reactivity series with water is very similar to the order of reactivity with oxygen (page 46). This is not surprising since the metal reacts to form its oxide in both cases.

e.g. metal + oxygen → metal oxide

2Mg + O_2 → 2MgO

e.g. metal + water → metal + hydrogen
(hydrogen oxide)
oxide

Mg + H_2O → MgO + H_2

14 Water

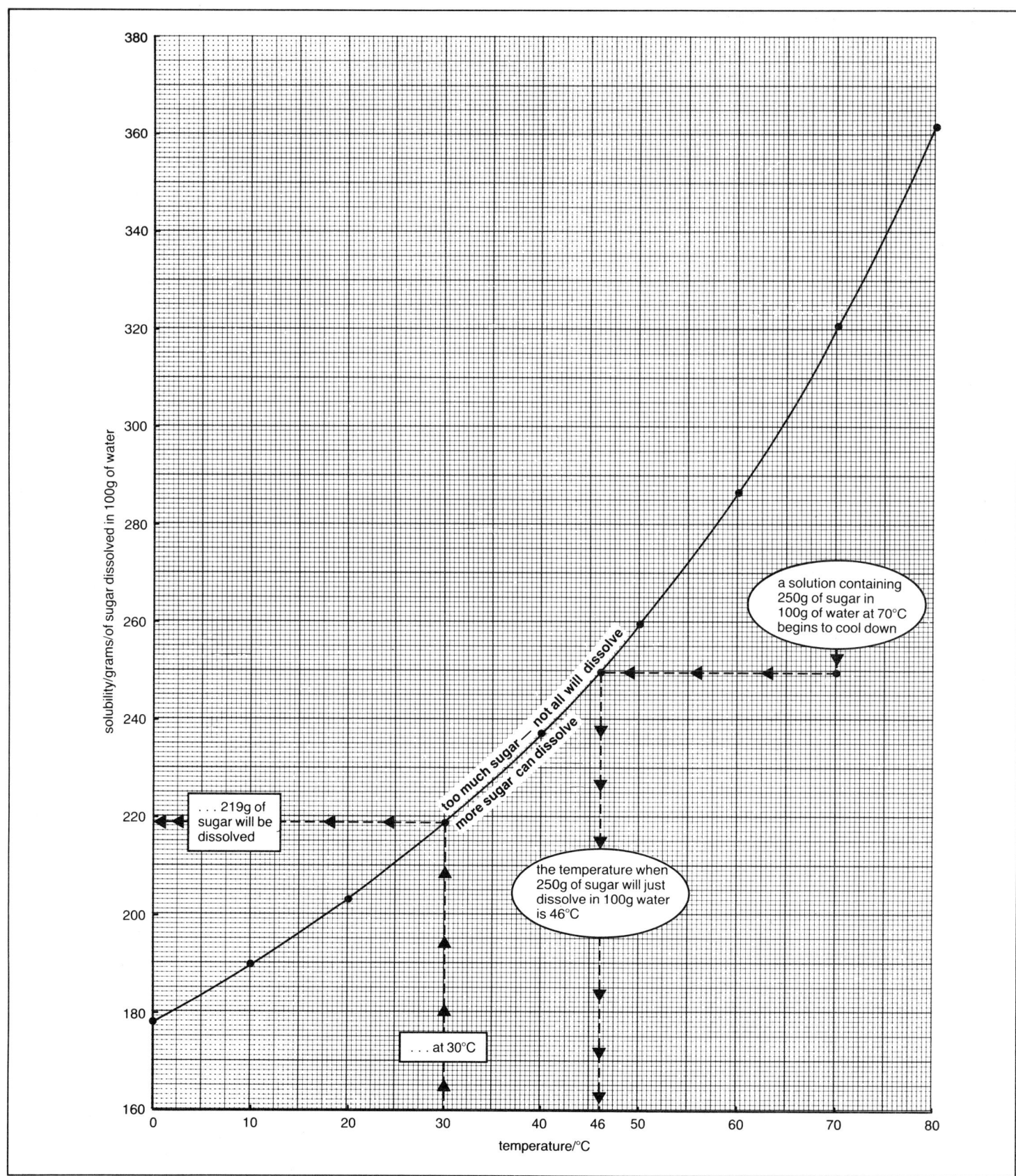

Figure 3.1 *The solubility of sugar at different temperatures.*

Table 3.2 *The reactions of metals with water.*

Metal	Reaction
Sodium (Na)	A vigorous reaction occurs. The sodium get so hot that it melts to a silvery bead which skates over the water surface. Hydrogen and sodium oxide are formed. The sodium oxide reacts with the water to form sodium hydroxide.
Calcium (Ca)	Sinks in the water and gives off a steady stream of hydrogen. The solution becomes alkaline and cloudy owing to the formation of calcium oxide, which then reacts with the water to form calcium hydroxide.
Magnesium (Mg)	Tiny bubbles of gas appear on the surface of the Mg after a few minutes. The solution slowly becomes alkaline.
Iron (Fe)	Rusts very slowly in water provided oxygen is present. The product is hydrated iron(III) oxide.
Copper (Cu)	No reaction.

Notice in table 3.2 that the reactive metals like sodium and calcium react with water to form their oxide and then the oxide reacts with more water to form the hydroxide.

$$Ca + H_2O \rightarrow CaO + H_2$$
$$CaO + H_2O \rightarrow Ca(OH)_2$$

Copper is the least reactive metal in the reactivity series shown in figure 3.2. Copper does not even react with steam, never mind water! Because of this, it is used for pipes and storage tanks for hot water.

Iron does not react with cold water. But when both water and air are present, iron reacts to form **rust**. This important reaction is covered in Chapter 2.

Water supplies

In Britain each person uses about 180 litres (two baths full) of water every day. Table 3.3 shows how this water is used. In some parts of Africa, where water is scarce, each person must survive on less than 10 litres per day.

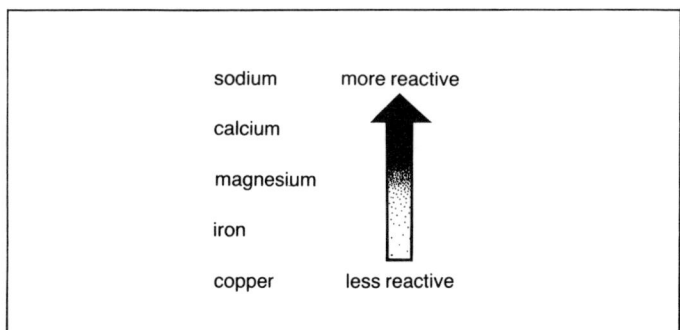

Figure 3.2 *The reactivity series.*

Table 3.3 *How we use water in our homes.*

Toilet flushing	65 litres
Personal washing	55 litres
Washing clothes	20 litres
Dish washing	15 litres
Gardening	12 litres
Cooking	10 litres
Drinking	3 litres
Total	**180 litres**

Industry uses even larger amounts of water than we do in our homes. Most of the water is used for cooling. A larger power station uses about 5 million litres of water per day. About 50 000 litres of water are used during the manufacture of a car! Sometimes the water used by industry needs to be fairly pure. In this case it is taken from the public water supply. Industry also uses large amounts of less pure water from rivers or from the sea.

Where does our water come from?

Most of the water in the public supply comes from rivers, lakes and underground wells. Figure 3.3 shows the main stages in the purification of this water before it can be used in our homes.

Despite all this, water from the public supply is not pure. Although water 'from the tap' looks pure, it is really a solution. It contains dissolved gases such as oxygen and carbon dioxide and also dissolved solids that are picked up by the water as it travels over rocks in rivers and streams. These solids may make the water 'hard' (see page 76).

We can trace our water supply even further back than rivers and underground wells. Water on the Earth's surface and underground comes originally from rain. The rain comes from clouds. The clouds come from water

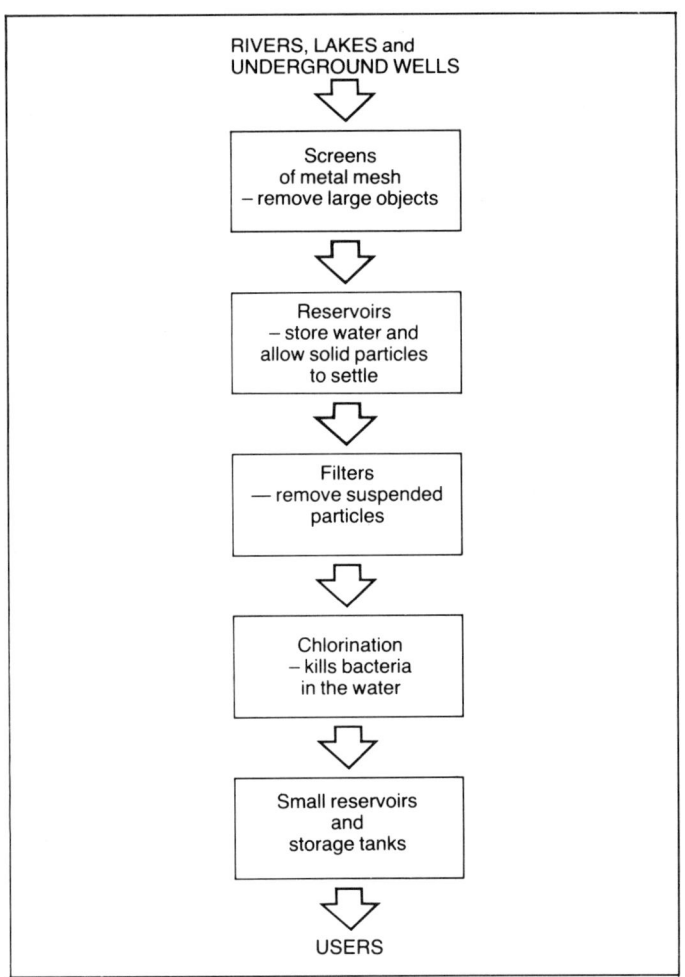

Figure 3.3 *The main stages in the purification of water.*

which has evaporated from rivers, lakes and oceans. This continuous movement of water from the Earth's surface to clouds and then back to the Earth as rain is called the **water cycle** (figure 3.4).

Water pollution

The main causes of water pollution together with their sources and effects are summarised in table 3.4. Sewage is the main cause of water pollution. At one time, sewage was just pumped into rivers and the sea. This led to diseases and it upset the balance of life in the water. To prevent this problem, sewage plants treat the waste before it is returned to rivers or the sea. The sewage is pumped into large tanks and mixed with air (aerated) so that it can be decomposed rapidly by bacteria.

Pollution control costs money. We need to cut down the amount of chemical waste that goes into our rivers. To do this, we must be prepared to spend more money on getting rid of the waste in some other way. This will make the goods from our factories more expensive as the costs of avoiding pollution get passed on to the customers. As a society we have to decide whether we want more pollution control and higher prices or less pollution control and lower prices.

Table 3.4 *The main causes of water pollution.*

Cause of pollution	Source	Effect
Sewage	Homes and factories	Bacteria grow on nutrients in sewage and use up all the dissolved oxygen. Bacteria and other living organisms then die and water becomes smelly.
Oil	Oil from refineries and ship-wrecked tankers	Covers birds with oil and pollutes beaches.
Fertilisers	Rain washes fertilisers into rivers	Bacteria and water plants grow rapidly, use up all the dissolved oxygen and then die.
Pesticides	Spraying crops with chemicals	Food may be contaminated. Poisonous substances build up in the bodies of animals and eventually in humans.
Industrial chemicals	Oils, metal compounds, acids, alkalis, dyes, etc. from factories	Poisonous to animals, plants and bacteria in the water.
Detergents	Homes and factories	Cause water to foam and are poisonous to living things.

Water pollution

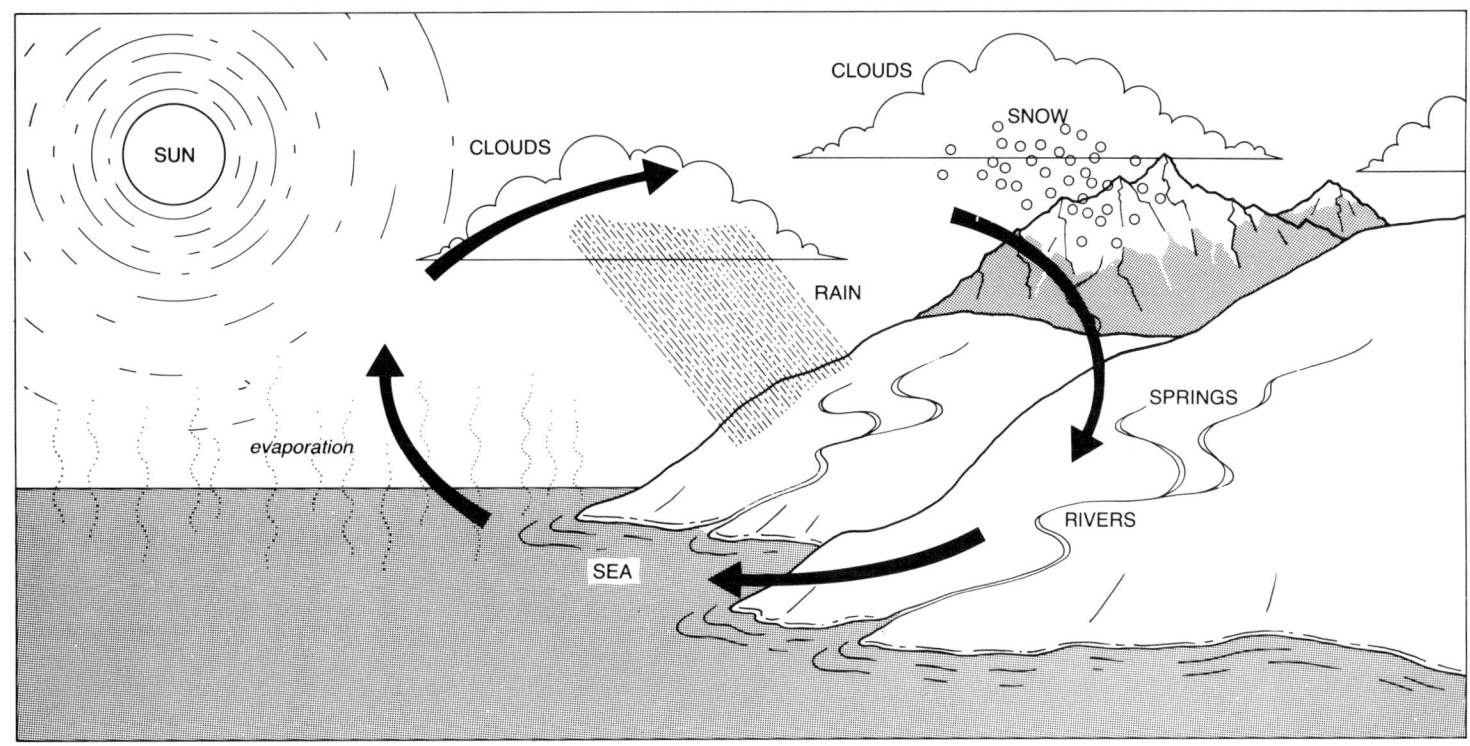

Figure 3.4 *The water cycle*

Self test

Questions 1–3

From the tubes **A** to **D** choose the *one* that
1. may contain a saturated solution.
2. contains an insoluble solid.
3. contains two miscible liquids.

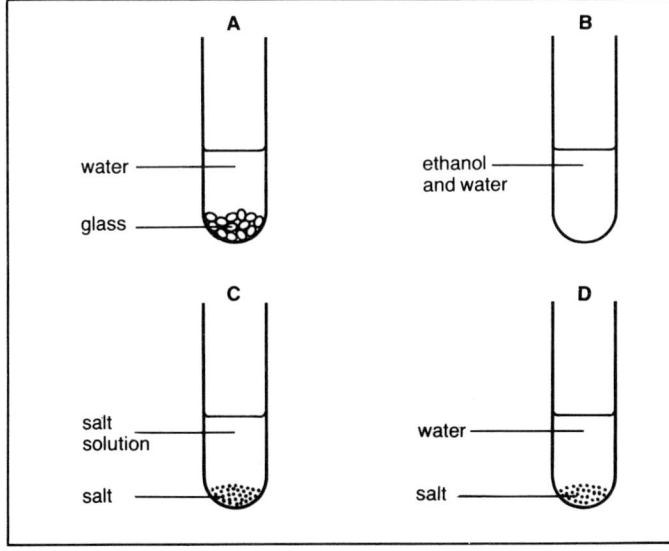

Questions 4–6

- **A** calcium
- **B** copper
- **C** iron
- **D** magnesium
- **E** zinc

From the list **A** to **E** choose the metal that
4. reacts most vigorously with water.
5. does not react with either water or steam.
6. reacts with cold water only when air is present.

Questions 7–11

Here is a list of substances that may get into natural waters.
- **A** crude oil
- **B** fertiliser
- **C** pesticide
- **D** detergent
- **E** treated sewage

From the list **A** to **E** choose the substance that
7. may cause river water to foam.
8. causes problems for birds and beaches.
9. may be washed off the land into rivers.
10. may build up in the bodies of some birds.
11. would not pollute river water.

18 Water

Questions 12–14

The graph below shows what happens to the percentage of oxygen dissolved in the water of a river when sewage is pumped into it.

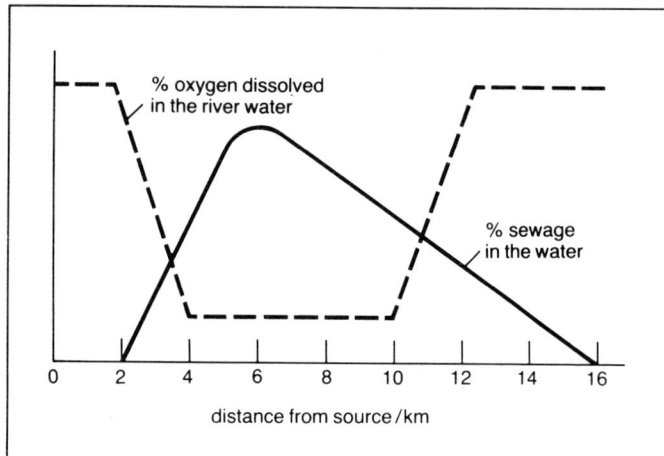

12 How far from the source of the river does the sewage enter it?
   A 2 km   B 4 km   C 6 km   D 10 km

13 When the sewage enters the river, the percentage of oxygen
   A falls rapidly to a constant low value.
   B falls rapidly to zero.
   C gradually falls to zero.
   D rises to a peak and then falls.

14 When a river flows over a weir, the water mixes with air. How far from the source does the river start to flow over a weir?
   A 6 km   B 10 km   C 12 km   D 16 km

15 Some solid grease dissolves in petrol to form a mixture M. M is a
   A residue   B solute   C solution   D solvent.

16 Which *one* of the following will usually increase the solubility of a solute in water?
   A adding more water
   B adding more solute
   C shaking the mixture
   D increasing the temperature

17 Rain occurs when water vapour in the sky forms drops of liquid. Geographers sometimes call this process precipitation. Chemists call this process
   A condensation   B distillation
   C evaporation   D sublimation

18 River water is purified for use in our homes by
   A boiling and chlorination.
   B boiling and filtration.
   C chlorination and filtration.
   D distillation and neutralisation.

19 Water is often stored in reservoirs before it passes into the public supply. Storing water in reservoirs helps to purify the water because it allows
   A bacteria to be killed.
   B dissolved substances to crystallise.
   C water plants to clean the water.
   D solid particles to settle.

4 Particles, formulas and equations

All matter is made up of tiny particles. These may be atoms, molecules or ions. Using the idea of particles, we can explain the way matter behaves.

The states of matter

All matter can exist in three states – solid, liquid and gas. **Solids** have a fixed shape. **Liquids** have no fixed shape, but their volume is fixed. **Gases** have no fixed shape or volume. They spread out (**diffuse**) to fill all the available space. Unlike solids and liquids, gases are easy to squeeze into a smaller space (**compress**).

The state of a substance can be changed by heating or cooling (figure 4.1).

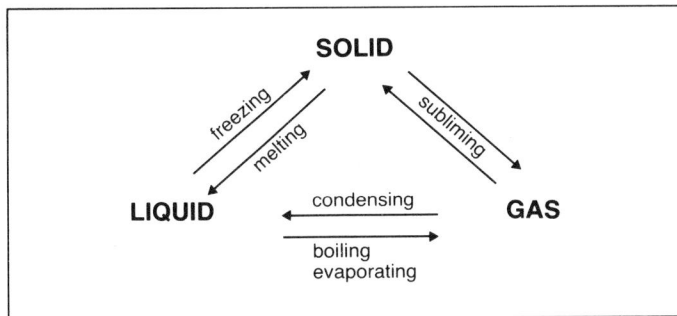

Figure 4.1 *Changes of state.*

State symbols are used to show the state of a substance. The state symbol is written after the formula of the substance.

- (s) indicates **solid**
- (l) indicates **liquid**
- (g) indicates **gas**
- (aq) indicates **a solid, liquid or gas dissolved in water**

Example: $H_2O(s)$ is ice, $H_2O(l)$ is liquid water and $H_2O(g)$ is steam.

Diffusion

All gases diffuse to fill the available space. This is why smells spread out, and why leaks of flammable gases can cause explosions. Liquids can also diffuse into one another, for example, when ink mixes with water. Solids can diffuse into liquids if they are soluble in the liquid. Figure 4.2 shows an example.

Some substances diffuse faster than others. The lighter the particles in the substance, the faster the substance

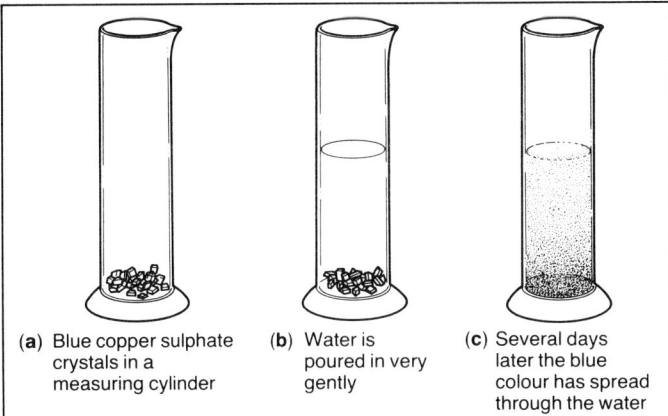

Figure 4.2 *Diffusion of copper sulphate in water.*

diffuses. Hydrogen has very light particles, so it diffuses very fast. This is why hydrogen-filled balloons go down quickly, as the hydrogen diffuses out through tiny holes in the rubber balloon.

The kinetic theory of matter

The kinetic theory helps to explain the way in which matter behaves. The main points of the theory are:
- All matter is made up of tiny, invisible particles. Different substances have different types of particles, with different sizes.
- The particles move all the time. The higher the temperature, the faster they move.
- Lighter particles move faster than heavier ones, at a given temperature.
- In a gas, there is a relatively large distance between the particles. They are free to move anywhere. They exert virtually no forces on each other. They move around at random, colliding with each other and with the walls of their container (figure 4.3a).

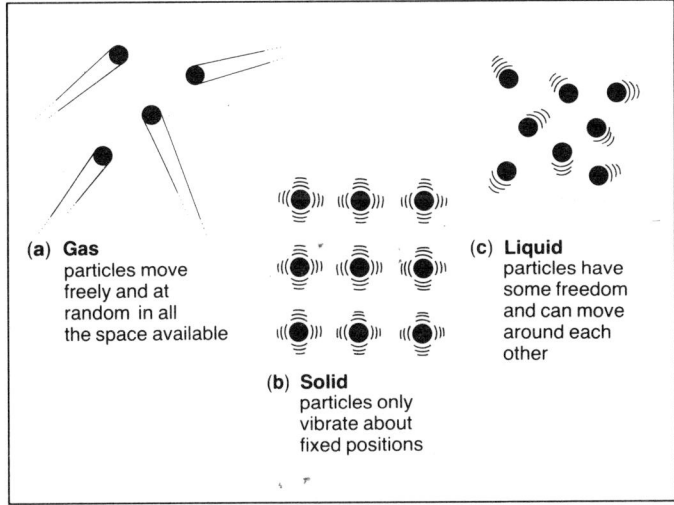

Figure 4.3 *Arrangement of particles in gases, solids and liquids.*

- In a solid, the particles attract one another strongly. They are arranged regularly, and very close together. They have little freedom of movement. They can only vibrate about fixed positions (figure 4.3b).
- In a liquid, the particles are close together, but the forces of attraction are weaker than in a solid. The particles can move more freely than in a solid (figure 4.3c).

Using the kinetic theory

We can use the kinetic theory to explain how matter behaves.

Explaining diffusion

The kinetic theory tells us that gases contain particles moving around at random. This explains why gases diffuse. The particles do not care where they go. Since they move around at random all the time, sooner or later they are bound to spread out and fill all the space available.

The kinetic theory tells us that lighter particles move faster than heavier ones, at a given temperature. This explains why less dense gases diffuse faster than denser ones. Less dense gases have lighter particles, which move faster. For example, hydrogen, the least dense of all gases, diffuses four times faster than oxygen at a given temperature.

Explaining changes of state

We can use the kinetic theory to explain what happens when a solid melts. Look back at figure 4.3b. In a solid, the particles are held in their fixed positions by the strong forces between them. As the solid is heated, the particles vibrate faster and faster until they begin to break free from one another. The particles can now move around each other – the solid melts. If the liquid is heated even more, the particles move still faster. Eventually they are moving fast enough to break away from one another completely – the liquid becomes a gas.

Exactly the opposite happens when a gas is cooled and becomes a liquid, and when a liquid cools to form a solid.

Cooling curves

Suppose we melt a solid by heating it. We can then allow the molten substance to cool again until it solidifies. We can take the temperature of the substance at regular times as it cools. We can then plot a graph of temperature against time. This graph is called a **cooling curve** (figure 4.4).

Notice the level part of the curve. This happens as the solid freezes. When the liquid turns to solid, the particles get close enough to form **bonds** to each other. Forming these bonds gives out energy in the form of heat. Giving out heat slows down the rate of cooling and keeps the temperature constant. This explains the level part of the graph.

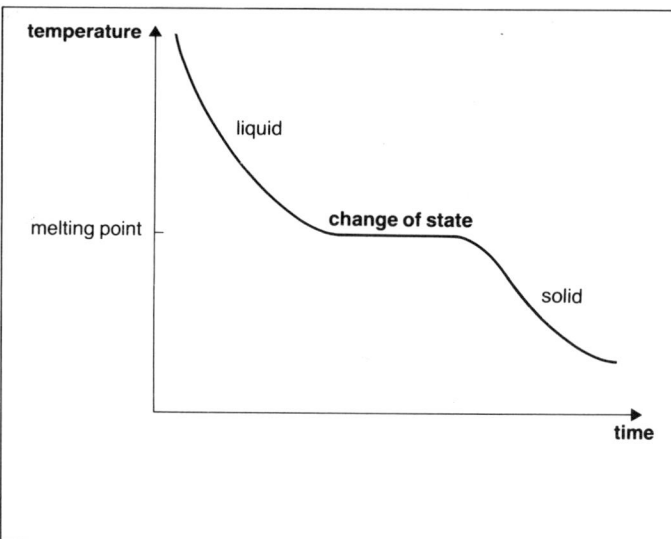

Figure 4.4 *A cooling curve.*

What kind of particles?

In this section we will be looking at three types of particles – atoms, molecules and ions. **Atoms** are the simplest. An atom is the smallest particle of an element. Often, atoms are joined together in groups called **molecules**. **Ions** are atoms, or groups of atoms, carrying an electric charge. Figure 4.5 gives some examples.

Atoms, molecules and ions are very, very small:
- the smallest atom, hydrogen, is about 10^{-10} m (0.000 000 0001 m) across;
- even quite large molecules, like sugar, are only about 10^{-9} m across – there are about 10^{19} molecules (10 000 000 000 000 000 000) in one grain of sugar!

Formulas

Formulas are a short way of showing what the particles in a substance are like. They use the symbols of the atoms (see page 1). For example, the formula of water is H_2O. This shows that a molecule of water contains two hydrogen atoms and one oxygen atom.

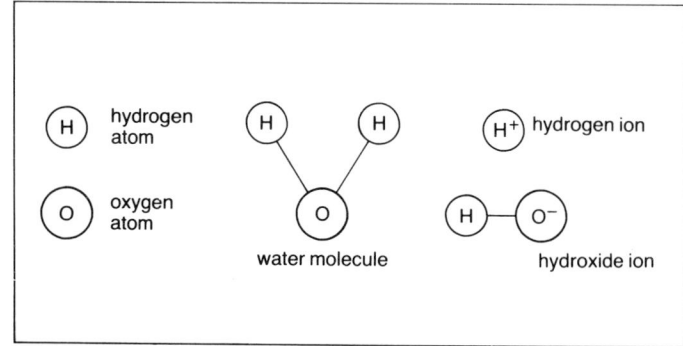

Figure 4.5 *Atoms, molecules and ions.*

The **empirical formula** is the simplest formula. It shows the *ratio* between the numbers of each type of atom.

The **molecular formula** shows the *actual* numbers of each type of atom in a molecule.

The **structural formula** shows how the atoms are actually joined together in one molecule. Figure 4.6 gives examples.

For a substance that contains molecules, the formula that we use is normally the molecular formula.

Example: Carbon dioxide contains molecules, with one carbon atom and two oxygen atoms in each molecule. The molecular formula of carbon dioxide is therefore CO_2.

For a compound that contains ions the empirical formula is used.

Example: Calcium chloride contains calcium ions, Ca^{2+}, and chloride ions, Cl^-. There are twice as many chloride ions as calcium ions. The formula of calcium chloride is therefore $CaCl_2$.

Formulas can be found by experiments. You can find out more about this on page 27.

Formulas can be predicted if you know a little about the elements involved. You can find out more about this on page 34.

Chemical equations

When a chemical reaction occurs, substances react together. These reacting substances are called the **reactants**. They form new chemicals, called the **products**.

Word equations give the *names of reactants and products*, but *not* their formulas or the amounts involved.

Example: When hydrogen burns in oxygen (or air), it forms water. The word equation for this simple reaction is:

$$\text{hydrogen} + \text{oxygen} \rightarrow \text{water}$$

Balanced equations go further than word equations. They give the *formulas* of the reactants and products. They also show the *relative numbers of particles* of each of the reactants and products.

Example: The balanced equation for hydrogen burning is:

$$2H_2 + O_2 \rightarrow 2H_2O$$

The number '2' in front of the H_2 shows that two hydrogen molecules are needed to react with one oxygen molecule.

CH_2O $C_2H_4O_2$

$$H-\underset{\underset{H}{|}}{\overset{\overset{H}{|}}{C}}-\underset{\underset{O}{\|}}{C}-O-H$$

empirical formula molecular formula structural formula

Figure 4.6 *The empirical formula, molecular formula and structural formula of ethanoic acid (acetic acid).*

The '2' in front of the H_2O shows that two water molecules are formed.

Balanced equations often include state symbols as well:

$$2H_2(g) + O_2(g) \rightarrow 2H_2O(l)$$

Writing balanced equations

The only way to be sure of the balanced equation for a reaction is to do experiments. First you need to find out exactly what the reactants and products are. Then you need to find their relative amounts (see page 28). But chemists write lots of equations, and it isn't possible to do experiments every time. Fortunately, if we know the reactants and products we can work out their formulas and then *predict* the equation. Here are the rules for predicting balanced equations.

Rules for predicting balanced equations

STEP 1. Make sure you know what the reactants and products are. Suppose we take the burning of magnesium in oxygen, which forms magnesium oxide.

STEP 2. Write a word equation for the reaction.

$$\text{magnesium} + \text{oxygen} \rightarrow \text{magnesium oxide}$$

STEP 3. Write symbols for elements and formulas for compounds. Remember that the common gases (nitrogen, oxygen, hydrogen and the halogens) are diatomic. This means that when they are not combined with other elements they exist as molecules containing two atoms. Thus oxygen is O_2, not O, and chlorine is Cl_2, not Cl.

Our example is now:

$$Mg + O_2 \rightarrow MgO$$

STEP 4. Balance the equation. There must be the same numbers of each type of atom on both sides. In the equation above there are two O atoms on the left-hand side, but only one on the right. To balance the numbers of O atoms, we need to double the amount of MgO:

$$Mg + O_2 \rightarrow 2MgO$$

But now there are two Mg atoms on the right-hand side, and only one on the left. Therefore we need to double the amount of Mg on the left:

$$2Mg + O_2 \rightarrow 2MgO$$

22 Particles, formulas and equations

Table 4.1 *Two examples of balanced equations.*

	Example 1	Example 2
Step 1 Make sure you know the reactants and products	Methane and oxygen react to form carbon dioxide and water	Zinc reacts with hydrochloric acid to form zinc chloride and hydrogen
Step 2 Write a word equation	methane + oxygen → carbon dioxide + water	zinc + hydrochloric acid → zinc chloride + hydrogen
Step 3 Write symbols and formulas	$CH_4 + O_2 \rightarrow CO_2 + H_2O$	$Zn + HCl \rightarrow ZnCl_2 + H_2$
Step 4 Balance the equation	$CH_4 + 2O_2 \rightarrow CO_2 + 2H_2O$	$Zn + 2HCl \rightarrow ZnCl_2 + H_2$

The equation is now balanced, with equal numbers of each type of atom on each side.

Remember that *equations cannot be balanced by altering formulas*. This would create an entirely different substance. You can only balance equations by putting a number *in front* of a formula.

Table 4.1 gives two more examples of writing balanced equations.

● Self test

Questions 1–4
The graph below shows the change in temperature of a solid when it is heated steadily from room temperature.

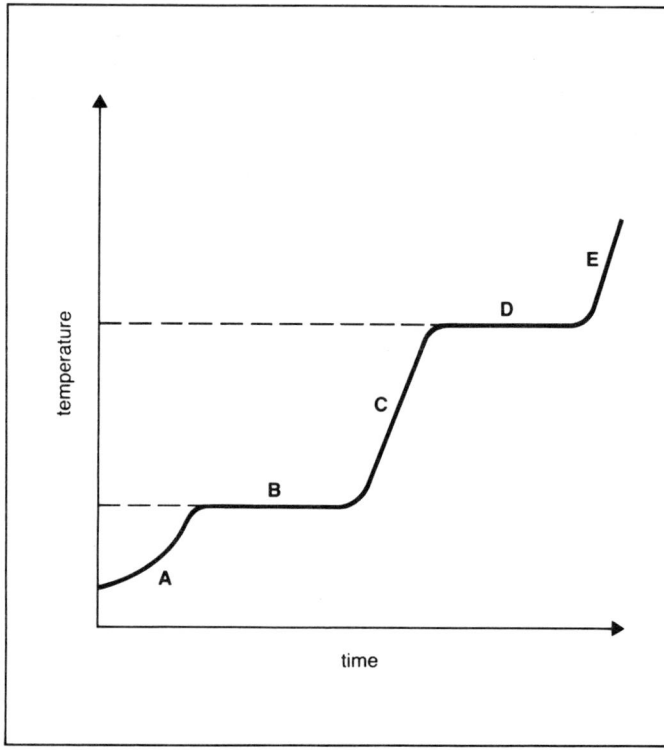

Which of the letters **A** to **E** corresponds to
1. solid changing to liquid?
2. liquid changing to gas?
3. solid warming up?
4. gas warming up?

Questions 5–8
In the diagrams below, ○ represents an atom of oxygen and ● represents an atom of hydrogen.

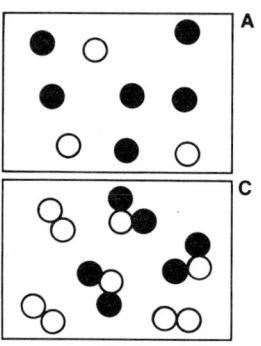
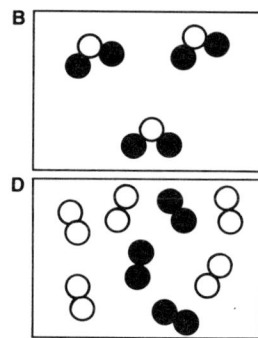

Choose from **A** to **D** the diagram that shows
5. oxygen and hydrogen atoms.
6. oxygen and hydrogen molecules.
7. water molecules.
8. oxygen and water molecules.

9. Which *one* of the following terms describes what happens when moving particles mix together?
   - **A** Brownian motion
   - **B** condensation
   - **C** diffusion
   - **D** evaporation.

10. When water is changing to ice at its freezing point, the water molecules
    - **A** gain energy.
    - **B** move closer.
    - **C** become more ordered.
    - **D** begin to move faster.

11. Diffusion does *not* occur in solids because the particles:
    - **A** are not moving.
    - **B** are moving too slowly.
    - **C** are in a regular order.
    - **D** only vibrate at fixed points.

12 The molecular formula of glucose is $C_6H_{12}O_6$.
    The empirical formula of glucose is
    A $C_6H_{12}O_6$ **B** $C_3H_6O_3$ **C** $C_2H_4O_2$ **D** CH_2O

13 Slug pellets contain metaldehyde. Metaldehyde is made from ethanal (C_2H_4O). Each molecule of metaldehyde is formed when four molecules of ethanal add together. The molecular formula of metaldehyde is
    A C_2H_4O **B** $C_4H_8O_2$ **C** $C_8H_{16}O_4$ **D** $4C_2H_4O$

Questions 14–18
Write the *names* of the substances that would replace the numbers in the following word equations.

zinc + oxygen → ___(14)___

magnesium + copper oxide → ___(15)___ + ___(16)___

Questions 17–20
Write the state symbols that would replace the numbers in the following equation.

Na(17) + H_2O (18) → NaOH (19) + ½H_2 (20)

Question 21
Balance the following equations by suggesting numbers to replace the letters (**a**) to (**g**).

(**a**) Fe + (**b**) Cl_2 → (**c**) $FeCl_3$

(**d**) C_3H_8 + (**e**) O_2 → (**f**) CO_2 + (**g**) H_2O

5 Chemical calculations

Chemists often need to ask the question 'How much?' How much of a substance is used up or formed in a chemical reaction? To answer the question, we need a way of counting atoms, molecules and ions.

Counting atoms

Atoms are far too small to count in the usual way. Instead, they are counted out by *weighing*. This is similar to the way bank clerks count coins by weighing them.

Because atoms are so small, they have to be weighed out in enormous numbers. The unit in which atoms are weighed out is called the **mole**. A mole of an element contains 6×10^{23} atoms of the element.

Example: One mole of iron, Fe, contains 6×10^{23} Fe atoms.

The number 6×10^{23} is called the **Avogadro constant**.

Relative atomic mass

Each element has its own type of atom. Atoms of different elements have different sizes, and different masses. To count atoms by weighing, we need to know the masses of the atoms. Atoms are far too small to weigh separately. Instead, we compare their masses *relative to one another*.

The basis of this **relative atomic mass scale** is the carbon atom, which is given a mass of exactly 12.

Relative atomic mass of C = 12.

It is possible to compare the masses of all other atoms with the mass of carbon atoms.

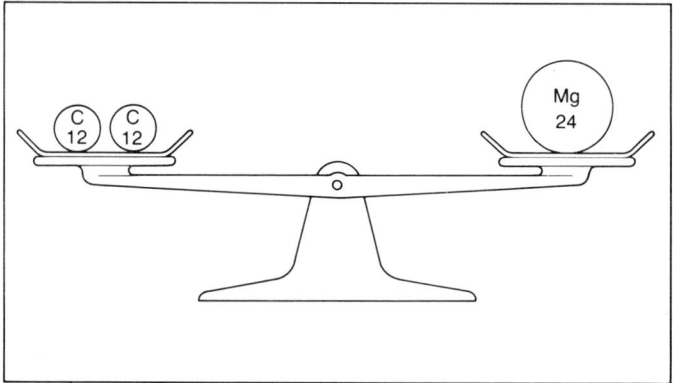

Figure 5.1 *Magnesium atoms are twice as heavy as carbon atoms, therefore the relative atomic mass of magnesium is 24.*

Example: Measurements show that magnesium atoms are twice as heavy as carbon atoms. So the relative atomic mass of magnesium is twice that of carbon, or $2 \times 12 = 24$ (figure 5.1).

In this way we can find the relative atomic masses (A_r) of all the elements. Table 5.1 gives the relative atomic masses of some of the more common elements.

Table 5.1 *Relative atomic masses of some elements.*

Element	Symbol	Relative atomic mass
aluminium	Al	27
bromine	Br	80
calcium	Ca	40
carbon	C	12
chlorine	Cl	35.5
copper	Cu	63.5
fluorine	F	19
gold	Au	197
helium	He	4
hydrogen	H	1
iodine	I	127
iron	Fe	56
lead	Pb	207
magnesium	Mg	24
nitrogen	N	14
oxygen	O	16
phosphorus	P	31
potassium	K	39
silicon	Si	28
silver	Ag	108
sodium	Na	23
sulphur	S	32
uranium	U	238
zinc	Zn	65

Finding the numbers of moles from relative atomic masses

Experiments show that the relative atomic mass of an element in grams (i.e. 12 g of carbon, 24 g of magnesium, etc.) always contains 6×10^{23} atoms (i.e. one mole of atoms). The relative atomic mass in grams is called the **molar mass**.

The molar mass of an element contains one mole of the element, which is 6×20^{23} atoms.

Example: A mole of iron, containing 6×10^{23} iron atoms, weighs 56 g, because the relative atomic mass of iron is 56. A mole of sulphur, containing 6×10^{23} sulphur atoms, weighs 32 g.

Knowing the relative atomic mass of an element, we can work out the number of moles in a certain mass of the element:

$$\text{number of moles} = \frac{\text{mass of element}}{\text{molar mass}}$$

Examples:
1. How many moles of sulphur atoms (S) are there in 64 g of sulphur? (A_r of S = 32)

   $$\text{number of moles} = \frac{\text{mass of element}}{\text{molar mass}} = 64/32 = \mathbf{2}$$

2. How many moles of helium atoms (He) are there in 1 g of helium? (A_r of He = 4)

   $$\text{number of moles} = \frac{\text{mass of element}}{\text{molar mass}} = 1/4 = \mathbf{0.25}$$

3. How many magnesium atoms (Mg) are there in 12 g of magnesium? (A_r of Mg = 24). First, find the number of moles:

   $$\text{number of moles} = \frac{\text{mass of element}}{\text{molar mass}} = 12/24 = 0.5$$

   But one mole of an element contains 6×10^{23} atoms.

   0.5 mole contains $0.5 \times 6 \times 10^{23} = \mathbf{3 \times 10^{23}}$ **atoms**

We can use the same idea to convert moles to masses. It is just a matter of doing the same thing backwards.

Examples:
1. What is the mass of 2 moles of iron atoms, Fe? (A_r of Fe = 56)

   $$\text{mass} = (2 \times 56) = \mathbf{112\,g}$$

2. What is the mass of 0.1 mole of sodium atoms, Na? (A_r of Na = 23)

   $$\text{mass} = (0.1 \times 23) = \mathbf{2.3\,g}$$

Relative molecular mass

So far we have talked about elements and atoms, but what about compounds?

With compounds we use the same ideas, but instead of relative *atomic* mass, we use **relative *molecular* mass** (M_r). Relative molecular mass measures the mass of a compound's molecules relative to the mass of an atom of carbon. To find the relative molecular mass of a compound, you just add up the relative atomic masses of all the atoms in the molecular formula. (In the case of an ionic compound, just add up the relative atomic masses in the *empirical* formula.)

Examples:
1. What is the relative molecular mass of water (H_2O)?
   $M_r = 2 \times$ (relative atomic mass of H) +
   (relative atomic mass of O)
   $= (2 \times 1) + 16$
   $= \mathbf{18}$

2. What is the relative molecular mass of sulphuric acid (H_2SO_4)?
   $M_r = (2 \times 1) + 32 + (4 \times 16)$
   $= \mathbf{98}$

3. What is the relative molecular mass of sodium carbonate (Na_2CO_3)?
   $M_r = (2 \times 23) + 12 + (3 \times 16)$
   $= \mathbf{106}$

Finding the number of moles from relative molecular masses

We can work out the number of moles of a compound in the same way as we did for elements, using the molar mass. For a compound, the molar mass is the relative molecular mass in grams.

Example: How many moles of carbon dioxide (CO_2) are there in 176 g of carbon dioxide?

$$M_r = 12 + (2 \times 16) = 44$$
$$\text{molar mass of } CO_2 = 44\,g$$
$$\text{number of moles} = \frac{\text{mass of compound}}{\text{molar mass}} = 176/44 = \mathbf{4}$$

Measuring moles of gases

Sometimes we want to find the number of moles of a gas. This *can* be done by weighing, if we know the relative molecular mass of the gas. But it is easier to measure gases by *volume* than by mass.

Fortunately there is a simple rule that we can use (figure 5.2).

1 mole of any gas occupies 24 dm³ (24 litres) at room temperature and pressure.

This rule applies to *all* gases. This makes it easy to convert moles of gas to volumes, and volumes to moles.

The general formula to use is:

$$\text{number of moles of gas} = \frac{\text{volume of gas in dm}^3 \text{ at room temperature and pressure}}{24 \text{ dm}^3}$$

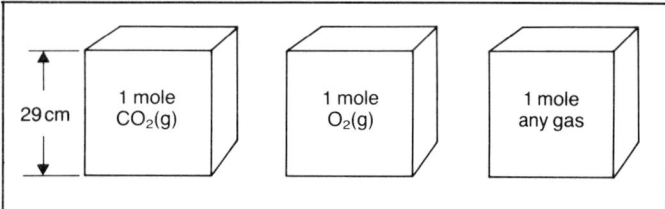

Figure 5.2 1 mole of any gas occupies 24 dm³ at room temperature and pressure. This is the volume of a cube with each side about 29 cm long.

Example:
1. How many moles of carbon dioxide are there in 72 dm³ of the gas at room temperature and pressure?

$$\text{number of moles of } CO_2 = \frac{\text{volume of } CO_2 \text{ in } dm^3}{24\ dm^3} = \frac{72}{24} = \mathbf{3}$$

Measuring out moles of substances in solution

In chemistry we often use solutions of substances in water. It is useful to know how many moles of the solute there are in a certain volume of the solution.

To do this, we need to know the **concentration** of the solution. Concentration is usually measured in moles per cubic decimetre (mol/dm³). Remember, 1 dm³ = 1 litre = 1000 cm³.

A solution of concentration 1 mol/dm³ has one mole of solute dissolved in 1 dm³ of solution. A solution of concentration 0.1 mol/dm³ has 0.1 mole of solute dissolved in 1 dm³ of solution (figure 5.3). The symbol 'M' is sometimes used to represent the unit mol/dm³. For example, a solution of concentration 2 mol/dm³ is sometimes said to be 2M.

Knowing the concentration, it is possible to work out the number of moles in a particular volume of solution.

$$\text{Number of moles} = \frac{\text{concentration of}}{\text{solution in mol/dm}^3} \times \frac{\text{volume of}}{\text{solution in dm}^3}$$

Examples:
1. The dilute hydrochloric acid (HCl(aq)) used in school laboratories usually has a concentration of 2 mol/dm³. How many moles of HCl are there in 250 cm³ of this acid?

   $250\ cm^3 = 0.25\ dm^3$
   number of moles = concentration × volume in dm³
   number of moles = 2 × 0.25 = **0.5**

2. A solution of sodium hydroxide contains 0.1 mole in 1 dm³. What volume of this solution would contain 1 mole?
   There is 0.1 mole in 1 dm³
   ⇒ There is 1 mole in (1/0.1)dm³ = **10 dm³**

Concentrations measured in g/dm³

Sometimes the concentration of a solution is given in grams per cubic decimetre (g/dm³). This is not as useful as having the concentration in moles per cubic decimetre, because different solutes have different relative molecular masses.

However, it is quite simple to convert concentrations in g/dm³ to mol/dm³, provided you know the molar mass of the solute.

$$\text{concentration in mol/dm}^3 = \frac{\text{concentration in g/dm}^3}{\text{molar mass}}$$

Example: The concentration of a solution of sulphuric acid (H_2SO_4) is 9.8 g/dm³. What is its concentration in mol/dm³? (A_r: H = 1; S = 32; O = 16)

molar mass of H_2SO_4 = 98 g/mol

$$\text{concentration in mol/dm}^3 = \frac{\text{concentration in g/dm}^3}{\text{molar mass}}$$

= 9.8/98 mol/dm³
= 0.1 mol/dm³

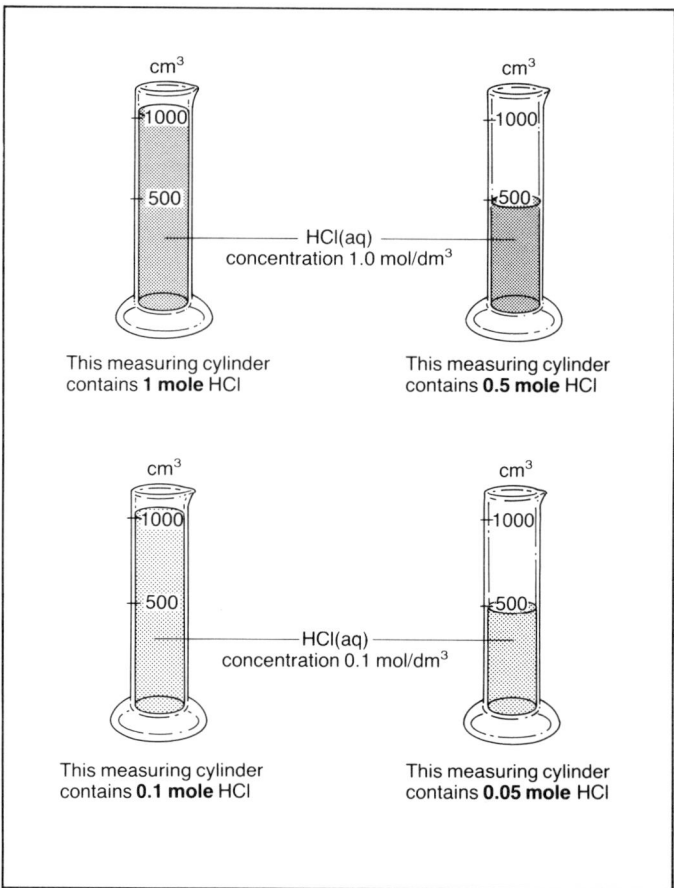

Figure 5.3

Finding formulas

The formula of a compound shows the number of atoms of each element in the compound. It also shows the number of *moles* of each element in the compound.

Example: The formula of methane is CH_4. This means:
- one molecule of methane contains one carbon atom and four hydrogen atoms;
- one mole of methane contains one mole of carbon (C) and four moles of hydrogen (H).

The masses of elements present in a compound can be found experimentally. These masses can then be used to work out the formula. This is done by calculating the number of moles of each element present.

Example – An experiment to find the formula of magnesium oxide: A piece of magnesium ribbon weighing 0.24 g was heated strongly in a crucible (figure 5.4). It burned, forming magnesium oxide. The mass of magnesium oxide formed was 0.40 g. What is the formula of magnesium oxide?

mass of magnesium oxide = 0.24 g
mass of oxygen combined with the magnesium = (0.40 − 0.24) g = 0.16 g

We can find the numbers of moles of magnesium and oxygen in these masses by using the formula:

$$\text{number of moles} = \frac{\text{mass}}{\text{molar mass}}$$

For the magnesium,

number of moles = 0.24/24 = 0.01

For the oxygen,

number of moles = 0.16/16 = 0.01

Therefore, the magnesium oxide contained 0.01 moles of magnesium and 0.01 moles of oxygen. This is a 1 : 1 ratio, so the formula of magnesium oxide is MgO.

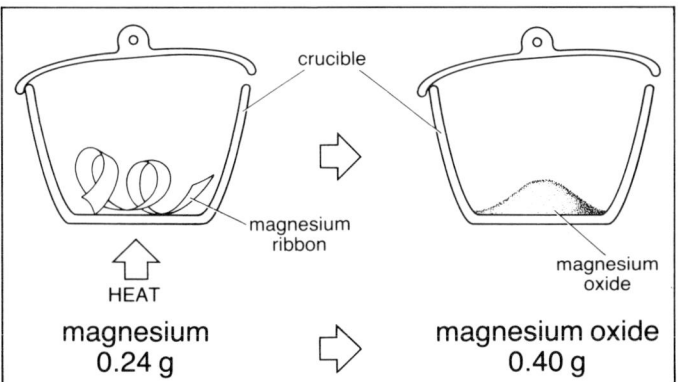

Figure 5.4 *Finding the formula of magnesium oxide.*

It is helpful to set out this kind of calculation in a table. Table 5.2 summarises the calculation we have done for magnesium oxide.

Table 5.2 *Finding the formula of magnesium oxide.*

	Mg	O
Combining mass	0.24 g	0.16 g
Molar mass	24 g	16 g
⇒Number of moles	0.01	0.01
⇒Simplest ratio	1 :	1
⇒Formula	MgO	

Here is another example to illustrate the use of the table.

Example: A hydrocarbon was analysed. It was found to contain 43 g of carbon combined with 7.2 g of hydrogen. Find the formula of the hydrocarbon.

	C	O
Combining mass	43 g	7.2 g
Molar mass	12 g	1 g
Number of moles	3.58	7.2
Simplest ratio	1 :	2
Formula	CH_2	

As a matter of fact, the formula CH_2 calculated in the last example does not exist as a compound. But compounds with formulas C_2H_4, C_3H_6, C_4H_8 and so on *do* exist. For each of these compounds, the formula can be reduced to the simplest ratio CH_2. This 'simplest ratio' formula is called the **empirical formula** (see page 21). The formula which shows the *actual* number of atoms in one molecule is the **molecular formula.**

Example: Ethene is an important hydrocarbon. Experiments show that the empirical formula of ethene is CH_2. The relative molecular mass of ethene is 28. What is its molecular formula? (C = 12; H = 1).

The molecular formula *could* be C_2H_4, C_3H_6, C_4H_8, etc. Knowing the relative molecular mass is 28, we can decide which of these it is.

relative molecular mass of CH_2 = (12 + 2) = 14
relative molecular mass of ethene = 28

Ethene must have twice as many of each type of atom as CH_2, therefore ethene is C_2H_4.

Chemical equations and moles

When we write a balanced chemical equation, we are showing the numbers of moles involved in the chemical reaction.

Examples:
1. The equation   Fe + S → FeS   tells us that:
   1 mole of iron reacts with 1 mole of sulphur to give 1 mole of iron sulphide.

2. The equation $N_2 + 3H_2 \rightarrow 2NH_3$ tells us that:
   1 mole of nitrogen reacts with 3 moles of hydrogen to give 2 moles of ammonia.

Once we know the equation for a reaction, we can use the mole idea to work out the *quantities* of different chemicals involved. For example, we could use the first equation above to work out the mass of iron sulphide that could be formed from 5.6 g of iron (figure 5.5).

The next three sections explain how these sort of calculations can be done. The general method is the same in each case:

STEP 1. First convert the given data to moles.
STEP 2. Work out the answer in moles.
STEP 3. Convert the answer in moles to the units you need.

Calculations involving reacting masses

Many chemical calculations involve working out the masses of the reactants or the products. In this type of calculation, we need to know the molar masses involved, so we can convert masses to moles and back.
Remember:

$$\text{number of moles} = \frac{\text{mass of substance}}{\text{molar mass}}$$

Examples:
1. What mass of iron sulphide (FeS) can be formed from 5.6 g of iron? (Assume there is more than enough sulphur to react with the iron.) (A_r: Fe = 56; S = 32)

   STEP 1 First convert the given data to moles.
   molar mass of iron = 56 g/mol

   $$\text{number of moles} = \frac{\text{mass of iron}}{\text{molar mass}}$$

   = 5.6/56 mole = 0.1 mole

   STEP 2 Work out the answer in moles.
   The equation tells us:
   1 mole Fe → 1 mole FeS
   ⇒ 0.1 mole Fe → 0.1 mole FeS

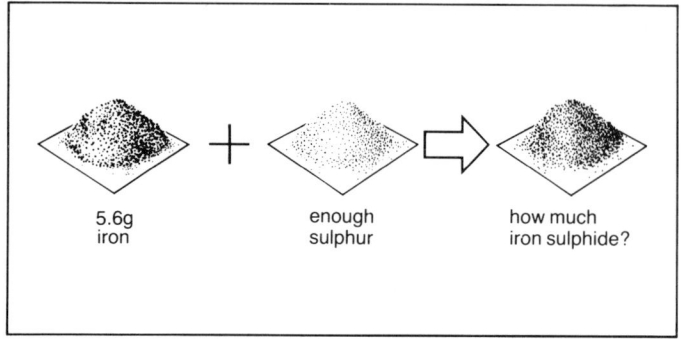

Figure 5.5

   STEP 3 Convert the answer in moles to the units you need.
   molar mass of FeS = 56 + 32 = 88 g/mol
   0.1 mole FeS is (0.1 × 88) g = **8.8 g**

2. What mass of aluminium can be made by electrolysis of 1 kg of pure aluminium oxide (Al_2O_3)?
   (A_r: Al = 27; O = 16)

   $$2Al_2O_3 \rightarrow 4Al + 3O_2$$

   STEP 1 First convert the given data to moles.
   molar mass of Al_2O_3 = 102 g/mol
   1 kg Al_2O_3 = 1000 g Al_2O_3 = 1000/102 mole = 9.8 mole

   STEP 2 Work out the answer in moles.
   The equation tells us:

   2 moles Al_2O_3 → 4 moles Al
   ⇒ 1 mole Al_2O_3 → 2 moles Al
   ⇒ 9.8 moles Al_2O_3 → 19.6 moles Al

   STEP 3 Convert the answer in moles to the units you need.
   molar mass of Al = 27 g/mol
   ⇒ 19.6 moles Al = (19.6 × 27) g = **529 g**

Calculations involving gas volumes

For calculations involving gas volumes, the general steps are the same. But remember to use the fact that 1 mole of gas occupies 24 dm^3 at room temperature and pressure.

Examples:
1. 10 g of calcium carbonate ($CaCO_3$) were heated strongly in a lime kiln. All the calcium carbonate decomposed to calcium oxide (CaO) and carbon dioxide (CO_2).

   $$CaCO_3 (s) \rightarrow CaO (s) + CO_2(g)$$

What volume of carbon dioxide, measured at room temperature and pressure, would be formed? (A_r: Ca = 40; C = 12; O = 16. 1 mole of carbon dioxide occupies 24 dm^3 at room temperature and pressure.)

STEP 1 **First convert the given data to moles.**
molar mass of CaCO$_3$ = 100 g/mol
10 g CaCO$_3$ = 10/100 mole = 0.1 mole

STEP 2 **Work out the answer in moles.**
The equation tells us:
1 mole CaCO$_3$ → 1 mole CO$_2$
⇒ 0.1 mole CaCO$_3$ → 0.1 mole CO$_2$

STEP 3 **Convert the answer in moles to the units you need.**
1.0 mole CO$_2$ occupies 24 dm^3
⇒ 0.1 mole occupies (0.1 × 24) dm^3 = **2.4 dm^3**

2 4.8 dm^3 of hydrogen (measured at room temperature and pressure) was burned in an excess of oxygen. What mass of water would be formed? (A_r: H = 1; O = 16; 1 mole of hydrogen occupies 24 dm^3 at room temperature and pressure)

$$2H_2(g) + O_2(g) \rightarrow 2H_2O(l)$$

STEP 1 **First convert the given data to moles.**
1 mole of H$_2$(g) = 24 dm^3
⇒ 4.8 dm^3 = 4.8/24 mole = 0.2 mole

STEP 2 **Work out the answer in moles.**
The equation tells us:
2 moles H$_2$ → 2 moles H$_2$O
⇒ 0.2 moles H$_2$ → 0.2 moles H$_2$O

STEP 3 **Convert the answer in moles to the units you need.**
molar mass of H$_2$O = 18 g/mol
⇒ 0.2 moles = (0.2 × 18) g = **3.6 g**

Calculations involving reacting volumes of solutions

In chemistry we often do reactions using solutions of substances. If we know the concentration of the solution, we can find the reacting quantities using the same general method as before.

Examples:
1 Sulphuric acid (H$_2$SO$_4$) reacts with magnesium to give magnesium sulphate, MgSO$_4$, and hydrogen.

$$Mg(s) + H_2SO_4(aq) \rightarrow MgSO_4(aq) + H_2(g)$$

A solution of dilute sulphuric acid has concentration 1 mol/dm^3. What volume of this solution would be just enough to react with 12 g of magnesium? (A_r: Mg = 24)

STEP 1 **First convert the given data to moles.**
molar mass of magnesium = 24 g/mol
⇒ 12 g Mg = 12/24 mole = 0.5 mole

STEP 2 **Work out the answer in moles.**
The equation tells us 1 mole of Mg reacts with 1 mole of H$_2$SO$_4$
⇒ 0.5 mole Mg reacts with 0.5 mole of H$_2$SO$_4$.

STEP 3 **Convert the answer in moles to the units you need.**
Concentration of sulphuric acid is 1 mol/dm^3
⇒ 0.5 mole is contained in 0.5 dm^3 = **500 cm^3**

2 A solution of dilute hydrochloric acid (HCl (aq)) contains 0.02 mol/dm^3. A solution of sodium hydroxide (NaOH(aq)) contains 0.1 mol/dm^3. The two solutions can be used to neutralise one another, forming sodium chloride and water.

$$HCl(aq) + NaOH(aq) \rightarrow NaCl(aq) + H_2O(l)$$

What volume of the hydrochloric acid solution would react with 10 cm^3 of the sodium hydroxide solution?

STEP 1 **Convert the given data to moles.**
10 cm^3 = 0.01 dm^3
number of moles of NaOH = concentration × volume in dm^3
⇒ number of moles = (0.1 × 0.01) mole
= 0.001 mole

STEP 2 **Work out the answer in moles.**
The equation tells us 1 mole NaOH reacts with 1 mole HCl
⇒ 0.001 mole NaOH reacts with 0.001 mole HCl.

STEP 3 **Convert the answer in moles to the units you need.**
Concentration of HCl is 0.02 mol/dm^3
⇒ 0.02 mole is contained in 1 dm^3
⇒ 0.001 mole is contained in 0.05 dm^3 = **50 cm^3**.

Notice that there is a simpler way of getting this answer. We could have just said:

1 mole of NaOH reacts with 1 mole of HCl. But the NaOH is five times more concentrated than the HCl (0.1 mol/dm^3 compared with 0.02 mol/dm^3). Therefore we will need five times the volume of HCl to get the same number of moles as NaOH.

⇒ volume of HCl needed = 5 × 10 cm^3 = **50 cm^3**

30 Chemical calculations

• Self test

Questions 1–4
The graph below shows the masses of bromine and copper which combine to form a compound.

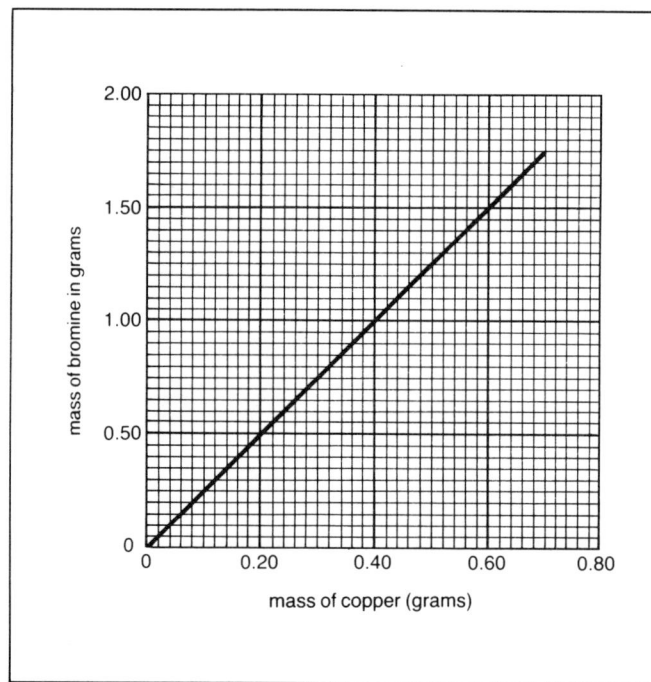

1. What mass of copper combines with 0.60 g of bromine?
   A 0.24 g **B** 0.30 g **C** 0.60 g **D** 1.50 g

2. What mass of compound will be formed from 0.30 g of copper?
   A 0.60 g **B** 0.75 g **C** 0.90 g **D** 1.05 g

3. An experiment shows that 1.60 g of bromine combines with 0.64 g of copper. How many moles of bromine (Br) combine with 64 g of copper? (Cu = 64, Br = 80)
   A 1.0 **B** 2.0 **C** 2.5 **D** 160

4. What is the formula of the compound formed?
   A Cu_2Br **B** $CuBr_4$ **C** $CuBr_2$ **D** $CuBr$

5. A solution of X has a concentration of 1 mole per dm^3. This means that the solution contains 1 mole of X in
   A 1 mole of solvent. **B** 1 dm^3 of solvent.
   C 1 mole of solution. **D** 1 dm^3 of solution.

6. Atoms of element X are one-third as heavy as atoms of potassium (K = 39). The relative atomic mass of X is therefore
   A 13 **B** 39 **C** 52 **D** 117

7. What is the order of *increasing* relative molecular mass for nitrogen (N_2), ammonia (NH_3) and neon (Ne)? (H = 1, N = 14, Ne = 20)
   A Ne, N_2 NH_3 **B** N_2, Ne, NH_3
   C NH_3, Ne, N_2 **D** NH_3, N_2, Ne

8. Two moles of the element Y react with three moles of Br_2. The empirical formula of the product is therefore
   A YBr_3. **B** Y_2Br_6. **C** Y_2Br_3. **D** Y_3Br_2.

9. Ammonium nitrate (NH_4NO_3) can be dissolved in water and used as a fertiliser at a concentration of 0.1 mole per dm^3. The number of grams of NH_4NO_3 per dm^3 of solution is (N = 14, H = 1, O = 16):
   A $\frac{0.1}{80}$ **B** 0.1×80 **C** $\frac{80}{0.1}$ **D** 0.1×66

Questions 10–12
Biogas contains 32 per cent by mass of methane. The equation for the complete combustion of methane is:

$$CH_4 + 2O_2 \rightarrow CO_2 + 2H_2O$$

10. What is the mass of methane in 1 kg of biogas?
11. What is the mass of carbon dioxide produced by complete combustion of this mass of methane? (H = 1, C = 12, O = 16)
12. What volume of oxygen reacts with 16 g of methane at room temperature and pressure? (1 mole of gas occupies 24 dm^3 at room temperature and pressure.)

Questions 13–18
Iron is manufactured by reducing iron ore in a blast furnace. Iron ore is mainly iron oxide (Fe_2O_3). The reducing agent is carbon monoxide (CO). The equation for the reaction is:

$$Fe_2O_3 + 3CO \rightarrow 2Fe + 3CO_2$$

(Fe = 56, C = 12, O = 16)

13. How many moles of Fe are produced from 1 mole of Fe_2O_3?
14. What is the mass of 1 mole of Fe_2O_3?
15. How many moles of Fe_2O_3 are there in 80 g of Fe_2O_3?
16. How many moles of Fe would be formed from 80 g of Fe_2O_3?
17. What mass of Fe would be produced from 80 g of Fe_2O_3?
18. What mass of Fe would be produced from 80 tonnes of Fe_2O_3?

6 Electrical currents and electrolysis

Electrical currents cause lightning flashes, they form the 'messages' which travel through our nerves and they enable us to use thousands of electrical gadgets. Using electricity, we can also decompose compounds by electrolysis and manufacture elements including aluminium, copper and chlorine.

Inside atoms

Atoms are composed of three particles – protons, neutrons and electrons. These are the building blocks for atoms. The centre of the atom, called the **nucleus**, contains protons and neutrons. **Protons** and **neutrons** have roughly the same mass but protons are positively charged and neutrons have no charge. **Electrons** are much smaller and lighter. They are negatively charged and occupy the outer parts of the atom. The negative charge on one electron just balances the positive charge on one proton. Thus atoms have equal numbers of protons and electrons (figure 6.1).

Electric currents

In metals, like copper, iron and aluminium, the electrons in the outer parts of the atoms can move from one atom to another. This makes metals **electrical conductors**. When these metal conductors are connected to a battery, electrons are attracted to the positive terminal of the battery as more electrons are repelled into the metal from the negative terminal (figure 6.2).

An electrical current is simply a flow of electrons.

Because of these properties, metals are used for cables, fuses and wiring in electrical machinery. On the other hand, plastics such as polythene and PVC are used as insulators because they do not allow electrons to move through them and they do not conduct electricity.

A few substances with special conducting properties are called **semiconductors**. Silicon and germanium containing a trace of impurity are two of the best-known semiconductors. These substances provide a very high resistance to the flow of electrons in one direction and a very low resistance to the flow of electrons in the other direction. Devices made with semiconductors of this kind form an important part of any transistor.

Which solids conduct electricity?

The circuit in figure 6.3 can be used to test whether a solid conducts electricity.

- Experiments show that **the only solids which conduct electricity well are metals and graphite.** No solid compound will conduct electricity. This experiment is therefore a good way of testing for metals.

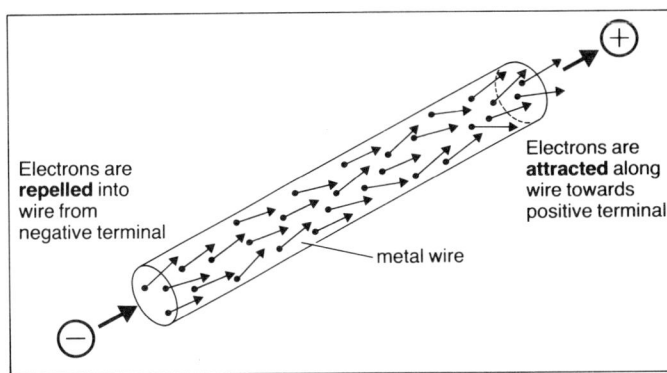

Figure 6.2 *An electrical current is a flow of negatively charged electrons.*

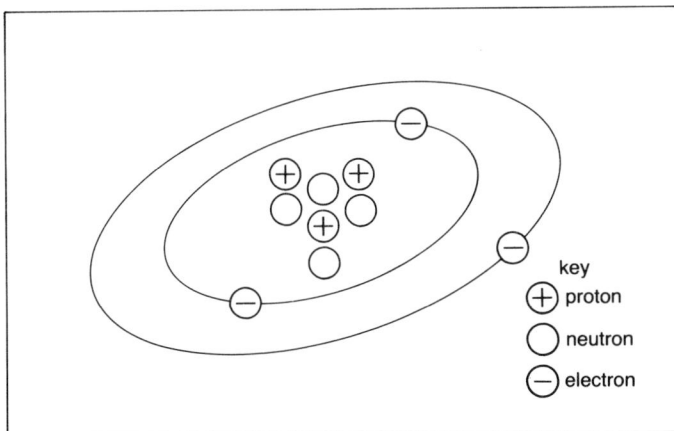

Figure 6.1 *Protons, neutrons and electrons in a lithium atom.*

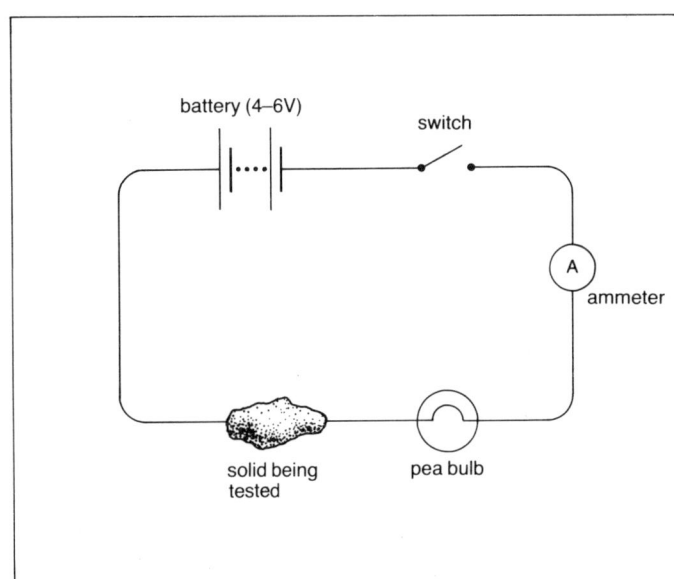

Figure 6.3 *Testing the conductivity of a solid.*

32 Electrical currents and Electrolysis

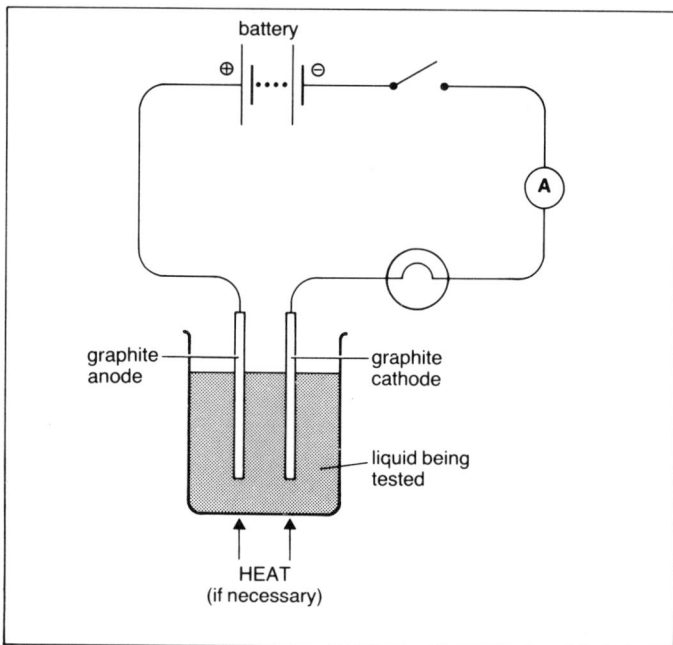

Figure 6.4 *Testing the conductivity of a liquid.*

Which liquids conduct electricity?

The circuit in figure 6.4 can be used to test whether different liquids conduct electricity. The results of tests on various substances are summarised in table 6.1. The experiments show that:
- metal/non-metal compounds conduct electricity as pure liquids and in aqueous solution;
- non-metal compounds do not conduct electricity as pure liquids or in aqueous solution (except aqueous solutions of acids).

When metal/non-metal compounds conduct electricity they are decomposed by the electric current. For example, when molten sodium chloride conducts electricity, it is decomposed into sodium and chlorine.

The decomposition of a substance, such as sodium chloride, by electricity is called **electrolysis**. The compound that is decomposed is called an **electrolyte**. The terminals through which the current enters and leaves the electrolyte are called **electrodes**. The electrode connected to the positive terminal of the battery is called the **anode**. The electrode connected to the negative terminal of the battery is called the **cathode**.

How do electrolytes conduct electricity?

When molten sodium chloride conducts electricity, sodium forms at the cathode and chlorine forms at the anode. Sodium particles in the electrolyte must be positive because they are attracted to the negative cathode. Chloride particles in the electrolyte must be negative because they are attracted to the positive anode.

The formula of sodium chloride is NaCl, so we can think of this as Na^+ particles and Cl^- particles. Charged particles, like Na^+ and Cl^-, which move to the electrodes during electrolysis are called **ions**.

When Na^+ ions reach the cathode, they combine with negative electrons on the cathode to form neutral sodium atoms.

$$Na^+ \quad + \quad e^- \quad \rightarrow \quad Na$$
sodium ion in electrolyte — electron from cathode — sodium atom

When Cl^- ions reach the anode, they lose their extra electron to the positive anode leaving a chlorine atom.

$$Cl^- \quad \rightarrow \quad e^- \quad + \quad Cl$$
chloride ion in electrolyte — electron given to anode — chlorine atom

In this way, Na^+ ions take electrons from the cathode, whilst Cl^- ions give up electrons to the anode. The electric current is being carried through the molten sodium chloride by Na^+ and Cl^- ions.

Investigating electrolysis

How can we investigate the products at the electrodes when aqueous solutions are electrolysed? Figure 6.5

Table 6.1 *The conduction of electricity by liquids.*

	Metal/non-metal compounds	Non-metal compounds (except acids)	Acids
Examples	Sodium chloride (NaCl) Copper sulphate ($CuSO_4$) Lead bromide ($PbBr_2$)	Water (H_2O) Ethanol (C_2H_6O) Tetrachloromethane (CCl_4) Sugar ($C_{12}H_{22}O_{11}$)	Acetic acid (CH_3COOH) Sulphuric acid (H_2SO_4) Nitric acid (HNO_3)
Does the pure liquid conduct?	Yes	No	No
Does the aqueous solution conduct?	Yes	No	Yes

Investigating electrolysis

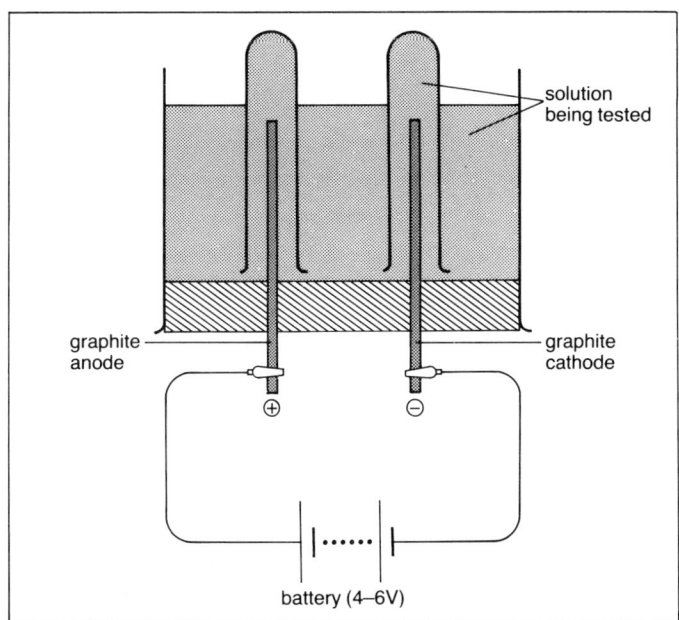

Figure 6.5 *Investigating the products at the electrodes.*

shows the apparatus that can be used. The results of six experiments are shown in table 6.2. These show that:
- metals and hydrogen are produced at the cathode and so metals and hydrogen have positive ions (cations);
- non-metals (except hydrogen) are produced at the anode and so non-metals (except hydrogen) have negative ions (anions).

Measuring the amount of charge on an ion

How much charge is required to deposit 1 mole of copper (63.5 g) when copper sulphate is electrolysed? This can be measured using the apparatus in figure 6.6. Here are the results of one experiment.

mass of dry copper cathode before electrolysis = 54.47 g
mass of dry copper cathode after electrolysis = 54.56 g
mass of copper deposited = 0.09 g
time of electrolysis = 45 min = 2700 seconds
current = charge per second = 0.1 A = 0.1 coulombs per second

Table 6.2 *Products at the electrodes during electrolysis.*

Solution tested	Product at anode	Product at cathode
Sulphuric acid	Oxygen	Hydrogen
Sodium chloride	Chlorine	Hydrogen
Copper sulphate	Oxygen	Copper
Zinc bromide	Bromine	Zinc
Potassium iodide	Iodine	Hydrogen
Silver nitrate	Oxygen	Silver

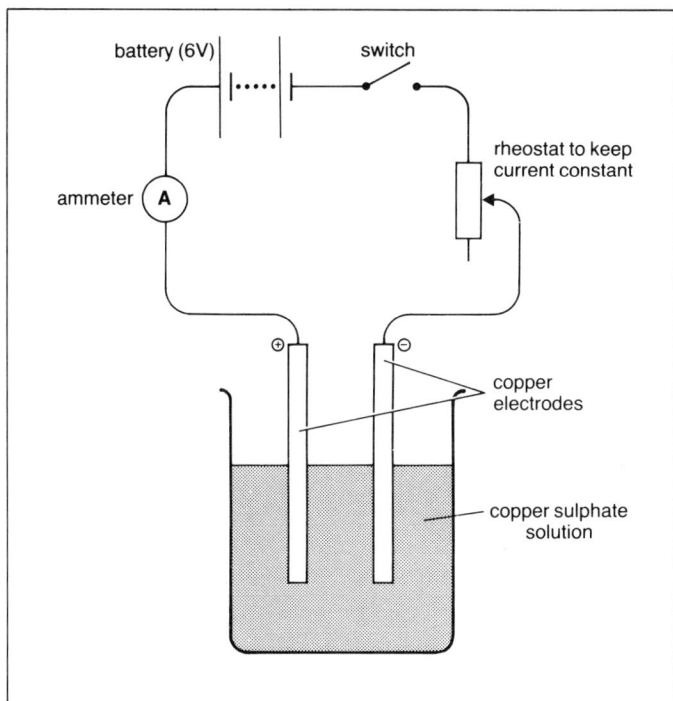

Figure 6.6 *Measuring the amount of charge which deposits 1 mole of copper.*

$$\therefore \text{quantity of charge used} = \text{current} \times \text{time}$$
$$= 0.1 \times 2700$$
$$= 270 \text{ coulombs}$$

So, 0.09 g of copper are deposited by 270 coulombs

$\therefore$ 1 g of copper is deposited by $270/0.09$ coulombs
$\Rightarrow$ 1 mole of copper (63.5 g) is deposited by $270/0.09 \times 63.5$ coulombs
$= 190\,500$ coulombs

Accurate experiments show that one mole of copper is deposited by 193 000 coulombs. Table 6.3 shows the quantity of charge required to produce 1 mole of atoms of five different elements. Notice that twice as much charge is required to produce 1 mole of copper as 1 mole of sodium. This means the copper ion must carry twice as much charge as a sodium ion. Because of this, the copper ion is written as Cu^{2+} and the sodium ion as Na^+. Three times as much charge is required for aluminium, so the aluminium ion is written as Al^{3+}.

Table 6.3 *The quantity of charge required to produce 1 mole of some elements.*

Element	Number of coulombs required to produce 1 mole of atoms
Copper	193 000
Sodium	96 500
Silver	96 500
Lead	193 000
Aluminium	289 500

34 Electrical currents and Electrolysis

Table 6.4 *The charges on some common ions.*

Positive ions			Negative ions	
+1	+2	+3	−1	−2
Hydrogen H^+ Sodium Na^+ Potassium K^+ Silver Ag^+	Calcium Ca^{2+} Copper Cu^{2+} Iron(II) Fe^{2+} Lead Pb^{2+} Magnesium Mg^{2+} Nickel Ni^{2+} Zinc Zn^{2+}	Aluminium Al^{3+} Iron(III) Fe^{3+} Chromium Cr^{3+}	Hydroxide OH^- Nitrate NO_3^- Chloride Cl^- Bromide Br^- Iodide I^-	Oxide O^{2-} Sulphide S^{2-} Carbonate CO_3^{2-} Sulphate SO_4^{2-} Sulphite SO_3^{2-}

Table 6.4 shows some ions with their charges.
- **Most metals have a charge of 2+.** The only common metal ions with a different charge are Ag^+, Na^+, K^+, Cr^{3+}, Al^{3+} and Fe^{3+}.

The quantity of charge needed to produce one mole of atoms is always a multiple of 96 500 coulombs (i.e. 96 500, 193 000 or 289 500). Because of this, 96 500 coulombs is called the **Faraday constant** (F), in honour of Michael Faraday. Faraday was the first scientist to measure the masses of elements produced during electrolysis. 96 500 coulombs is the amount of charge carried by 1 mole of electrons (6×10^{23} electrons).

Ionic compounds

Salt, lime, limestone and fertilisers all contain ions. They are called **ionic compounds**.

Forming ionic compounds – electron transfer

Ionic compounds form when metals react with non-metals. For example, when sodium reacts with chlorine the elements combine to form sodium chloride which contains Na^+ and Cl^- ions.

$$Na + Cl \rightarrow Na^+Cl^-$$

During the reaction each sodium atom gives up one electron. The electron is taken up by a chlorine atom to form a chloride ion.

$$Na \rightarrow Na^+ + e^-$$
$$Cl + e^- \rightarrow Cl^-$$

Other ionic compounds form by **electron transfer** in the same way as sodium chloride. Metal atoms lose electrons and form positive ions (cations). Non-metals gain electrons and form negative ions (anions). There is more about the formation of ionic bonds by electron transfer on page 104.

Formulae and structure of ionic compounds

- Ionic compounds are held together by strong forces of attraction between positive and negative ions. This is called **ionic bonding (electrovalent bonding)**.

Strong ionic bonds hold the ions tightly together in the crystal and so *solid* ionic compounds cannot conduct electricity. But when they are *molten* (i.e. liquid), ionic compounds can conduct because now the ions are free to move.

In ionic compounds, the charges on the positive ions just balance the charges on the negative ions. This enables us to predict the formulas of ionic compounds. For example, the formula of aluminium oxide is Al_2O_3. In Al_2O_3, the charge on two Al^{3+} ions balances the charge on three O^{2-} ions.

X-ray analysis and electron microscope photographs show that the ions in ionic compounds are arranged in regular patterns. Sodium chloride (salt) and calcium oxide (lime) have a cubic structure of ions. Figure 6.7 shows the structure of sodium chloride. Although figure 6.7 shows only a few ions, there are millions in even the smallest crystal of sodium chloride. Because of this, ionic compounds are described as **giant ionic structures**. Ionic compounds like sodium chloride, are giant structures of ions in the same way that metals are giant structures of atoms (page 60). Each Na^+ ion in the structure attracts all the Cl^- ions around it, and vice versa.

Notice that each Na^+ ion in the structure is surrounded by six Cl^- ions, and each Cl^- ion is surrounded by six Na^+

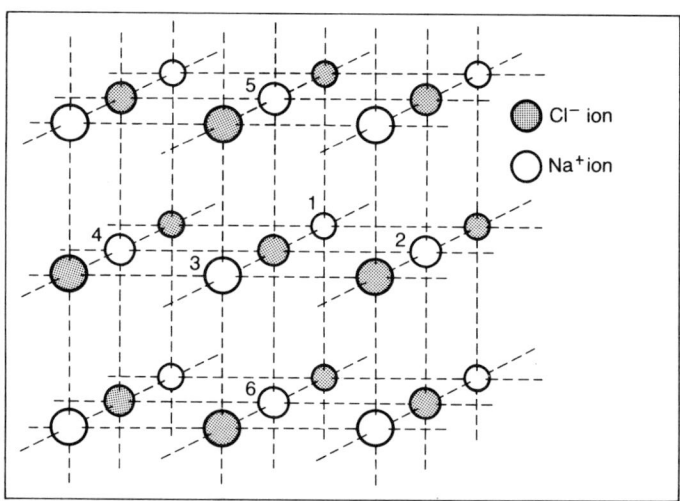

Figure 6.7 *The structure of sodium chloride. (Each dot shows the centre of an ion)*

ions. The six Na^+ ions around the central Cl^- ion in figure 6.7 are numbered from 1 to 6. Four of the Na^+ ions (numbered 1, 2, 3 and 4) are in the same horizontal layer as the central Cl^- ion. One Na^+ ion (number 5) is in the layer above. The sixth Na^+ ion (number 6) is in the layer below.

Forming molecular compounds – electron sharing

Metals *never* react with each other to form compounds. Unlike metals, two non-metals can react with each other and form a compound, even though they both want to gain electrons. These non-metal compounds consist of uncharged molecules. They do not contain ions. They are therefore called **molecular compounds**. Water (H_2O), carbon dioxide (CO_2) and sugar ($C_{12}H_{22}O_{11}$) are examples of simple molecular compounds.

When two non-metals react to form a molecule, their regions of electrons overlap. The positive nucleus of each atom then attracts the negative electrons in the region of overlap and this holds the atoms together. This type of bond formed by **electron sharing** is known as a **covalent bond** (figure 6.8). There is more about the formation of covalent bonds by electron sharing on page 104.

Covalent bonds hold the atoms together *within* a molecule. The bonds *between* different molecules are called **intermolecular bonds**. They hold the molecules together in molecular solids like sugar and molecular liquids like water. The strength of the intermolecular bonds determines the state of a substance. For example, carbon dioxide has very weak intermolecular bonds, so it is a gas at room temperature.

Properties of ionic and molecular compounds

Salt and sugar have very different properties because of their different structures and bonding. The differences between them are typical of the differences between ionic compounds and simple molecular compounds. These differences are shown in table 6.5.

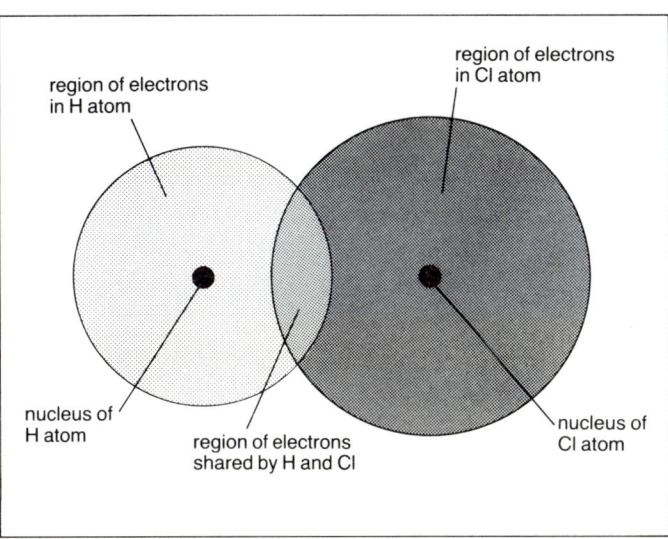

Figure 6.8 *A simple model of the structure of hydrogen chloride.*

Electrolysis in industry

Electrolysis is used in industry to manufacture certain chemicals. It is also used to manufacture and purify metals, and for electroplating.

Manufacturing chemicals by electrolysing sodium chloride solution

When sodium chloride solution (brine) is electrolysed, hydrogen is formed at the cathode and chlorine is formed at the anode. A solution of sodium hydroxide is left behind.

sodium chloride + water $\xrightarrow{electrolysis}$ hydrogen + chlorine + sodium hydroxide

$2NaCl(aq) + H_2O(l) \longrightarrow \underset{\text{at cathode}}{H_2(g)} + \underset{\text{at anode}}{Cl_2(g)} + \underset{\text{left behind}}{2NaOH(aq)}$

Table 6.5 *Typical properties of ionic and simple molecular compounds.*

	Ionic compounds	**Simple molecular compounds**
Examples	NaCl, CaO, $CuSO_4$	H_2O, $C_{12}H_{22}O_{11}$ (sugar), CO_2
Structure	Giant structure of ions	Separate small molecules
Bonding	Attraction of positive ions for negative ions – strong ionic bonds	Strong covalent bonds between atoms *within molecules*, weak intermolecular bonds *between separate molecules*
Properties Melting point	High – solids at room temperature	Low – usually liquids or gases at room temperature
Hardness	Hard solids	Soft when solid
Conduction of electricity	Conduct when liquid or aqueous, do *not* conduct when solid	Do *not* conduct when liquid, aqueous or solid

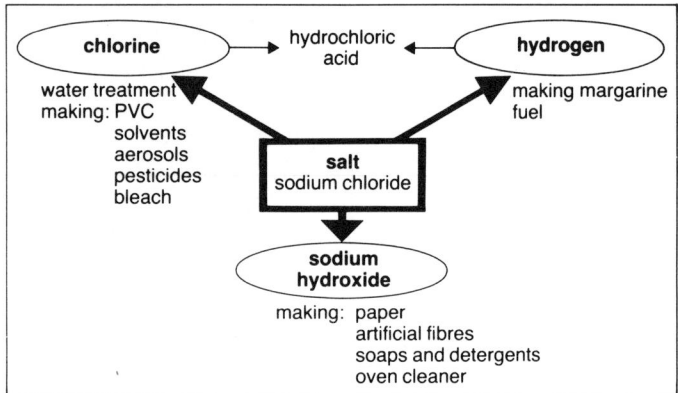

Figure 6.9 *Some uses of the chemicals made from salt.*

This is a very important industrial process. All three products have major industrial uses (figure 6.9). Notice that hydrogen and chlorine are used together to make hydrochloric acid, an important acid with many uses.

The process is carried out on a huge scale. The sodium chloride (salt) for the process can be obtained from the sea, or from underground salt deposits. In Britain, the major salt deposits are in Cheshire. The salt is obtained by pumping water underground to dissolve the salt, then pumping the brine back to the surface.

Manufacturing aluminium by electrolysis

Reactive metals, like aluminium, are manufactured by electrolysis of their molten compounds. These metals *cannot* be obtained by:
- electrolysis of their aqueous compounds; or
- reduction of their oxides with coke.

For example, aluminium is obtained by electrolysis of molten aluminium oxide obtained from bauxite (figure 6.10).

Aluminium ions are attracted to the carbon cathode lining the cell, where they accept electrons to form aluminium.

Cathode $(-)$ $Al^{3+} + 3e^- \rightarrow Al$

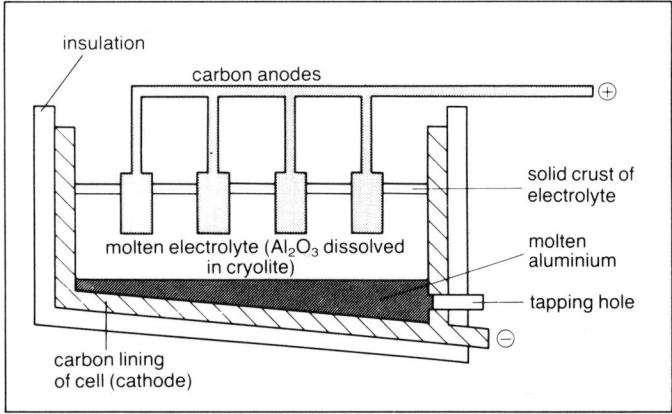

Figure 6.10 *The electrolytic cell for manufacturing aluminium.*

Oxide ions are attracted to the carbon anodes. Here, they give up electrons leaving oxygen atoms.

Anode $(+)$ $O^{2-} \rightarrow O + 2e^-$

The oxygen atoms then combine in pairs to form oxygen gas (O_2).

Purifying copper by electrolysis

Metals low in the activity series, like copper, can be purified by electrolysis of their aqueous solutions. For example, copper is purified by electrolysis of copper sulphate solution. Impure copper is used as the anode and the cathode is a sheet of pure copper (figure 6.11). Copper ions are attracted to the cathode from which they take electrons and deposit pure copper.

Cathode $(-)$ Cu^{2+} (aq) $+ 2e^- \rightarrow Cu(s)$

Sulphate ions are attracted to the anode, but they are *not* discharged. Instead, copper atoms in the impure anode go into solution as copper ions. Two electrons are left behind on the anode.

Anode $(+)$ $Cu(s) \rightarrow Cu^{2+}$ (aq) $+ 2e^-$

An electrolysis proceeds, the lump of impure copper at the anode dissolves away and pure copper deposits on the cathode.

Electroplating

The method described in the last section is also used for plating one metal on to another. If the cathode in figure 6.10 were made of steel, it would still get coated with copper. The steel bodywork of cars and bicycle frames are sometimes protected from corrosion by copper plating in this way. Car bumpers and kettles are protected in a similar way, but in this case a layer of chromium is plated on top of the metal to increase the protection and give a shiny finish.

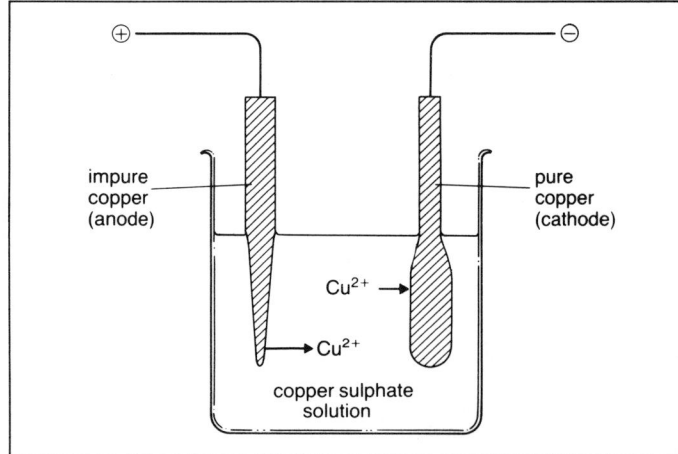

Figure 6.11 *Purifying copper by electrolysis.*

The metal coating is always deposited on the cathode, so the object to be plated must be the cathode during electrolysis. In addition, the electrolyte must contain ions of the metal that will form the coating.

Cells and batteries

Cells and batteries are a convenient source of electricity for calculators, watches, torches, radios, etc.

When a cell or a battery is used, a chemical change takes place and chemical energy is converted to electrical energy. This is the reverse of electrolysis, in which electrical energy is changed into chemical energy in the substances produced at the electrodes.

$$\text{chemical energy} \underset{\text{electrolysis}}{\overset{\text{use of cells/batteries}}{\rightleftarrows}} \text{electrical energy}$$

One of the most widely used simple cells is the **dry cell** (figure 6.12). When this is used, the zinc case acts as the negative terminal. The zinc gives up electrons, which form the electric current from the cell.

$$Zn \rightarrow Zn^{2+} + 2e^-$$

The positive terminal in the dry cell is the carbon rod and the powdered carbon around it. At this positive terminal, ammonium ions (NH_4^+) take electrons and form ammonia and hydrogen.

$$2NH_4^+ + 2e^- \rightarrow 2NH_3 + H_2$$

One dry cell can produce only 1.5 volts, but batteries containing many cells can give up to 100 volts.

Storage cells – accumulators

When dry cells produce electricity, materials in the cell are used up. The zinc casing becomes Zn^{2+} ions and eventually falls apart. Cells like this, which cannot be recharged and used again, are called **primary cells.** On the other hand, there are some cells that can be recharged and used again; these are called **secondary cells** or **accumulators**. Car batteries contain six lead–acid secondary cells connected in series. Each cell can produce about 2 volts, so the full battery gives 12 volts. The negative terminals are made of lead and the positive terminals are lead covered with lead (IV) oxide (PbO_2). The electrolyte is sulphuric acid.

When the lead–acid cells are used to produce electricity (**discharged**), reactions occur at the terminal. Chemical energy is changed into electrical energy.

When the battery is **recharged**, an electric current is forced through the cells in the opposite direction and the reactions at the terminals are reversed. This electrolysis changes electrical energy back into chemical energy. The lead–acid cell is then ready for use once again.

Figure 6.12 *A dry cell.*

Redox reactions and electron transfer

Whenever electrons are transferred from one atom to another, a redox (reduction–oxidation) reaction takes place.

On page 10, redox was described as the addition or removal of oxygen. When oxygen is added to a substance, the substance is oxidised. When oxygen is removed from a substance, the substance is reduced. But during redox, *electrons* are also transferred.

Consider the reaction of magnesium with oxygen:

$$\begin{array}{ccccc} \text{magnesium} & + & \text{oxygen} & \rightarrow & \text{magnesium oxide} \\ 2Mg & + & O_2 & \rightarrow & 2MgO \end{array}$$

The magnesium is oxidised and the oxygen is reduced.

During this reaction, two electrons are transferred from magnesium to oxygen. Magnesium ions and oxide ions are formed.

$$Mg \rightarrow Mg^{2+} + 2e^-$$
$$O + 2e^- \rightarrow O^{2-}$$

Magnesium, which is oxidised, loses electrons. Oxygen, which is reduced, gains electrons. So, we can say that:

Oxidation is the loss of electrons.
Reduction is the gain of electrons.

Figure 6.13 shows a simple way to remember this.

So we can look at redox in two ways – as loss and gain of oxygen, or as gain and loss of electrons.

OIL RIG helps you remember about redox

Oxidation
Is
Loss
} of electrons
Reduction
Is
Gain

Figure 6.13

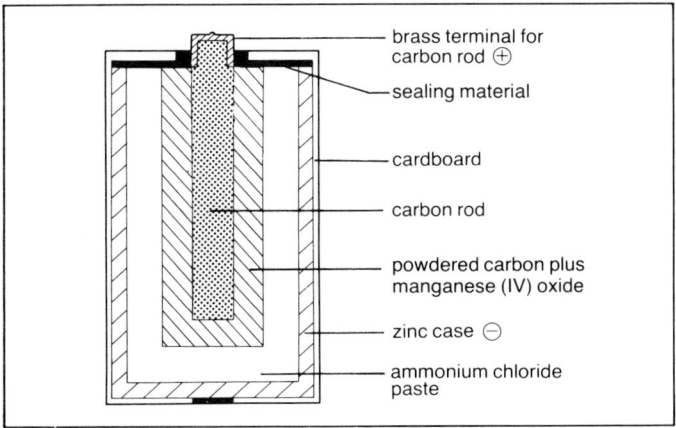

38 Electrical currents and Electrolysis

• Self test

Questions 1–2
The diagram below shows the electrolysis of concentrated sodium chloride solution.

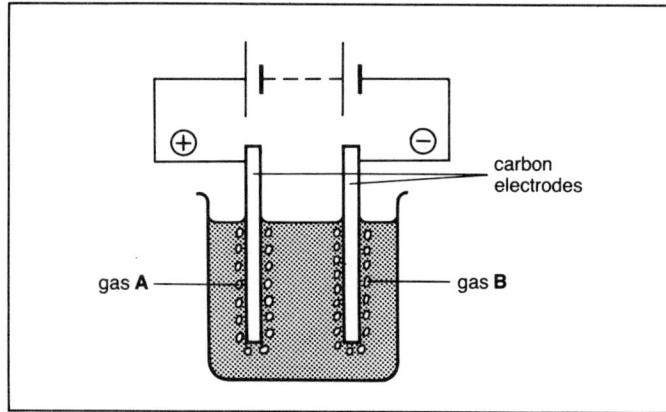

1. Gas A is
   - A carbon dioxide.
   - B chlorine.
   - C hydrogen.
   - D oxygen.

2. Gas B is
   - A carbon dioxide.
   - B chlorine.
   - C hydrogen.
   - D oxygen.

3. During electrolysis, electric charge is carried through the solution by
   - A atoms and ions.
   - B electrons and ions.
   - C electrons only.
   - D ions only.

4. Carbon anodes are used in the manufacture of aluminium by electrolysis of molten aluminium oxide. The carbon anodes wear away because the carbon reacts with
   - A aluminium.
   - B aluminium oxide.
   - C bauxite.
   - D oxygen.

Questions 5–9
From the list **A** to **E** below
- A calcium oxide (lime)
- B nickel
- C PVC
- D sugar
- E sulphur

choose the substance that
5. conducts electricity when solid or liquid.
6. conducts electricity when liquid, but not when solid.
7. is used as an insulator for electric wire.
8. is produced at the anode during electrolysis.
9. is a simple molecular compound.

Questions 10–13
From the list **A** to **E** below
- A electrode
- B electrolysis
- C electrolyte
- D electromagnet
- E electrovalent

choose the term that is used to describe
10. a bond between ions.
11. a solid conductor.
12. the breakdown of a substance by electricity.
13. a substance which is decomposed by electricity.

Questions 14–18
Complete the following passage by writing down words that would replace the numbers.

When a dry cell is used, ⑭ acts as the ⑮ terminal and gives up electrons which form the electric current.

A dry cell is an example of a ⑯ cell. When a dry cell is used ⑰ energy is converted to ⑱ energy.

7 The periodic table

Patterns in the properties of elements

If you collect stamps, your collection is probably divided into smaller sections containing all the stamps from one country. By arranging your stamps in this way, you know where the stamps on one page come from and what they will be like.

During the nineteenth century, chemists began to look closely at the properties of elements. They tried to group similar elements together in the same way that you might group similar stamps together. Most of the early classifications of the elements were very limited. Then, in 1869, the Russian chemist Dmitri Mendeléev put forward his periodic table. Mendeléev arranged the elements in a table in order of increasing relative atomic mass. He also arranged his table so that elements with similar properties were in the same vertical column. Mendeléev called his table a **'periodic table'** because elements with similar properties occurred periodically. Although the periodic table has been updated a little since Mendeléev's time, it is still the most important way of classifying elements.

The periodic table

A modern form of the periodic table is shown in figure 7.1. Notice the following points about the periodic table:

- Metals are clearly separated from non-metals. The 20 or so non-metals are all packed into the top right-hand corner above the thick stepped line in figure 7.1. A number of elements close to the steps have some properties like metals and some properties like non-metals. These elements are called **metalloids**.

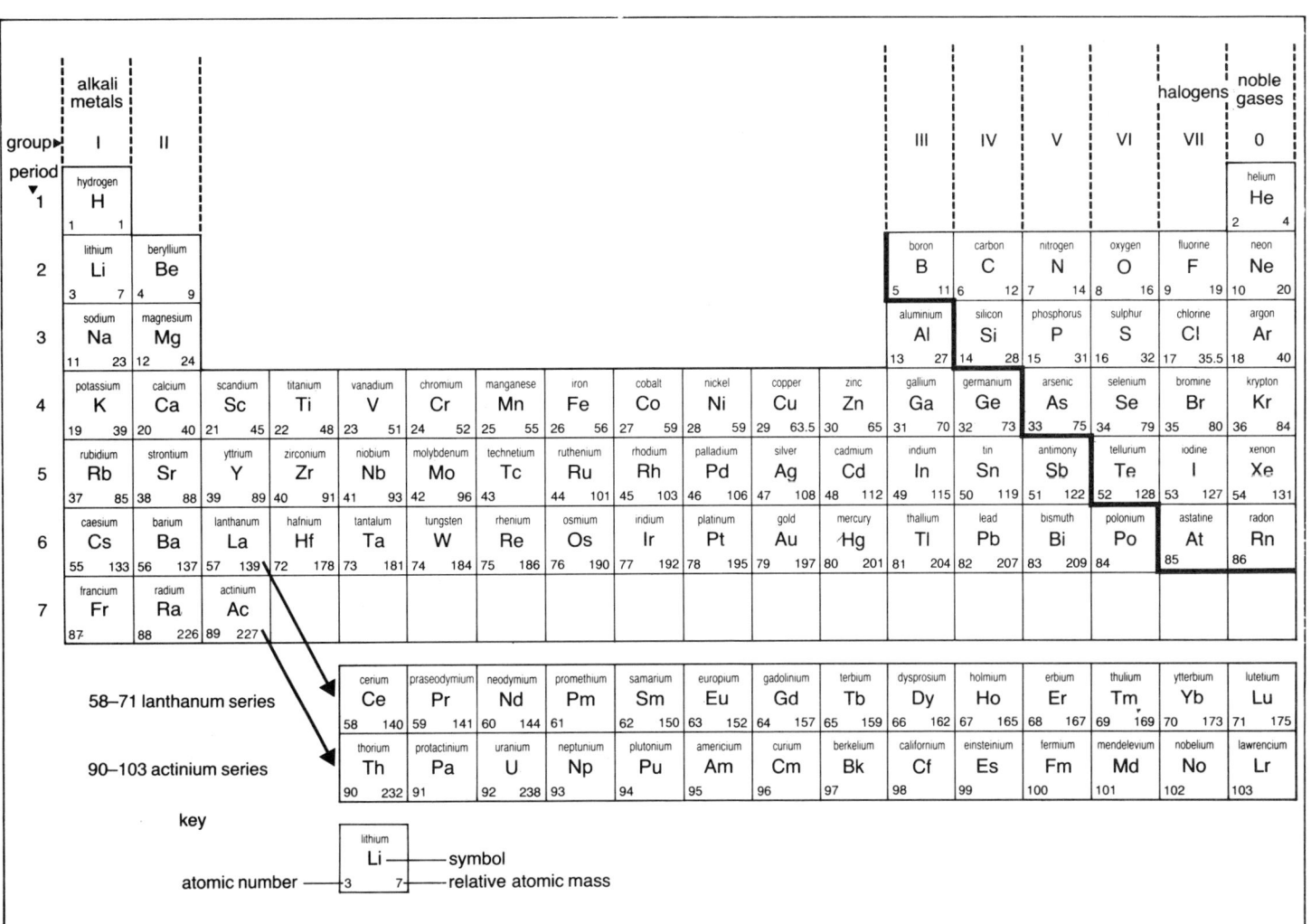

Figure 7.1 *The modern periodic table.*

- The vertical columns of similar elements are called **groups**. Some of these groups have names as well as numbers. For example, group I, which contains lithium, sodium and potassium, is called the **alkali metals**. Group VII, containing chlorine, bromine and iodine, is known as the **halogens**.
- Although the properties of the elements in one group are similar, they gradually change as you move down the group from one element to the next. Later in this section we shall study the changes in properties among the alkali metals, the halogens and the noble gases.
- The horizontal rows of elements in the table are called **periods**. Moving from left to right across a period, the elements change from reactive metals on the left (like sodium and potassium), through rather unreactive elements (like carbon and nitrogen) to reactive non-metals on the right (like oxygen and chlorine). Finally, there are the very unreactive noble gases in group 0.
- Reading across the table from left to right and from top to bottom, the elements are nearly always in order of relative atomic mass. There are, however, a few places in the periodic table where the elements are *not* in strict order of relative atomic mass. This is because the order of atomic masses would place them in the wrong group. For example, look at argon and potassium in figure 7.1. Argon ($A_r = 40$) is placed before potassium ($A_r = 39$), because argon is a noble gas and potassium is an alkali metal.
- The elements are numbered along each period, starting with period 1, then period 2, etc. The numbers are shown in the bottom left-hand corner of each box in figure 7.1. The number given to each element is called its **atomic number**. Thus, hydrogen has an atomic number of 1, helium 2, lithium 3, etc.

Group I – the alkali metals

The elements in group I are called alkali metals because they react with water to form alkaline solutions. The best-known alkali metals are lithium, sodium and potassium (figure 7.2).

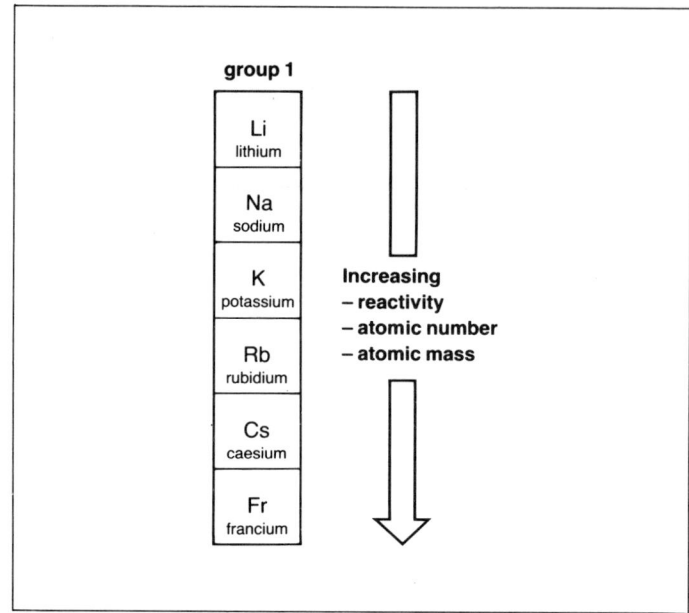

Figure 7.2 *The alkali metals.*

The alkali metals are so reactive that they must be stored under oil. This prevents them from reacting with oxygen and water vapour in the air. Alkali metals also have some other unusual properties:
- they float on water because their densities are less than 1 g/cm³;
- they are soft enough to cut with a knife;
- they melt and boil at very low temperatures compared with other metals.

Some of the chemical properties of lithium, sodium and potassium are summarised in table 7.1. Notice how the elements react in a similar way with air (oxygen).

$$\text{metal} + \text{oxygen} \rightarrow \text{metal oxide}$$

For example:

$$\text{sodium} + \text{oxygen} \rightarrow \text{sodium oxide}$$
$$4\text{Na} + \text{O}_2 \rightarrow 2\text{Na}_2\text{O}$$

Table 7.1 *Chemical properties of lithium, sodium and potassium.*

Element	Reaction with air	Reaction with water	Salts
Lithium	Tarnishes slowly to give an oxide layer: $4\text{Li} + \text{O}_2 \rightarrow 2\text{Li}_2\text{O}$	Reacts steadily to give $\text{H}_2(g)$ and an alkaline solution of LiOH(aq): $\text{Li} + \text{H}_2\text{O} \rightarrow \tfrac{1}{2}\text{H}_2 + \text{LiOH}$	All salts (chlorides, nitrates, carbonates, etc.) are white, ionic, solids, soluble in water
Sodium	Tarnishes rapidly to give an oxide layer: $4\text{Na} + \text{O}_2 \rightarrow 2\text{Na}_2\text{O}$	Reacts vigorously to give $\text{H}_2(g)$ and an alkaline solution of NaOH(aq): $\text{Na} + \text{H}_2\text{O} \rightarrow \tfrac{1}{2}\text{H}_2 + \text{NaOH}$	
Potassium	Tarnishes very rapidly to give an oxide layer: $4\text{K} + \text{O}_2 \rightarrow 2\text{K}_2\text{O}$	Reacts violently to give $\text{H}_2(g)$ and an alkaline solution of KOH(aq): $\text{K} + \text{H}_2\text{O} \rightarrow \tfrac{1}{2}\text{H}_2 + \text{KOH}$	

The elements also react in a similar manner with water:

metal + water → hydrogen + metal hydroxide

For example:

sodium + water → hydrogen + sodium hydroxide
Na + H_2O → ½H_2 + NaOH

Although these elements react in a similar way with air (oxygen) and water, the reactions get more vigorous from lithium to potassium. From the properties of lithium, sodium and potassium, we can make predictions about the properties of other alkali metals. This is one of the most important uses of the periodic table – predicting the properties of elements and their compounds.

The uses of alkali metals

The alkali metals are too reactive to have many uses. Liquid sodium is used as a coolant in some fast nuclear reactors and sodium vapour is used in yellow street lamps.

The transition metals

The **transition metals** lie in a broad rectangle between group II and group III in the periodic table (figure 7.3). All the transition metals have similar properties. The typical properties of transition metals like iron, copper, nickel and chromium are:
- high melting points and boiling points;
- high densities;
- hard with high tensile strength;
- fairly unreactive (none of them react with cold water);
- coloured compounds;
- form more than one kind of ion (e.g. iron has Fe^{2+} and Fe^{3+} ions; copper has Cu^+ and Cu^{2+} ions);
- show catalytic properties (transition metals and their compounds can act as catalysts).

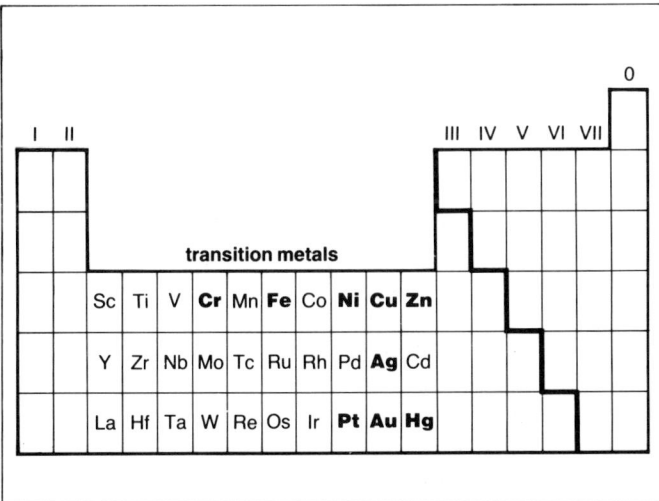

Figure 7.3 *The transition metals. (Symbols for the more common elements are in bolder print)*

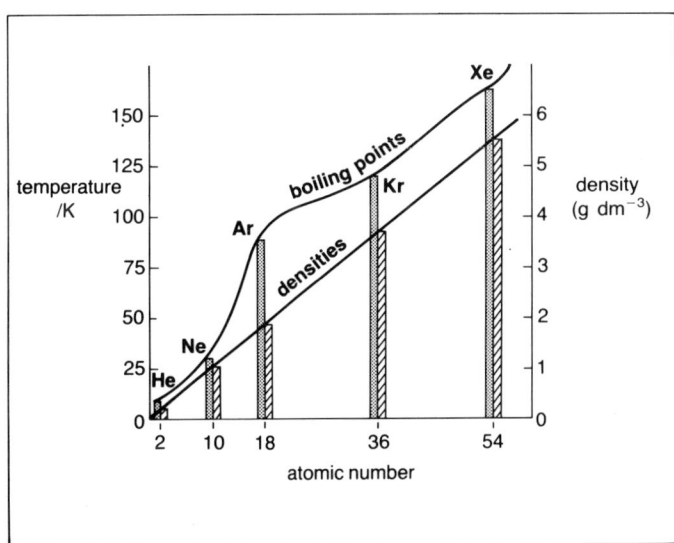

Figure 7.4 *The noble gases.*

Compare these properties of transition metals with those of alkali metals on page 40.

The most important transition metals are iron and copper. Iron is the most widely used metal. It is hard, strong, malleable and by far the cheapest metal to manufacture. It is used to make steel for cutlery, tools, machines, vehicles and girders. Copper is the third most used metal after iron and aluminium. Copper is malleable, ductile (can be made into wires) and a good conductor of heat and electricity. Because of these properties copper is used in electrical wires and cables and in hot-water pipes and radiators.

The noble gases

The **noble gases** are in group 0, on the extreme right of the periodic table (figure 7.4). All of them are gases at room temperature. The bar chart in figure 7.5 shows the boiling

Figure 7.5 *Boiling points and densities of the noble gases.*

points and densities of the noble gases. Notice how the values slowly increase with atomic number.

At one time, chemists thought that the noble gases were completely unreactive and formed no compounds. Because of this, they were once called the 'inert gases'. Since 1963, several compounds of krypton and xenon have been prepared so they have been renamed the 'noble gases'. Nevertheless, they are a group of very unreactive elements.

Uses of the noble gases

The special properties of the noble gases make them very useful.

- **Helium** is very light and it does not burn. It is now used in preference to hydrogen to fill weather balloons and airships. Helium is also used with oxygen for breathing in deep-sea diving apparatus. Helium is used in place of nitrogen because the latter gas dissolves in the blood under pressure. As the diver comes to the surface, the pressure falls and bubbles of nitrogen then form in the blood. This causes dizziness and pains – a condition called 'divers' bends'.
- **Neon** is used in advertising signs. Glass tubes are filled with neon at a low pressure and an electric spark is passed through the tube. This causes the neon to glow with a red light.
- **Argon** and argon/nitrogen mixtures are used in electric light-bulbs. This protects the tungsten filament, which glows white hot when an electric current passes through it. If the bulb contained oxygen, the filament would burn to form tungsten oxide. If the bulb was evacuated (i.e. had no gas in it), the filament would vaporise slowly.
- **Krypton** and **xenon** are used in high intensity lamps such as those for photography.

The halogens – a group of reactive non-metals

The halogens form group VII of the periodic table. They are fluorine (F), chlorine (Cl), bromine (Br) and iodine (I). The fifth halogen, called astatine (At), is radioactive and unstable.

Table 7.2 shows some information about fluorine, chlorine, bromine and iodine.

Table 7.2 *Some properties of the halogens.*

Halogen	Molecular formula	State at room temperature	Boiling point /°C	Colour
Fluorine	F_2	Gas	−188	Pale yellow
Chlorine	Cl_2	Gas	−34	Green
Bromine	Br_2	Liquid	58	Orange-red
Iodine	I_2	Solid	183	Dark purple

The halogens are another typical group of elements in the periodic table. They show similarities to one another, but there is a gradual change in properties as you move down the group.

All the halogens have simple molecular structures with diatomic molecules – Cl_2, Br_2, etc. Strong bonds hold the atoms together as a molecule, but there are relatively weak bonds between the separate molecules (figure 7.6). This means that the halogen molecules are easily separated and turned into gases. Moving down the group, the molecules get larger and forces between them increase. Therefore, from fluorine to iodine the halogens are gradually more difficult to vaporise. The boiling points increase down the group – at room temperature fluorine and chlorine are gases, bromine is a liquid and iodine is a solid.

There are graduations like this in all the properties of the halogens. Their colours become deeper and more intense moving down the group. Fluorine is pale yellow, chlorine is green and bromine is orange-red. Iodine is such a dark purple colour that the solid looks almost black.

The chemical reactions of the halogens also show a graduation. Fluorine is the most reactive of all non-metals and there are very few substances that do not react with fluorine. On the other hand, iodine is only moderately reactive. Table 7.3 shows how chlorine, bromine and iodine react with water and iron. Look at the table and notice how the halogens get less reactive down the group from chlorine to iodine.

A more reactive halogen will displace a less reactive halogen from its compounds. This is rather like the way more reactive metals displace less reactive ones.

Table 7.3 *The reactions of chlorine, bromine and iodine with water and iron.*

Halogen	Reaction with water	Reaction with iron
Chlorine	A mixture of hydrochloric acid and hypochlorous acid is produced; the solution is very acidic and is also a strong bleach	Iron reacts vigorously forming iron(III) chloride ($FeCl_3$)
Bromine	Bromine reacts less easily than chlorine forming hydrobromic acid and hypobromous acid; the solution is a bleach	Iron reacts slowly forming iron(III) bromide ($FeBr_3$)
Iodine	Iodine dissolves slightly in the water; the solution is slightly acidic and bleaches very slowly	Iron reacts very slowly forming iron(II) iodide (FeI_2)

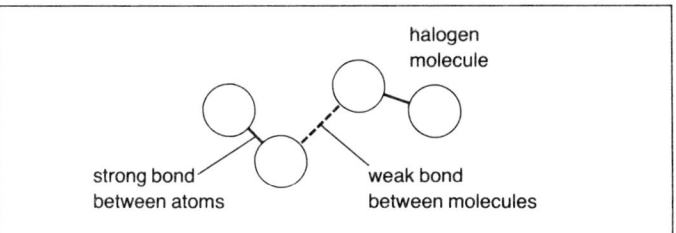

Figure 7.6 *Bonds between the atoms and molecules in halogens.*

For example, when chlorine is added to a solution of sodium bromide, the more reactive chlorine displaces the less reactive bromine.

chlorine + sodium → bromine + sodium
              bromide   chloride

$Cl_2(g) + 2NaBr(aq) \rightarrow Br_2(aq) + 2NaCl(aq)$

But when bromine is added to sodium chloride solution, nothing happens. The bromine is not reactive enough to displace the chlorine.

Uses of the halogens

Figure 7.7 summarises some of the uses of the halogens and their compounds. The halogens are reactive elements. They react with a wide variety of elements and compounds. In particular, they react with the substances in living things such as proteins and other compounds in our lungs, our eyes and our skin. Chlorine, for example, is very poisonous and has a choking smell. In fact it was used as a poison gas in the First World War.

The halogens can kill bacteria and viruses as well as human tissue. This makes them useful as antiseptics and disinfectants. Chlorine is added to drinking water and the water in swimming pools to prevent infection by bacteria. A solution of iodine is sometimes used as an antiseptic. Chlorine also reacts with many coloured compounds, turning them colourless, so it is used as a bleach.

Chlorine will bleach indicators like litmus or Universal Indicator. This provides a useful test for chlorine gas. A damp piece of indicator paper is held in the gas. If the indicator is bleached, the gas is probably chlorine.

Because of their reactivity, the halogens form many compounds. These compounds are usually unreactive and stable. For example, sodium chloride (salt) is an essential part of the human diet.

Many of the things we use every day are manufactured from halogens, particularly from chlorine. PVC (polychloroethene), pesticides such as BHC and DDT, photographic film, aerosol propellants and dry-cleaning liquids are all made from halogens (figure 7.7).

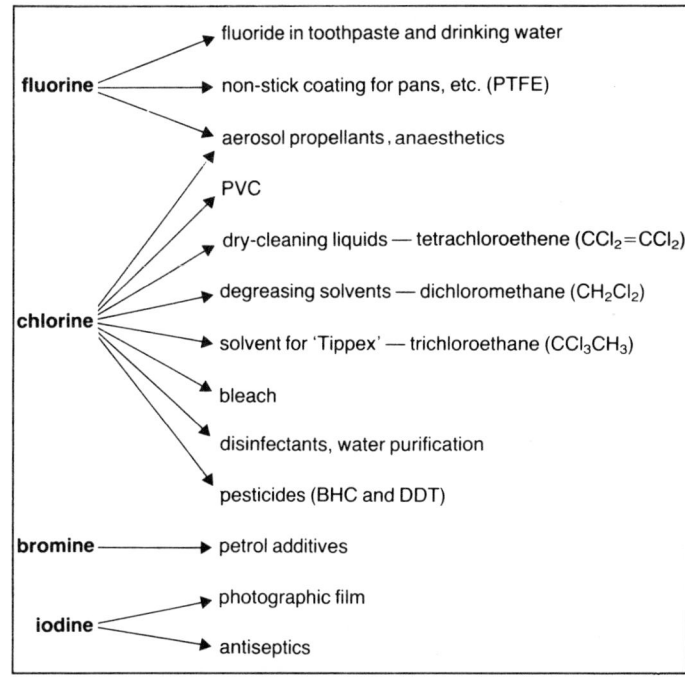

Figure 7.7 *Some uses of the halogens and their compounds.*

Self test

Questions 1–8

An outline of part of the periodic table is shown below. Certain elements are shown by letters **A** to **E**.

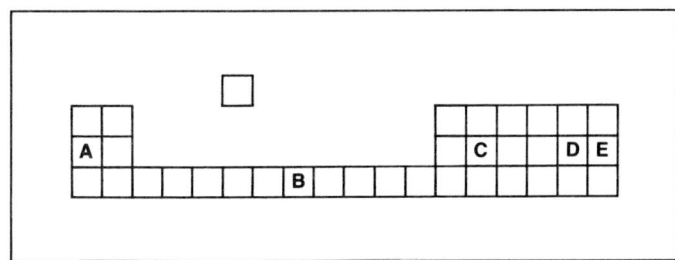

Choose the letter for an element that
1 is a transition element.
2 is present in dry air.
3 is a metalloid.
4 reacts vigorously with water to form hydrogen.
5 is obtained by electrolysis of its fused compounds.
6 forms no compounds.
7 forms an ion with one negative charge.
8 is used as a germicide or disinfectant.

9 Which *one* of the following sets contains elements from three different groups in the periodic table?
   A Na, K, Ca   **B** H, He, Ne
   C Na, Mg, Al **D** S, O, Cl

44 The periodic table

10 All elements in group 6 of the periodic table have the same
   A number of protons and neutrons.
   B number of electrons in their outer shell.
   C physical properties.
   D relative atomic mass.

11 Transition metals differ from group 1 metals because they
   A conduct electricity.
   B have coloured compounds.
   C form positive ions.
   D form basic oxides.

12 Which *one* of the following will displace bromine from a solution of sodium bromide?
   A chlorine   B iodine
   C sodium   D sodium chloride

13 Francium is an element in group 1 of the periodic table. It is likely that francium will
   A contain Fr_2 molecules.
   B react slowly with cold water.
   C form a chloride $FrCl_2$.
   D form an alkaline oxide.

Questions 14–19
Write down the names of the substances which would replace the numbers in the following word equations.

sodium + oxygen → (14)

sodium + water → (15) + (16)

iron + chlorine → (17)

chlorine + water → (18) + (19)

Questions 20–22

20 What is the name for the horizontal rows of elements in the periodic table?

21 What is the family name for elements in group 1 of the periodic table?

22 What property is used to determine the order of the elements in modern periodic tables?

8 Metals and hydrogen

Using metals and alloys

Metals are one of our most important materials. Our society, our lives and our industry all depend on the use of metals. Everyone's work involves metals, whether we use a lathe, a computer, a typewriter, a tractor, a saucepan or a pen.

The properties of metals were discussed in Chapter 1 and metals were compared with non-metals. The reactions of metals with oxygen and with water were studied in Chapters 2 and 3 respectively. We must now turn to the uses of metals and their reactions with acids.

The uses of metals depend on their properties (density, strength, conductivity, resistance to corrosion) and on their cost of production. Table 8.1 shows the properties, costs and uses of the three most commonly used metals.

Most metallic substances which we use nowadays are *mixtures* of two or more metals, called **alloys**. Alloys are formed by mixing molten metals and then allowing them to solidify. The alloys produced have more useful properties than the pure metals. For example, aluminium has a low density and it does not corrode like iron, but it is only moderately strong. On mixing with 4 per cent copper, it gives an alloy that is light, strong and resistant to corrosion. This makes it ideal for aircraft construction.

Pure copper is a very good conductor of electricity. This makes it useful for electrical wires and cables, but it is not very hard or strong. Brass is an alloy of copper and zinc. Bronze is an alloy of copper and tin. Alloying copper with zinc or nickel produces alloys that are strong enough for use in coins. 1p and 2p coins contain 97 per cent copper, 2.5 per cent zinc and 0.5 per cent tin, while 5p, 10p, 20p and 50p coins contain 75 per cent copper and 25 per cent nickel.

The most important alloys are those based on iron. Iron alloys are called **steels**. Steel contains about 1 per cent carbon. It is much harder and tougher than iron. Stainless steel contains about 20 per cent chromium and 10 per cent nickel. Chromium prevents the steel from rusting; nickel makes it harder and less brittle.

Table 8.1 *The properties, costs and uses of aluminium, iron and copper.*

Metal	Abundance of ores	Relative density	Relative strength	Relative electrical conductivity	Resistance to corrosion	Approximate cost of production per kg	Main uses
Aluminium	Most abundant metal in Earth's crust, but not worth extracting from most ores except bauxite	Low	Moderate	High	Forms an oxide layer which protects metal from further reaction	£0.9	Lightweight alloys for tent frames, bicycle frames, aircraft construction, saucepans, etc.
Iron	Very abundant High quality ores plentiful throughout the world	High	Strong	Moderate	Rusts steadily and the metal wears away	£0.1	Structural metal as steel for girders, bridges, buildings, vehicles, etc.
Copper	Most ores are of low quality (contain only a small amount of copper)	High	Weak	High	Does not corrode due to low reactivity	£1.0	Conducting metal in electrical wires, cables. Unreactive metal for hot water pipes, coins

Metals and Hydrogen

How do metals react with acids?

Table 8.2 shows what happens when five metals are added to dilute hydrochloric acid. Some metals, like aluminium and magnesium, react vigorously. Others, like iron and zinc, react steadily. Copper does not react at all. When the metals react, the products are hydrogen plus the chloride of the metal:

metal + hydrochloric acid → metal chloride + hydrogen

e.g.

zinc + hydrochloric acid → zinc chloride + hydrogen

$Zn + 2HCl \rightarrow ZnCl_2 + H_2$

A similar reaction occurs between metals and dilute sulphuric acid. In this case, the products are hydrogen plus a metal sulphate. In general, acids react with those metals that are above copper in the activity series. The products are a metal compound (salt) and hydrogen.

metal + acid → metal compound (salt) + hydrogen

Many foods, like pickled onions and citrus fruits, contain acids. These acids will attack saucepans and cutlery made of certain metals. Pans and cutlery are often made from aluminium, copper, iron (steel) and nickel. All of these metals, except copper, will react with acids in food. Unfortunately, copper is so expensive that aluminium and steel are used in most saucepans nowadays and cutlery is usually made of nickel or steel. This means that most saucepans and cutlery are attacked by vinegar (which contains acetic acid), lemon juice (which contains citric acid) and rhubarb (which contains oxalic acid).

Foods that contain acids are best stored in glass or plastic containers. These are not attacked by acids. Fruits like pineapple and grapefruits are also stored and sold in 'tin' cans. Tins are made of steel coated with a thin layer of tin and then lacquered on the inside. The lacquer acts as an unreactive layer between the tin and its contents.

Table 8.2 *The reactions of metals with hydrochloric acid.*

Metal	Reaction with dilute hydrochloric acid
Aluminium	No reaction at first, but vigorous after a few minutes: rapid effervescence as hydrogen is produced
Copper	No reaction
Iron	Slow reaction, bubbles of hydrogen form steadily
Magnesium	Very vigorous evolution of hydrogen: reaction is very exothermic
Zinc	Moderate reaction as bubbles of hydrogen are produced.

The reactivity series

When articles made of iron and steel are exposed to oxygen and water vapour in the air, they begin to rust quite quickly. Other metals such as copper are hardly affected by oxygen and water vapour in the air.

There are obvious differences in the reactivity of different metals. Sodium and potassium react with air and water vapour so rapidly that they must be stored under oil. Iron and aluminium are less reactive, but they form oxides slowly in moist air. Gold is so unreactive that it keeps its shine for years. Metals can be listed in order of their reactivity. The list is called the **reactivity series** or activity series. Table 8.3 shows a reactivity series for metals and summarises the reactions of metals with oxygen, water, steam and dilute acids. Experiments show that the order

Table 8.3 *A summary of the reactions of metals.*

Reactivity series	Reaction when heated in air or oxygen	Reaction with cold water	Reaction with steam	Reaction with dilute acids
K Na	Burn brightly and vigorously	React with decreasing vigour (K – violently, Mg – slowly)	React with decreasing vigour	React with decreasing vigour (K, Na violently, Fe steadily)
Ca Mg	Burn rapidly to form oxides			
Al Zn Fe		Do not react		
Cu	Only forms an oxide layer		Do not react	Do not react
Ag Au	Do *not* react			

of reactivity of the metals is the same with all four substances. This is not surprising because metal atoms react to form metal ions in each case. This is summarised in the equation below for a metal which forms ions with a 2+ charge.

$$M \rightarrow M^{2+} + 2e^-$$
metal → metal ion

Metals higher in the reactivity series form ions more easily and therefore they are more reactive.

Reaction with oxygen

When metals react with oxygen, metal oxides form. The metal oxide contains metal ions (M^{2+}) and oxide ions (O^{2-}).

$$\text{metal} + \text{oxygen} \rightarrow \text{metal oxide}$$
$$2M + O_2 \rightarrow 2M^{2+}O^{2-}$$

Reaction with water and steam

Here again the metals react to form metal oxides.

$$\text{metal} + \text{water} \rightarrow \text{metal oxide} + \text{hydrogen}$$
$$M + H_2O \rightarrow M^{2+}O^{2-} + H_2$$

Oxides of metals high in the reactivity series (e.g. Na_2O, CaO) react with more water to form solutions of their hydroxides.

Reaction with dilute acids

In this case, the metals react to form salts which contain metal ions.

$$\text{metal} + \text{acid} \rightarrow \text{salt} + \text{hydrogen}$$
e.g. $Fe + H_2SO_4 \rightarrow Fe^{2+}SO_4^{2-} + H_2$

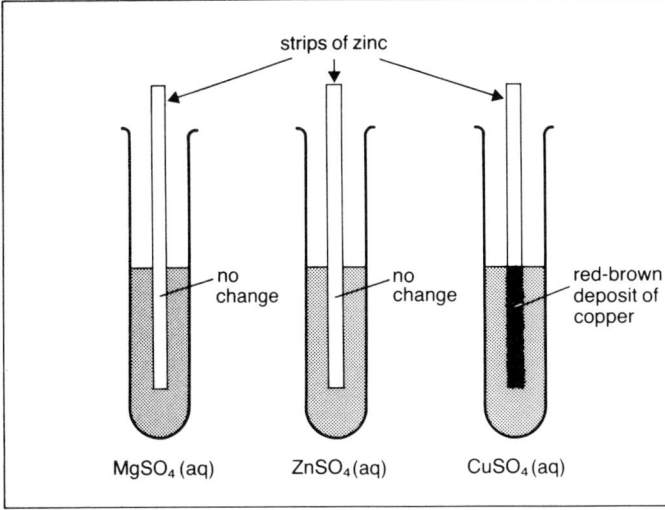

Figure 8.1 *Displacement reactions with zinc.*

Displacement reactions of metals

When metals react with acids, they form a salt and hydrogen. For example,

$$\text{zinc} + \text{sulphuric acid} \rightarrow \text{zinc sulphate} + \text{hydrogen}$$
$$Zn + H_2SO_4 \rightarrow Zn^{2+}SO_4^{2-} + H_2$$

In this case, zinc has displaced hydrogen from the acid.

If zinc can displace hydrogen from an acid, then it may also be able to displace metals from solutions of their salts. Figure 8.1 shows what happens when strips of zinc are placed in solutions of magnesium sulphate, zinc sulphate and copper sulphate.

Notice that zinc displaces copper from copper sulphate solution, but it does not displace magnesium from magnesium sulphate. Table 8.4 summarises the results of two other experiments in which magnesium and then copper are used in place of zinc.

Table 8.4 *Displacement reactions of metals.*

Metal used	Solution used		
	Magnesium sulphate $MgSO_4(aq)$	**Zinc sulphate** $ZnSO_4(aq)$	**Copper sulphate** $CuSO_4(aq)$
Magnesium		Dark grey deposit of zinc	Red-brown deposit of copper
Zinc		No reaction	Red-brown deposit of copper
Copper			

When zinc is placed in copper sulphate solution, it gets covered in a red-brown deposit of copper. At the same time, the blue colour of the solution fades.

Copper ions have been displaced from the solution forming copper atoms. Zinc has gone into solution as zinc ions. The equation for the reaction is:

$$\text{copper ions} + \text{zinc} \rightarrow \text{copper} + \text{zinc ions}$$
$$Cu^{2+}(aq) + Zn(s) \rightarrow Cu(s) + Zn^{2+}(aq)$$

Notice one important fact from table 8.4.
Each metal only displaces ions of a metal below it in the reactivity series.
- magnesium displaces zinc and copper;
- zinc displaces copper but not magnesium;
- copper does not displace magnesium or zinc.

These experiments provide more evidence that magnesium is more reactive than zinc and copper. Magnesium reacts and forms its ions, while the other metals are displaced from solution. Thus, magnesium is higher in the reactivity series than the other two metals.

In the same way, zinc is more reactive than copper and therefore higher than copper in the reactivity series.

Extracting metals

Only a few metals, like gold and silver, are found as free, uncombined elements in the Earth's crust. These metals are very low in the reactivity series. Most metals are too reactive to occur uncombined in the Earth's crust. They react with other elements to form **ores**. These ores contain compounds (mainly oxides, sulphides, chlorides and carbonates) from which the metal can be extracted. There are two main methods for extracting metals from their ores:

- chemical reduction of the metal compound using coke (carbon);
- electrolysis of the molten metal compound.

If possible, reduction with coke is used because it is cheaper than electrolysis. Chemical reduction methods are used to extract most metals in the middle of the reactivity series, such as zinc, iron, lead and copper. Once the metals are extracted they may require purification. The purification of impure copper by electrolysis was described on page 36. Metals at the top of the reactivity series, such as sodium, magnesium and aluminium, cannot be obtained by reduction of their compounds using coke. This is because the temperature needed to reduce their compounds is too high. The only way to extract these reactive metals is by electrolysis of their molten compounds. Electrolysis of their aqueous solutions cannot be used because hydrogen from the water is produced at the cathode instead of the metal.

The extraction of aluminium by electrolysis of molten aluminium oxide is described on page 36.

Table 8.5 shows how the methods of extracting metals can be related to the reactivity series.

Table 8.5 *Methods of extracting metals.*

Metal	Method of extraction
K, Na, Ca, Mg	Electrolysis of molten chloride
Al	Electrolysis of molten oxide
Zn, Fe	Reduction of oxides using coke
Cu	Reduction of oxide by sulphide
Ag, Au	Occur in Earth's crust as free elements

Extracting iron

Iron is probably the most important metal. It is made into steel and used for machinery, tools, vehicles, buildings, bridges and many other things. The main ore of iron is haematite, which is usually called iron ore. This contains iron (III) oxide mixed with sand and clay. The best quality ores are found in Scandinavia, Russia, Australia, North Africa and America. Iron is extracted from iron ore in a blast furnace. The furnace gets its name from the blasts of hot air blown in at the bottom (figure 8.2). Iron ore, coke and limestone are added at the top of the furnace.

Reactions in the furnace

Coke (carbon) reacts with oxygen in the blast of hot air to form carbon monoxide.

$$\text{carbon} + \text{oxygen} \rightarrow \text{carbon monoxide}$$
$$2C + O_2 \rightarrow 2CO$$

As the carbon monoxide rises up the furnace it reduces the iron ore (Fe_2O_3) to iron.

$$\text{iron (III) oxide} + \text{carbon monoxide} \rightarrow \text{iron} + \text{carbon dioxide}$$
$$Fe_2O_3 + 3CO \rightarrow 2Fe + 3CO_2$$
(iron ore)

The temperature inside the furnace rises to 2000°C and molten iron trickles to the bottom. Molten iron is tapped off from time to time. It solidifies in large chunks called 'pigs'. The name 'pig iron' is used for this impure metal straight out of the blast furnace.

Limestone is added to remove impurities, like clay and sand, from the furnace. The limestone decomposes to form calcium oxide at the high temperatures inside the furnace.

$$\text{calcium carbonate} \rightarrow \text{calcium oxide} + \text{carbon dioxide}$$
$$CaCO_3 \rightarrow CaO + CO_2$$
(limestone)

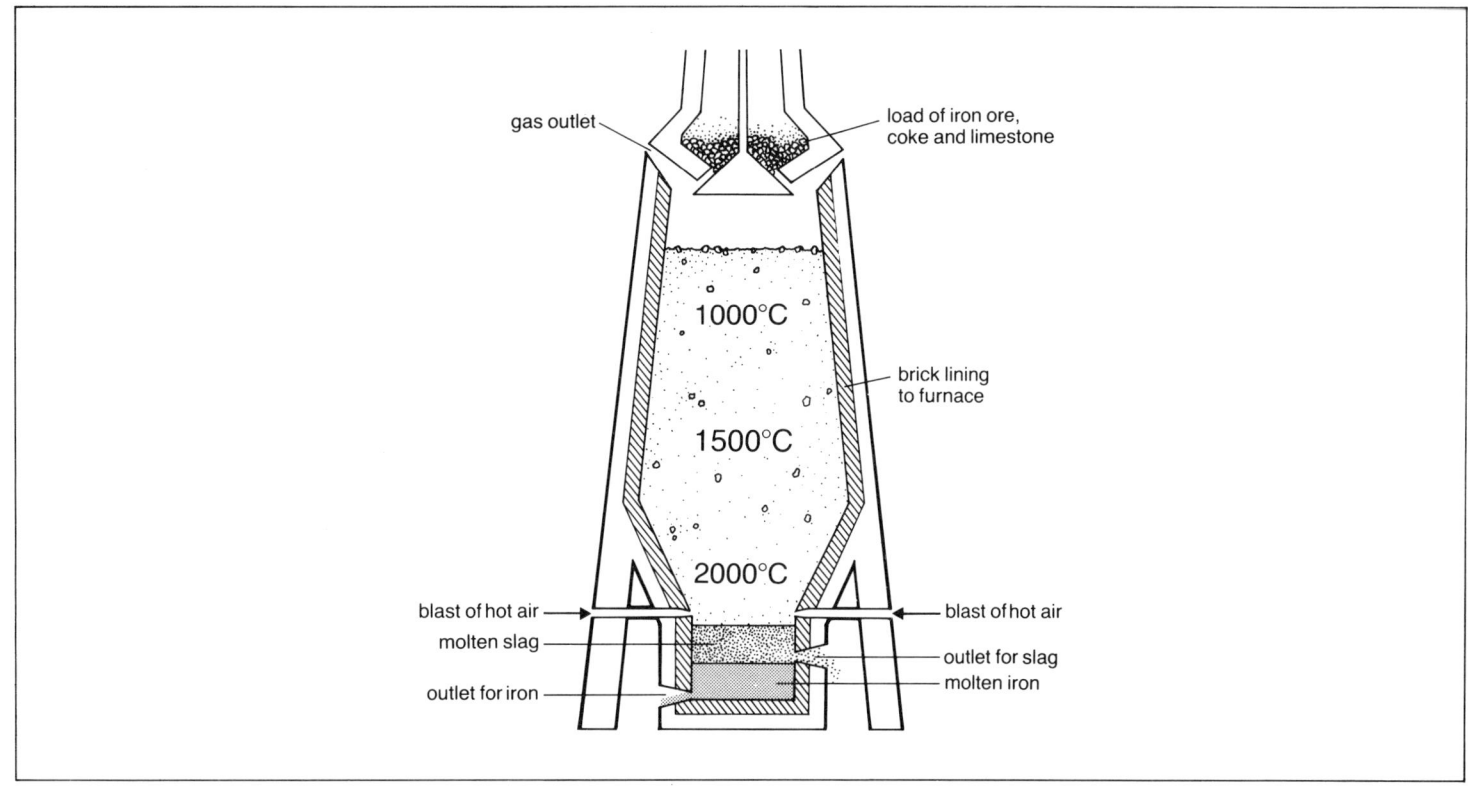

Figure 8.2 *A blast furnace.*

The calcium oxide then reacts with sand and other impurities to form a liquid 'slag'.

$$\begin{array}{ccccc} \text{calcium} & + & \text{silicon(IV)} & \to & \text{calcium} \\ \text{oxide} & & \text{oxide} & & \text{silicate} \\ \text{CaO} & + & \text{SiO}_2 & \to & \text{CaSiO}_3 \\ & & \text{(sand)} & & \text{(slag)} \end{array}$$

The 'slag' runs to the bottom of the furnace and floats on top of the iron. It is drained off from time to time.

Steelmaking

The 'pig iron' from a blast furnace contains 5–10 per cent impurities. The main impurities are carbon, sulphur, silicon and phosphorus. These impurities make the 'pig iron' hard and brittle compared with iron and steel. In order to make steel most of the impurities must be removed. This is done in a **basic oxygen furnace**. Pure oxygen is blown onto the molten 'pig iron'. The oxygen converts carbon and sulphur to CO_2 and SO_2, which escape as gases. Silicon and phosphorus are oxidised to solid oxides (SiO_2 and P_2O_5). These combine with lime in the basic oxygen furnace to form more 'slag'.

Recycling metals

When a car is no longer useful, it is sold for scrap. Iron and steel can be separated from the scrap car by magnets. They are sent to the steelworks to be **recycled**. At the steelworks, the scrap iron is melted down and mixed with new iron.

All metals can be recycled. Recycling makes sense because:

- It saves money.
- It means we need to dig up less metal ore. Resources of ores are limited, and cannot last forever. Recycling metals means we use up the ores less quickly.
- It solves the problem of waste disposal. Recycling metals stops them causing a litter problem and spoiling the environment.

However, it is impossible to recycle *all* the metal we use. There are problems with collecting the scrap metal, separating it from other materials, and transporting it to the place where it will be processed.

Recycling other materials

Glass, paper, cloth and plastics can all be recycled. For example, old glass bottles can be melted down to make new bottles. This saves resources and solves a litter problem.

Hydrogen

Hydrogen is formed when metals react with acids. The reaction of zinc with acid provides a useful way of making hydrogen in the laboratory (figure 8.3).

50 Metals and Hydrogen

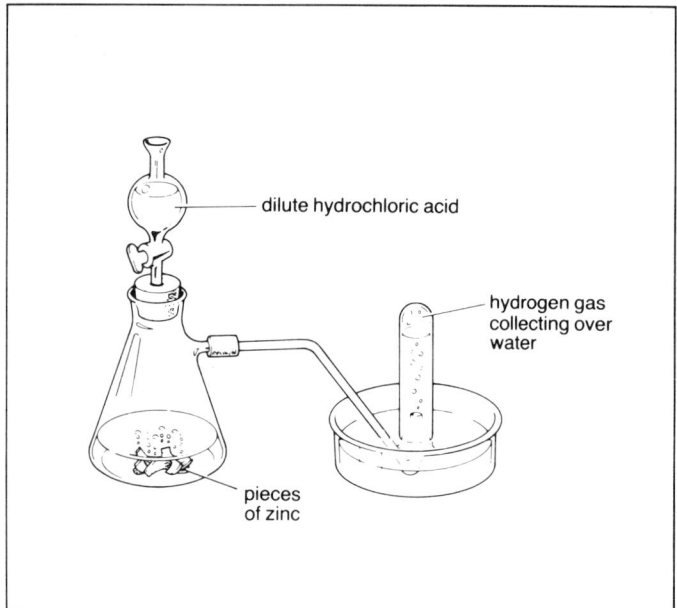

Figure 8.3 *Making and collecting hydrogen in the laboratory.*

Properties of hydrogen

In some ways hydrogen behaves like a metal in its chemical reactions. Like metals, it forms positive ions and is given off at the cathode in electrolysis. But in appearance hydrogen is not at all like a metal – it is a colourless, odourless gas, lighter than air. Figure 8.4 summarises some important properties of hydrogen.

Mixtures of hydrogen and air explode when ignited. This can be very dangerous, and a safety screen should always be used when experimenting with hydrogen. But small quantities of hydrogen explode harmlessly, and this provides a useful test for the gas. If you hold a flame over the mouth of a tube containing hydrogen, the gas explodes with a squeaky 'pop'.

Manufacture and uses of hydrogen

Hydrogen has many important industrial uses. Table 8.6 gives some of them.

Industrially, hydrogen is manufactured in a number of ways. Two of the most important are:

- as a by-product of the electrolysis of sodium chloride solution (page 35);
- by the reaction of natural gas with steam in the presence of a catalyst.

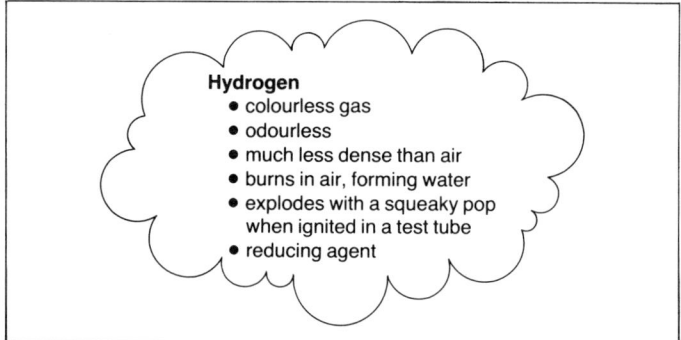

Figure 8.4 *Important properties of hydrogen.*

Table 8.6 *Important uses of hydrogen.*

Hydrogen is used
• As a fuel – it burns very clearly and causes little pollution, though it has an explosion risk
• For making ammonia (page 91)
• For making margarine – hydrogen reacts with oils, turning them into solid fats
• In some lighter-than-air balloons – but only where there is no danger of explosion

• Self test

Questions 1–5

From the list **A** to **E** below
- **A** copper
- **B** lead
- **C** magnesium
- **D** iron
- **E** zinc

choose the metal that is used
1. to make light alloys.
2. to galvanize steel.
3. as a protective shield from radiation.
4. for the hot-water pipes in a house.
5. as the major structural material in buildings.

Questions 6–10

From the list **A** to **D** below
- **A** electrolysis of a fused compound of the metal
- **B** reduction of the metal oxide by the metal sulphide
- **C** reaction of the metal oxide with carbon in a furnace
- **D** occurs as a free element in the Earth's crust and only needs purifying

choose the method that is used to produce
6. aluminium
7. copper
8. silver
9. potassium
10. zinc

Questions 11–13
From the list **A** to **E** below
- **A** calcium
- **B** iron
- **C** magnesium
- **D** silver
- **E** zinc

choose the metal that
11. does *not* react with dilute hydrochloric acid.
12. displaces iron from iron oxide, but not magnesium from magnesium oxide.
13. reacts vigorously with cold water.

14. Which *one* of the following is an alloy?
    - **A** bauxite
    - **B** iron ore
    - **C** nichrome
    - **D** platinised asbestos

15. Which *one* of the following pairs of substances will react?
    - **A** copper and magnesium nitrate solution
    - **B** gold and aluminium sulphate solution
    - **C** iron and potassium chloride solution
    - **D** zinc and silver nitrate solution

16. Which *one* of the following equations correctly represents the formation of tin from its Sn^{4+} ion?
    - **A** $Sn \rightarrow Sn^{4+} + 4e^-$
    - **B** $Sn^{4+} + 4e^- \rightarrow Sn$
    - **C** $Sn^{4+} - 4e^- \rightarrow Sn$
    - **D** $Sn^{4+} \rightarrow Sn + 4e^-$

17. Which *one* of the following substances is used to remove the impurities from pig iron to make steel?
    - **A** coke   **B** iron ore   **C** oxygen   **D** sand

Questions 18–22
Write down the names of the substances which would replace the numbers in the following word equations. The equations concern the extraction of iron.

iron (III) oxide + carbon monoxide → ⑱ + ⑲

calcium carbonate $\overset{heat}{\rightarrow}$ ⑳ + ㉑

calcium oxide + silicon (IV) oxide → ㉒

9 Acids, bases and salts

Introducing acids

Most people expect acids to be dangerous and corrosive chemicals. Some acids, like hydrochloric acid, nitric acid and sulphuric acid, are obviously dangerous. They attack tough materials like metals and stone, and their effect on our flesh and clothing can be disastrous. **Always wear safety spectacles when you are using these strong acids.**

However, not all acids are dangerous. Many acids occur naturally. These are usually weak or so dilute that they are not harmful. They include carbonic acid in soda water, acetic acid in vinegar, lactic acid in milk and citric acid in lemonade and citrus fruits. Table 9.1 lists the main properties of acids.

Indicators and pH

The easiest way to tell whether a substance is an acid is to test its solution with **indicator**.

Indicators are substances that change colour depending on whether they are in acidic or alkaline solution.

For example, **Litmus** is red in acid and blue in alkali; it is purple in neutral solution. **Universal indicator** is red or orange in acid and green or blue in alkali. It is green/yellow in neutral solution. It is very useful because it will turn different colours depending on the acidity or alkalinity of a solution. The colour can be related to the **pH scale** to give a measure of acidity or alkalinity. Most solutions have pH values between 0 and 14. On the pH scale:

acids have a pH less than 7;
neutral solutions, like water, have a pH of 7;
alkalis have a pH greater than 7.

Table 9.1 *The main properties of acids.*

Acids:
● Turn litmus red
● Turn universal indicator orange or red
● Have a pH less than 7
● Conduct electricity
● React with metals above copper in the activity series to give hydrogen
● React with bases to form salts; this reaction is called neutralisation
● React with carbonates to give carbon dioxide

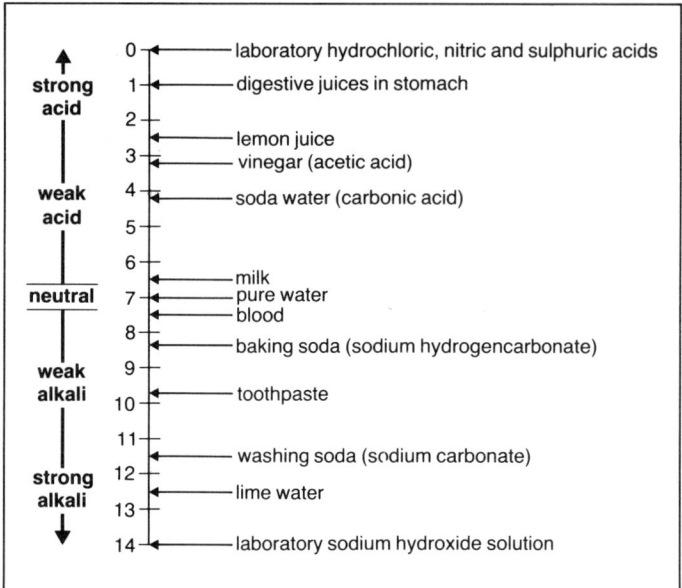

Figure 9.1 *The pH of some common substances.*

The stronger an acid, the lower is its pH. The stronger an alkali, the higher is its pH. Figure 9.1 shows the pH of some common substances. Look at table 9.1 again. Notice that:

● acids conduct electricity; this shows that solutions of acids contain ions;
● acids combine with reactive metals to form hydrogen; this suggests that all acids contain hydrogen.

In fact, acids have similar properties because they all contain hydrogen ions (H^+). When acids react with metals, hydrogen ions are converted to hydrogen gas (see pages 46–7):

metal + acid → salt + hydrogen
(above Cu in
activity series)

Strong and weak acids

Experiments show that some acids (such as hydrochloric acid) conduct electricity very well. The pH of their solutions is low. These are called **strong acids**. Other acids (such as acetic acid) do not conduct electricity so well and the pH of their solutions is higher. They are called **weak acids** (table 9.2).

Table 9.2 *Strong acids and weak acids.*

Strong acids		Weak acids	
Hydrochloric acid	HCl	Acetic acid	CH_3COOH
Nitric acid	HNO_3	Carbonic acid	H_2CO_3
Phosphoric acid	H_3PO_4	Sulphurous acid	H_2SO_3
Sulphuric acid	H_2SO_4		

Strong acids split up (dissociate) completely into ions in solution. This is why they conduct electricity better than weak acids and give a lower pH.

For example, hydrochloric acid (HCl(aq)) is a strong acid. It is completely split up into ions, H^+(aq) and Cl^-(aq). Hydrochloric acid is made by dissolving hydrogen chloride (HCl(g)) in water. Hydrogen chloride is a gas that contains molecules, not ions. But when hydrogen chloride dissolves in water, it becomes completely ionised:

$$\text{hydrogen chloride} \xrightarrow{\text{water}} \text{hydrogen ions} + \text{chloride ions}$$

$$HCl(g) \xrightarrow{H_2O} H^+(aq) + Cl^-(aq)$$

Weak acids, on the other hand, are only partly dissociated into ions. They conduct less well and have a higher pH value (figure 9.2).

For example, acetic acid (CH_3COOH) is a weak acid.

$$\text{acetic acid} \xrightleftharpoons{\text{water}} \text{hydrogen ions} + \text{acetate ions}$$

$$CH_3COOH(l) \xrightleftharpoons{\text{water}} H^+(aq) + CH_3COO^-(aq)$$

(The half-arrows in opposite directions show that some of the acetic acid remains undissociated in the solution.)

Concentrated strong acids, such as concentrated hydrochloric acid and concentrated sulphuric acid, burn our skin. This is because they dissociate into ions in the water in our flesh and this reaction is very exothermic.

Sulphuric acid – a typical strong acid

Sulphuric acid (H_2SO_4) is an important example of a strong acid. It is used in two forms: concentrated and dilute.

Concentrated sulphuric acid is 98 per cent H_2SO_4 and only 2 per cent water. It has a strong attraction for water,

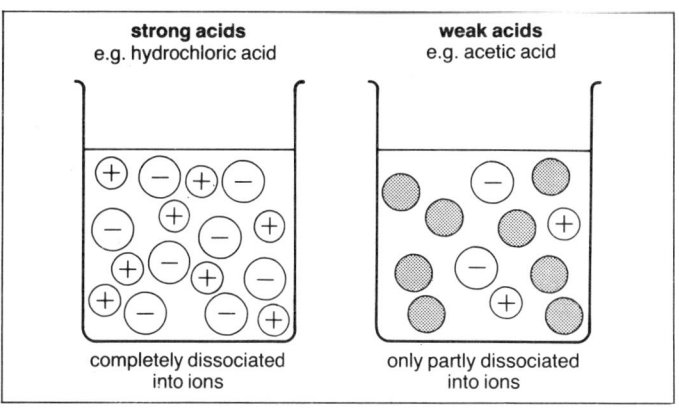

Figure 9.2 *The dissociation (splitting up) of strong acids and weak acids.*

because water helps the acid to ionise. This makes concentrated sulphuric acid a powerful **dehydrating agent**. It will take the water out of many substances.

For example, concentrated sulphuric acid turns blue hydrated copper sulphate to white anhydrous copper sulphate:

$$\text{hydrated copper sulphate} \xrightarrow{\text{minus water}} \text{anhydrous copper sulphate}$$

$$CuSO_4 \cdot 5H_2O \xrightarrow{-5H_2O} CuSO_4$$
$$\text{blue} \qquad\qquad\qquad \text{white}$$

It removes water from carbohydrates like sugar, turning them to black carbon.

$$\text{sugar} \xrightarrow{\text{minus water}} \text{carbon}$$

$$C_{12}H_{22}O_{11} \xrightarrow{-11H_2O} 12C$$

Dilute sulphuric acid contains more water than the concentrated acid. The acid used in school laboratories is usually about 10 per cent H_2SO_4 and 90 per cent water.

The water enables the sulphuric acid to ionise completely, so dilute sulphuric has all the properties of a strong acid. Table 9.3 shows some reactions of dilute sulphuric acid.

Table 9.3 *Some reactions of dilute sulphuric acid as a typical strong acid.*

Reaction	Example
Reacts with bases to form salts (sulphates) and water	With potassium hydroxide: potassium hydroxide + sulphuric acid → potassium sulphate + water $2KOH + H_2SO_4 \rightarrow K_2SO_4 + 2H_2O$
Reacts with carbonates to form salts (sulphates), carbon dioxide and water	With sodium carbonate: sodium carbonate + sulphuric acid → sodium sulphate + carbon dioxide + water $Na_2CO_3 + H_2SO_4 \rightarrow Na_2SO_4 + CO_2 + H_2O$
Reacts with metals to form salts (sulphates) and hydrogen	With magnesium: magnesium + sulphuric acid → magnesium sulphate + hydrogen $Mg + H_2SO_4 \rightarrow MgSO_4 + H_2$

Bases and alkalis

If you have suffered from indigestion you may have taken 'anti-acid' ('antacid') medicine to cure it. Acid indigestion is caused by too much hydrochloric acid in the stomach. The 'antacid' medicine contains a **base** which removes the excess acid.

Bases are substances that neutralise acids.

Bases are the chemical opposites of acids. When a base neutralises an acid a **salt** is formed (table 9.1).

Table 9.4 lists some important bases and their uses. Notice that **bases include the oxides, hydroxides and carbonates of metals.** All the bases in table 9.4 except magnesium oxide, are soluble. These soluble bases are called **alkalis**. Table 9.5 summarises the solubilities of bases.

Strong alkalis can be corrosive and dangerous like acids. Sodium hydroxide is sometimes called 'caustic soda' (caustic means burning). As with acids, **never let alkalis get on your skin and always wear eye protection when using them.**

Table 9.4 *Some important bases.*

Name	Formula	Example of use
Sodium hydroxide (caustic soda)	NaOH	Grease remover, oven cleaner
Ammonia	NH_3	Bath and sink cleaner, fertiliser manufacture
Sodium hydrogencarbonate (bicarbonate of soda)	$NaHCO_3$	Baking powder, anti-acid medicine
Calcium hydroxide (slaked lime)	$Ca(OH)_2$	Added to the soil to neutralise acidity
Magnesium oxide	MgO	Anti-acid medicine (Milk of Magnesia)

Table 9.5 *The solubilities of common bases.*

All	metal oxides	are insoluble *except*	Na_2O, K_2O, $Ca(OH)_2$
All	metal hydroxides	are insoluble *except*	NaOH, KOH, $Ca(OH)_2$
All	carbonates	are insoluble *except*	Na_2CO_3, K_2CO_3

Neutralisation

How do bases neutralise acids? Acidity is due to hydrogen ions, H^+. Bases remove acidity by reacting with these H^+ ions. So:

acids give up H^+ ions and bases take H^+ ions.

For example, look at these two neutralisation reactions:

magnesium + sulphuric → magnesium + water
oxide   acid   sulphate
MgO   + H_2SO_4 → $MgSO_4$ + H_2O

sodium   + hydrochloric →   sodium   + water
hydroxide   acid   chloride
NaOH   +   HCl   →   NaCl   + H_2O

During neutralisation, H^+ ions in the acid are converted to water. The other product of neutralisation is a salt. When sodium hydroxide is used to neutralise hydrochloric acid, sodium chloride is formed. Sodium chloride is a salt – the common salt we put on our food. But **scientists use the word salt to mean any compound formed by the reaction between an acid and a base.** Therefore, neutralisation can be summed up as:

acid + base → salt + water

This reaction is shown in figure 9.3.

Carbonates act as bases when they react with acids. The carbonates take H^+ ions from the acid to form a salt plus water. Carbon dioxide is also formed.

acid + carbonate → salt + H_2O + CO_2

For example:

hydrochloric + calcium → calcium + water + carbon
acid   carbonate   chloride   dioxide
2HCl   + $CaCO_3$ → $CaCl_2$ + H_2O + CO_2

Salts

Salts are formed when acids react with metals or bases.

Salts are ionic compounds (e.g. Na^+Cl^-, $Cu^{2+}SO_4^{2-}$, $NH_4^+NO_3^-$). They contain metal or ammonium ions,

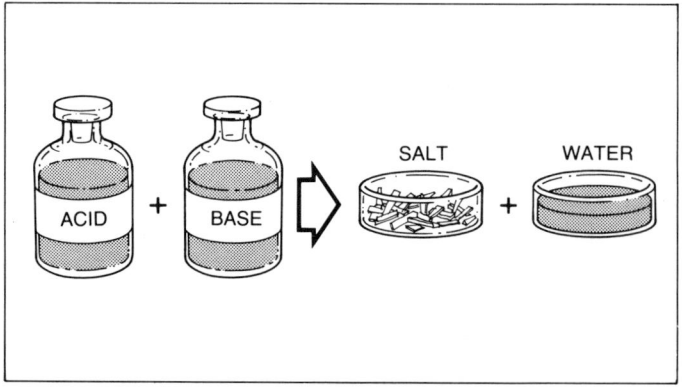

Figure 9.3 *Neutralisation.*

which are positive, and non-metal ions, which are negative. Many ores and minerals are salts. These include anhydrite (calcium sulphate), fluorite (calcium fluoride), rock salt (sodium chloride) and galena (lead sulphide). Some salts, such as those in table 9.6 have important uses. Salt crystals, such as those of sodium chloride, are often formed by crystallisation from aqueous solution. When this happens, water molecules sometimes form part of the crystal structure. This happens with washing soda ($Na_2CO_3.10H_2O$) and copper sulphate ($CuSO_4.5H_2O$). The water that forms part of the crystal structure is called **water of crystallisation**. Salts containing water of crystallisation are called **hydrates** or hydrated salts.

Preparing salts

It is important to know whether a salt is soluble or insoluble before you make it or use it. Table 9.7 summarises the solubilities of common salts.

When you are making a salt, the first question to ask is 'Is the salt soluble or insoluble?' If the salt is insoluble, it is usually prepared by precipitation. If the salt is soluble, it is usually prepared by reacting an acid with a metal or a base.

The flow diagram in figure 9.4 will help you to decide how to prepare a particular salt.

Table 9.6 *Some important salts.*

Name	Formula	Use
Sodium chloride	NaCl	Common salt – used in cooking
Calcium sulphate	$(CaSO_4)_2.H_2O$	Plaster of Paris – setting broken limbs
Iron(II) sulphate	$FeSO_4$	Iron tablets – to cure anaemia (lack of haemoglobin)
Ammonium nitrate	NH_4NO_3	'Nitram' – fertiliser

Table 9.7 *The solubilities of common salts.*

All {sodium, potassium, ammonium}	salts are soluble	
All nitrates	are soluble	
All sulphates	are soluble *except*	$BaSO_4$, $CaSO_4$, $PbSO_4$
All chlorides	are soluble *except*	$AgCl$, $PbCl_2$
All {carbonates, sulphides, sulphites}	are insoluble *except* those of sodium, potassium and ammonium	

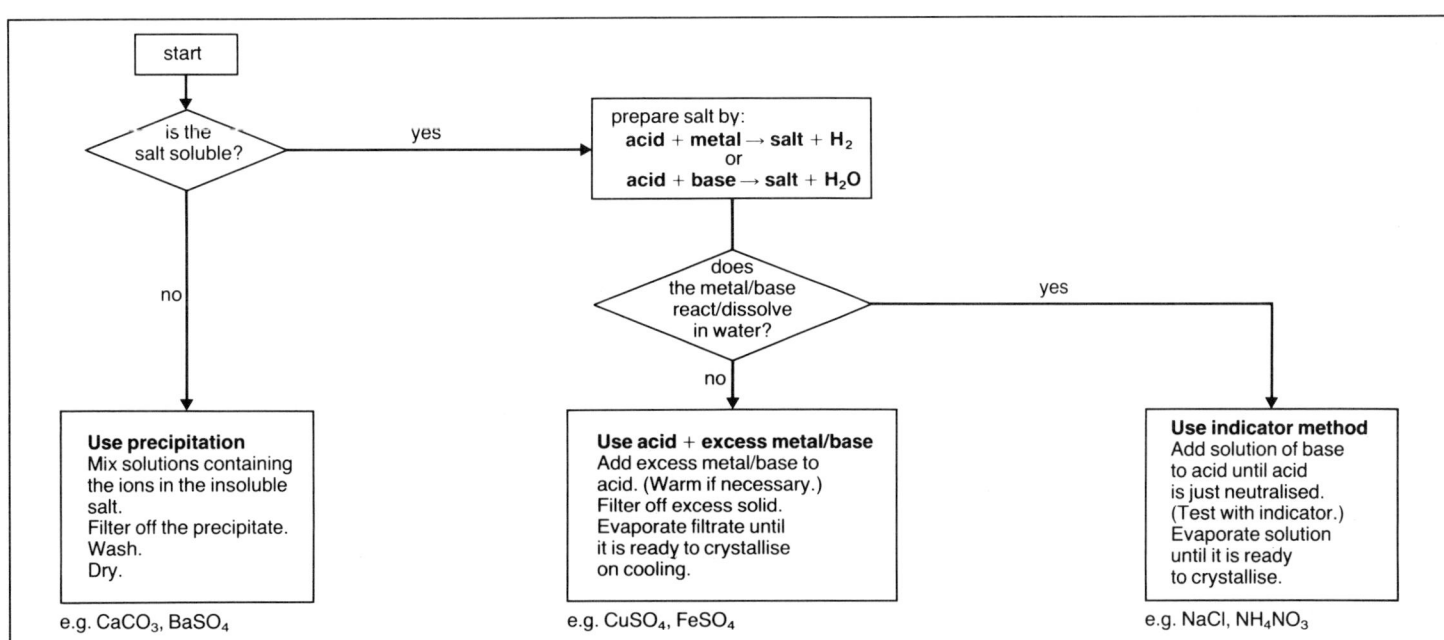

Figure 9.4 *How to prepare a particular salt.*

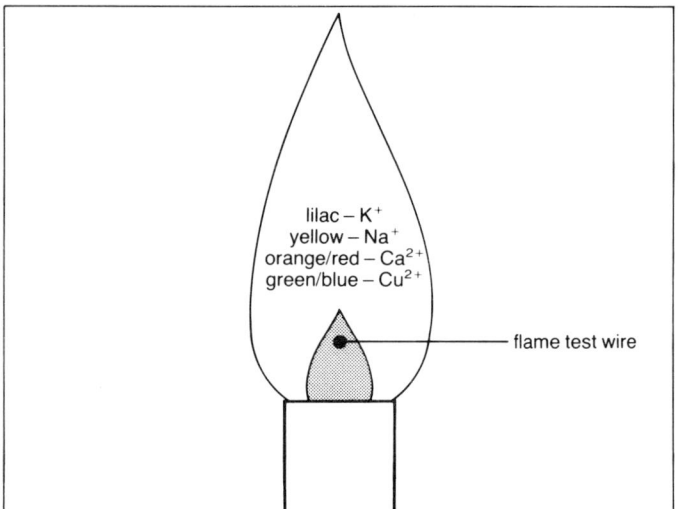

Figure 9.5 *The flame colours of some cations.*

Analysing salts – testing for cations and anions

Salts are ionic compounds. They contain cations (positive ions) and anions (negative ions). Sometimes we want to analyse a salt and find out what is in it. A simple way to analyse a salt is to test for the cations and anions that it might contain.

Tests for cations

- **Flame tests.** Dip a nichrome wire in concentrated hydrochloric acid and then in the substance to be tested. Now heat the wire in a hot bunsen flame. Figure 9.5 shows the colours which certain cations give to the flame.

- **Tests with sodium hydroxide solution.** The hydroxides of all metals (except those in groups 1 and 2 of the periodic table) are insoluble. These insoluble hydroxides are precipitated when sodium hydroxide solution is added to a solution of the metal ions. For example:

copper ions + hydroxide ions → blue precipitate of
in solution   in NaOH(aq)   copper hydroxide

$$Cu^{2+}(aq) + 2OH^-(aq) \rightarrow Cu(OH)_2(s)$$

Some of these insoluble hydroxides dissolve when excess sodium hydroxide solution is added.

Figure 9.6 shows a key for identifying cations using the colour and solubility of their hydroxides.

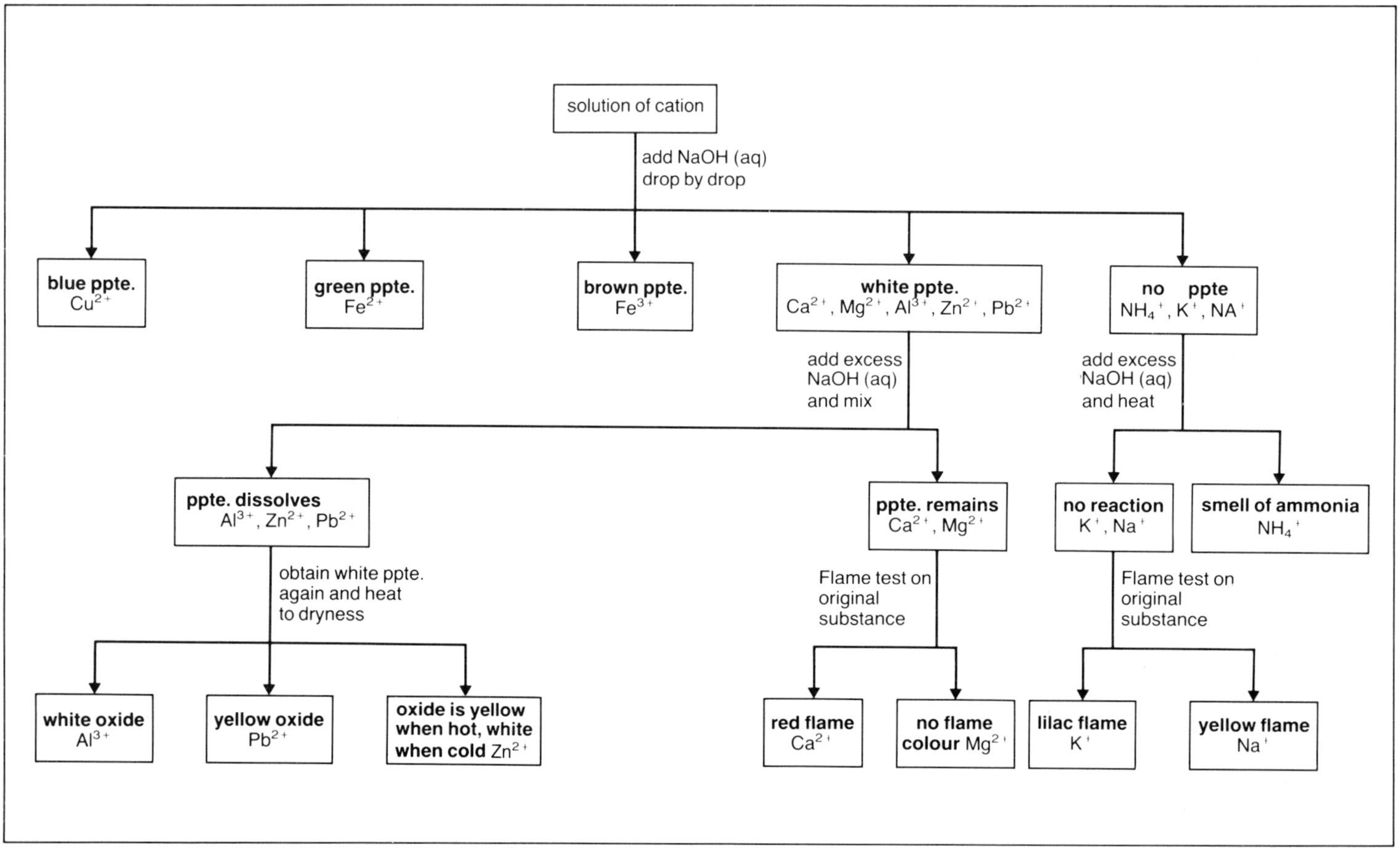

Figure 9.6 *A key for identifying cations.*

Table 9.8 *Tests for anions.*

Test	Observation	Conclusion
Test for carbonate (CO_3^{2-}) sulphide (S^{2-}) and sulphite (SO_3^{2-}) Add dil. HCl to the solid salt. If no reaction occurs heat carefully	Gas turns lime-water milky	CO_2 from **carbonate** $2H^+ + CO_3^{2-} \rightarrow H_2O + CO_2$
	Gas smells of bad eggs	H_2S from **sulphide** $2H^+ + S^{2-} \rightarrow H_2S$
	Gas is acidic with a pungent smell	SO_2 from **sulphite** $2H^+ + SO_3^{2-} \rightarrow H_2O + SO_2$
Test for chloride (Cl^-) Make a solution of the salt. Add dil. HNO_3 and then silver nitrate solution	White ppte. of silver chloride (AgCl)	**Chloride** $Ag^+ + Cl^- \rightarrow AgCl$
Test for sulphate (SO_4^{2-}) Make a solution of the salt. Add dil. HNO_3 and then barium nitrate solution	White ppte. of barium sulphate ($BaSO_4$)	**Sulphate** $Ba^{2+} + SO_4^{2-} \rightarrow BaSO_4$
Test for nitrate (NO_3^-) Make a solution of the salt. Add an equal volume of $FeSO_4$(aq) and then **(care)** pour conc. H_2SO_4 down the side of the test tube	Brown ring forms where conc. H_2SO_4 meets the solution	**Nitrate**

Tests for anions

Table 9.8 shows a series of tests that can be used to identify common anions.

Anions of weak acids (carbonate (CO_3^{2-}); sulphide (S^{2-}) and sulphite (SO_3^{2-})) can be identified by the gas produced when dilute hydrochloric acid is added to the salt.

Chloride (Cl^-) and sulphate (SO_4^{2-}) can be identified by precipitation reactions.

Nitrate ions (NO_3^-) are identified by the brown ring test.

• Self test

Questions 1–5

    A ammonia
    B sulphur dioxide
    C magnesium oxide
    D sodium hydrogencarbonate
    E sodium hydroxide

From the list of substances **A** to **E** choose the substance that
1. is insoluble in water.
2. turns universal indicator red.
3. is used as a grease remover and oven cleaner.
4. is used in baking cakes and bread.
5. is used to manufacture nitrogen-containing fertilisers.

Questions 6–9

The table below shows the results of tests on four gases.

Gas	Colour of damp litmus paper in the gas	Effect on lighted splint
A	Blue	Splint goes out
B	Purple	Gas burns
C	Purple	Splint burns brighter
D	Red	Splint goes out

Which *one* of the gases **A, B, C** or **D** is
6. ammonia?
7. hydrogen?
8. hydrogen chloride?
9. oxygen?

Questions 10–13

The table below shows the results of tests on four solutions.

Solution	Flame test	Add sodium hydroxide solution
A	No colour	White precipitate
B	Lilac flame	No precipitate
C	No colour	Brown precipitate
D	Red flame	White precipitate

Which *one* of the solutions **A, B, C** or **D** could contain
10. calcium nitrate?
11. iron (III) nitrate?
12. potassium nitrate?
13. zinc nitrate?
14. Salts always
    A dissolve in water.   **B** conduct electricity.
    C contain ions.   **D** form white solids.

15 Some nitric acid has been spilled. When it is neutralised by adding limestone (calcium carbonate)
   A the pH decreases.   **B** a gas is produced.
   C a precipitate forms.   **D** an alkali forms.

16 An insoluble salt has been precipitated by mixing two solutions. Which *one* of the following series shows the correct order of the processes used to purify the salt?
   A filter, wash, dry   **B** evaporate, filter, dry
   C dissolve, crystallise, dry   **D** evaporate, crystallise, dry

17 Which *one* of the following series shows the correct order of processes to obtain crystals of ammonium phosphate fertiliser after neutralising phosphoric acid with excess ammonia?
   A filter, evaporate, crystallise
   B evaporate, crystallise
   C evaporate, filter, crystallise
   D filter, crystallise

18 Which *one* of the following equations represents an acid–base reaction?
   A $Zn + CuSO_4 \rightarrow ZnSO_4 + Cu$
   B $Zn + H_2SO_4 \rightarrow ZnSO_4 + H_2$
   C $ZnO + H_2SO_4 \rightarrow ZnSO_4 + H_2O$
   D $ZnO + H_2O \rightarrow Zn(OH)_2$

Questions 19–20

A test was made for chloride ions in sea water. Dilute nitric acid was added to some sea water. Then silver nitrate solution was added and a precipitate formed.

19 What colour was the precipitate?
20 What is the name of the precipitate?

10 The structure of elements and compounds

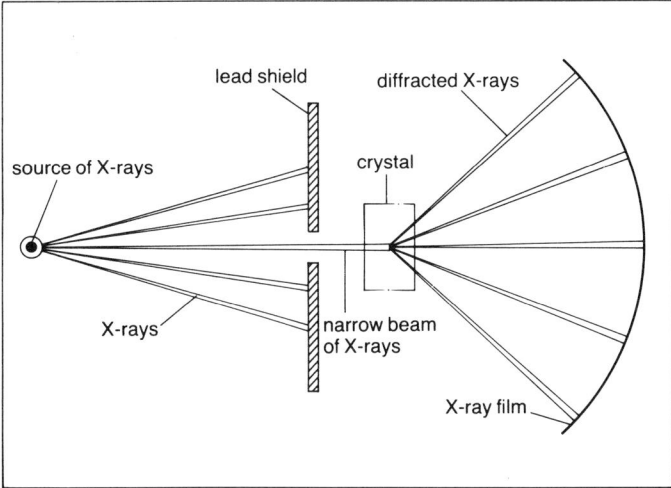

Figure 10.2 *Diffraction of X-rays by a crystal.*

How are the particles packed in solids?

Substances are made up from three kinds of particles – atoms, ions and molecules. All the crystals of one substance have roughly the same shape. This suggests that the particles of one substance always pack in a regular way to give the same crystal shape (figure 10.1). For example, snow flakes (water crystals) always look hexagonal and salt crystals (sodium chloride) are always cubic.

The shape of a crystal can give only a general idea of the way in which particles are arranged. Chemists can get better evidence for the packing of particles using:
- **X-ray photographs.** X-rays are directed at the solid. Some X-rays get reflected by particles in the crystal. The reflected rays make patterns, called diffraction patterns. From these patterns, it is possible to find the way in which the particles are arranged (figure 10.2).
- **Electron microscopes.** Electron microscopes use beams of electrons in the way that ordinary microscopes use beams of light. Using electron microscopes it is possible to identify particles as small as atoms. So, electron microscopes can help us to understand how the particles are packed in solids.

The properties of a substance depend on its structure. By 'structure', we mean the particles the substance contains (atoms, ions or molecules) and the way in which these particles are arranged and held together. In this section we shall be looking at the structure of substances. We will see how the structure of a substance is related to its properties and its uses.

Looking at the structure of metals

Look carefully at the surface of some tinplate or galvanised iron (i.e. iron coated with zinc). You may be able to see small, irregular-shaped areas separated from each other by clear boundaries. These areas are called **grains**. They are crystals of the metal. The boundaries between the grains are called **grain boundaries**.

Unlike tin and lead, the grains in most metals are too small to see. But they can often be seen under a microscope. In general, the smaller the grains in a metal, the stronger the metal will be. Scientists can control the size of grains in a metal by heating and cooling the metal in a carefully controlled way.

When metal grains are investigated using X-rays, the results show that metal atoms are packed regularly. The results also show that the atoms of most metals are packed together as close as possible. This arrangement is called **close packing**.

Figure 10.3 shows a few atoms in one layer of a metal crystal. Notice that each atom in the middle of the layer touches six others. When a second layer is placed on top of the first layer, atoms in the second layer sink into the depressions between atoms in the first layer (figure 10.4). This means that one atom in the first layer can touch three atoms in the layer above it. It also touches three in the layer below it and, of course, six in its own layer. So each metal atom in a close-packed structure touches twelve other atoms. The crystal grains in metals are made up of millions and millions of close-packed atoms. This type of structure is called a **giant structure**.

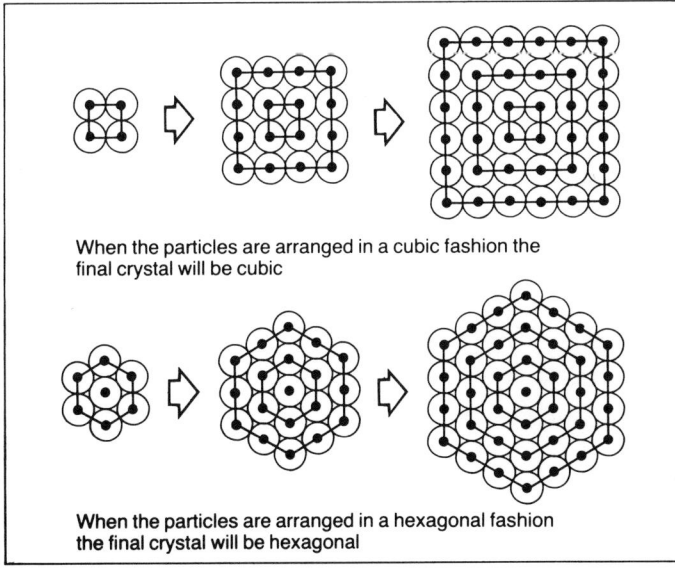

When the particles are arranged in a cubic fashion the final crystal will be cubic

When the particles are arranged in a hexagonal fashion the final crystal will be hexagonal

Figure 10.1.

60 The structure of elements and compounds

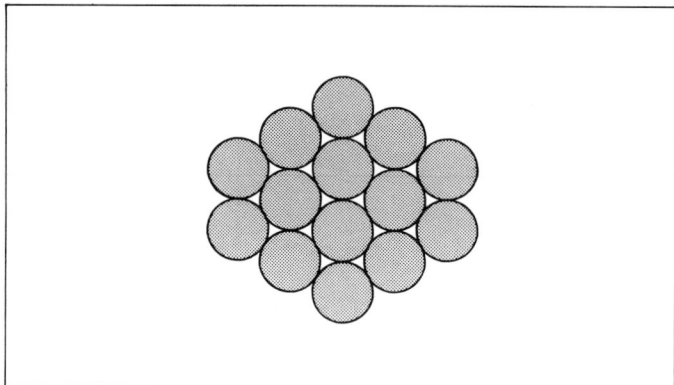

Figure 10.3 *A few atoms in one layer of a close-packed metal crystal.*

Explaining the properties of metals

We can explain the properties of metals in terms of their giant structures of close-packed atoms.

- **High melting points and boiling points.** The outermost electrons of each metal atom can move about freely. Thus, metals consist of positive ions surrounded by moving electrons (figure 10.5). The negatively charged electrons attract *all* the positive ions and hold them strongly together as a single unit. These strong forces between the atoms account for the high melting points and high boiling points of metals.
- **Good conductivity.** Metals are good conductors of electricity. Freely moving electrons in the metal will move to a positive terminal while an equal number of electrons are fed in from the negative terminal. This flow of electrons through the metal forms the electric current.
- **High density.** Most metals have a close-packed structure of atoms. This explains why they have a higher density than other substances.

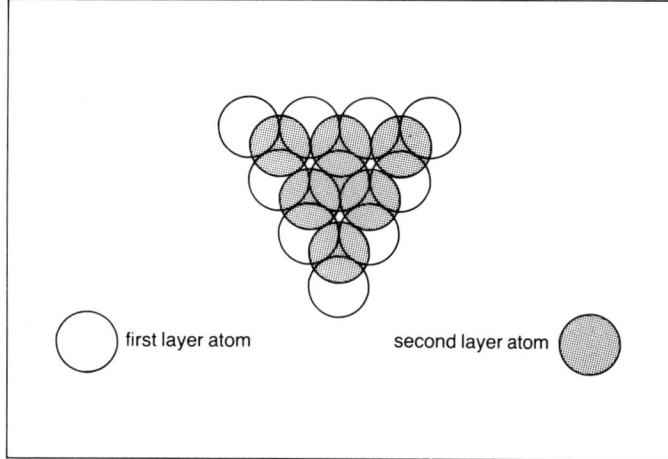

Figure 10.4.

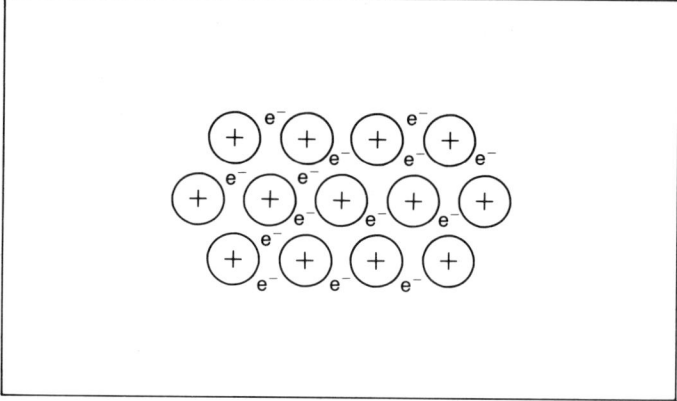

Figure 10.5 *The arrangement of positive ions and freely moving outer electrons in a metal structure.*

- **Malleable and ductile.** The bonds between atoms in a metal are strong, but they are not rigid. So, when a force is applied to a metal, rows of atoms can 'slide' over each other. This is known as **slip**. After slipping, the atoms settle into position touching their new neighbours and the close-packed structure is reformed (figure 10.6). 'Slip' means that metals are malleable (can be hammered into different shapes) and ductile (can be drawn into wires).

Comparing sulphur with metals

Look at table 10.1. This compares the properties of sulphur and copper. Sulphur has properties that are typical of non-metals.
- low melting point and low boiling point;
- poor conductivity;
- low density;
- brittleness.

X-ray analysis shows that sulphur crystals contain S_8 molecules. These S_8 molecules have eight sulphur atoms joined in a ring (figure 10.7). Notice in figure 10.6 that the centres of the sulphur atoms lie at the points on a crown.

The eight sulphur atoms are joined together in the ring by strong covalent bonds. But *between* the separate S_8 molecules there are relatively weak bonds (**intermolecular forces**). The weak forces between S_8 molecules make

Table 10.1 *The properties of sulphur and copper.*

Property	Sulphur	Copper
Melting point	119°C	1083°C
Boiling point	445°C	2600°C
Electrical conductivity	Poor	Good
Malleable or brittle	Brittle	Malleable
Density	2.1 g/cm³	9.0 g/cm³

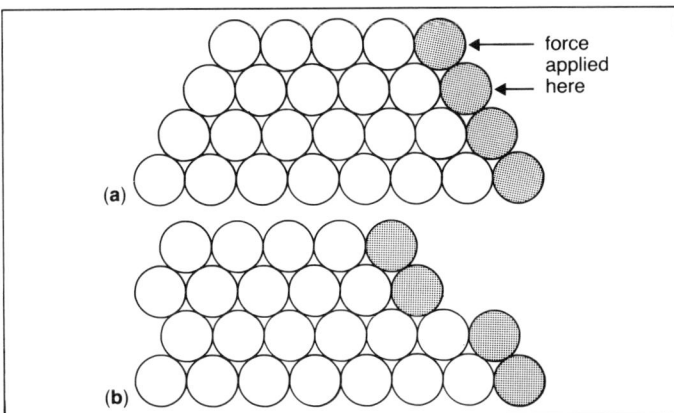

Figure 10.6 *The positions of atoms in a metal crystal (a) before and (b) after slip has taken place.*

them easy to separate. That is why sulphur has a low melting point and a low boiling point. The weak forces cannot pull the S_8 molecules close together, so sulphur has a low density. Unlike metals, sulphur has no freely moving electrons so it is a poor conductor of electricity.

Allotropes of sulphur

There are two different forms of solid sulphur, called **monoclinic sulphur** and **rhombic sulphur**. When an element like sulphur has two or more forms in the same state, the phenomenon is called **allotropy**. The different forms are called **allotropes** or **allotropic forms**.

The structure and properties of the two allotropes of sulphur are shown in table 10.2.

What are the uses of sulphur?

The most important use of sulphur is sulphuric acid manufacture (page 92). Other major uses of sulphur are for vulcanisation (hardening) of rubber and fireworks and match manufacture. Rubber tyres contain about 2 per cent sulphur.

Smaller quantities of sulphur are used as fungicides to kill fungus on crops such as vines and hops. The sulphur is sprayed on to the crops as a fine powder or as a suspension in water.

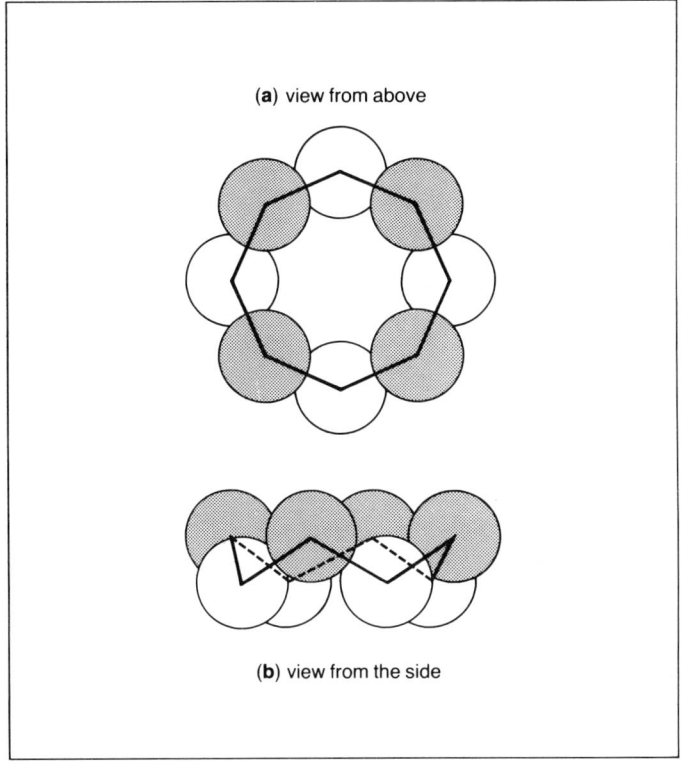

Figure 10.7 *A molecule of sulphur – a ring of eight atoms bonded together.*

How is sulphur obtained for industry?

Millions of tonnes of sulphur are required each year by the chemical industry. Sulphur occurs in volcanic areas throughout the world. The largest deposits occur below the ground in Texas and Louisiana in the USA. The sulphur deposits are obtained by first melting the sulphur below ground with hot steam at 170°C. The molten sulphur is then forced to the surface with hot compressed air.

Large quantities of sulphur are also extracted from crude oil and from natural gas. Sulphur occurs in natural gas as hydrogen sulphide, and in crude oil as various compounds.

Table 10.2 *Comparing monoclinic and rhombic sulphur.*

	Monoclinic sulphur	**Rhombic sulphur**
Crystal shape	Long, thin, monoclinic crystals	Rhombic-shaped crystals
Constituent particles	S_8 molecules	S_8 molecules
Preparation	Allow hot, molten sulphur to crystallise	Allow solutions of sulphur (e.g. sulphur in carbon disulphide) to evaporate and crystallise at room temp.
Temperatures when stable	Below 96°C	96°C to 119°C

62 The structure of elements and compounds

Looking at the structure of non-metals

Most non-metals are composed of simple molecules. For example, sulphur contains S_8 molecules, oxygen contains O_2 molecules and chlorine contains Cl_2 molecules. Because of this, the structure of these non-metals is described as **simple molecular**.

In these simple molecular substances, there are strong covalent bonds between the atoms *within* a molecule. But *between* the separate molecules there are only weak **intermolecular forces** (van der Waal's bonds) (figure 10.8). The structures of a few non-metals are shown in table 10.3. Each covalent bond is shown by a line in the molecular structure. So '–' indicates a single bond, '=' indicates a double bond and '≡' indicates a triple bond. (The electronic structures of covalent bonds are discussed further in Chapter 16.)

The *weak forces between simple molecules* in these non-metals give them similar properties to sulphur:
- low melting points and low boiling points;
- poor conductivity;
- low density as solids.

Carbon – an unusual non-metal

Carbon is another element that has allotropes. One of the allotropes is **diamond**. The other is **graphite**. (Charcoal and soot have the same structure as graphite.) The differences between these allotropes are very noticeable. They have different uses, different properties and different structures (table 10.4, figures 10.9 and 10.10). Notice in table 10.4 how the uses of these allotropes are related to their properties. In turn, the properties are related to structure.

The allotropes of carbon are unusual for non-metals as they have giant structures. This gives them very high melting points and very high boiling points. A further unusual property of graphite is that it conducts electricity. The electrons in the bonds *between* the layers are weakly held and can move along the layers.

Table 10.3 *The structures of some non-metals.*

Name	Molecular formula	Molecular structure	Model of structure
Chlorine	Cl_2	Cl – Cl	
Oxygen	O_2	O = O	
Nitrogen	N_2	N ≡ N	
Sulphur	S_8	(ring of S)	

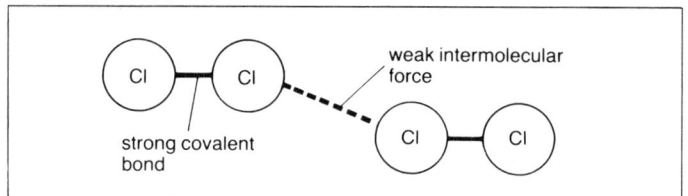

Figure 10.8 *Covalent bonds and intermolecular forces in chlorine.*

Table 10.4 *Comparing the uses, properties and structures of diamond and graphite.*

	Diamond	Graphite/charcoal
Uses	• As gems • In glass cutters • In diamond-studded saws • As abrasives	• In pencils and charcoal sticks • Crucibles for molten metals • Electrodes in cells • As a lubricant • Graphite fibres to reinforce metals and plastics
Properties	• Hard • Clear • Very high melting point • Non-conductor	• Soft • Black • Very high melting point • Conductor
Structure	Carbon atoms are linked by very strong covalent bonds in a **giant molecule**. Each carbon atom is joined to four other atoms. The carbon atoms are arranged tetrahedrally. Outer electrons are held firmly in covalent bonds (figure 10.9).	Carbon atoms are arranged in hexagons in parallel layers. There are strong covalent bonds between the carbon atoms within a layer. Therefore, each layer is a **giant molecule**. Each carbon atom is joined to three other atoms in its own layer (figure 10.10). Bonds between the layers are weak and the electrons in these bonds can move along the layers. The layers can slide over one another

The structure of compounds

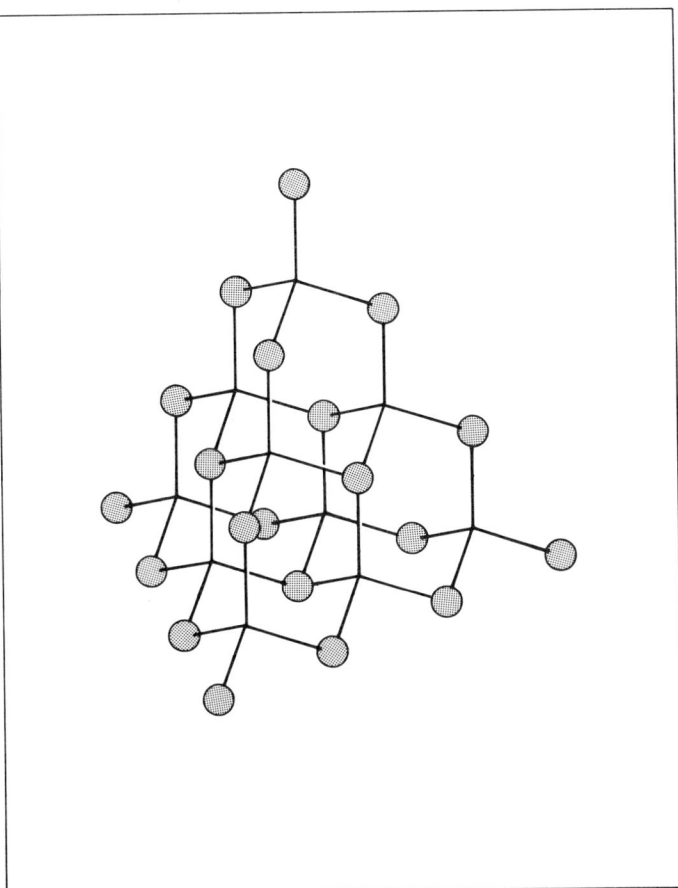

Figure 10.9 *A model of the diamond structure.*

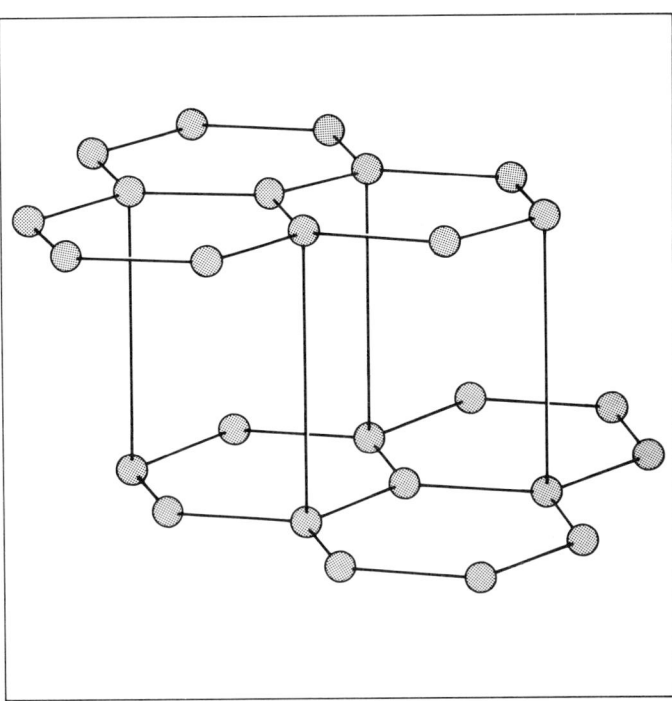

Figure 10.10 *A model of the graphite structure.*

The structure of elements

Table 10.5 summarises the structures and properties of elements. Notice that there are only three different structures for elements – giant metallic, giant molecular or simple molecular.

The structure of compounds

X-ray photographs and electron microscopes can be used to investigate the structures of *compounds* as well as elements. As with elements, the properties of compounds depend on their structures.

Look at the boiling points and conductivities of the compounds in table 10.6. The top four compounds in the table have low boiling points. They can be boiled by heating with a bunsen burner. These four compounds are non-metal compounds with simple molecular structures. The bonding and properties of simple molecular compounds are discussed on page 35. The bottom three

Table 10.5 *A summary of the structures and properties of metals and non-metals.*

Element	Structure	Examples	Properties
Metals	Giant metallic	Aluminium Iron Copper	High melting point High boiling point High density Conduct electricity
Non-metals	Giant molecular	Diamond Graphite	High melting point High boiling point Low density (Graphite conducts, diamond does not)
	Simple molecular	Sulphur Chlorine Oxygen Nitrogen	Low melting point Low boiling point Low density when solid Do not conduct electricity

64 The structure of elements and compounds

Table 10.6 *The boiling points and conductivities of some common compounds.*

Compound	Formula	Boiling point/°C	Does the compound conduct when liquid?
Water	H_2O	100	No
Methane (natural gas)	CH_4	−160	No
Octane (in petrol)	C_8H_{18}	126	No
Ethanol (alcohol)	C_2H_5OH	79	No
Salt (sodium chloride)	NaCl	1465	Yes
Lime (calcium oxide)	CaO	2850	Yes
Potassium chloride (fertiliser)	KCl	1407	Yes

compounds in table 10.6 have high boiling points and conduct electricity when liquid. These properties show that the compounds have giant ionic structures. This is what we would expect for metal – non-metal compounds. The structure and properties of ionic compounds are discussed on pages 34 and 35.

The structure, bonding and properties of ionic compounds and simple molecular compounds were compared in table 6.5 (page 35).

● Self test

Questions 1–5
- **A** diamond
- **B** graphite
- **C** steel
- **D** sulphur
- **E** tin

Choose from **A** to **E** the substance that is used
1. to protect steel from rusting.
2. to lubricate the moving parts of machines.
3. to make rubber harder.
4. to make wire fencing.
5. as an abrasive

Questions 6–10
The properties of substances **A** to **E** are shown in the table below.

Substance	Electrical conductivity		Melting point/°C
	solid	liquid	
A	Poor	Poor	−210
B	Poor	Poor	170
C	Good	Good	660
D	Poor	Poor	softens over a range of temps.
E	Poor	Good	2850

Which *one* of the substances **A** to **E** could be
6. aluminium?
7. calcium oxide (lime)?
8. nitrogen?
9. polythene?
10. sugar?

Questions 11–14
The structures of substances **A** to **D** are shown below.

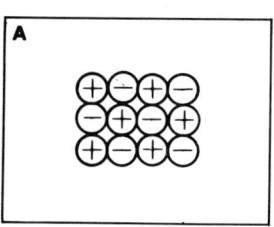
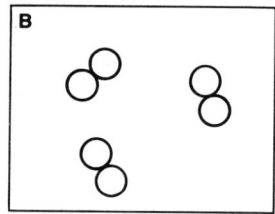
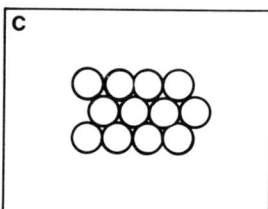
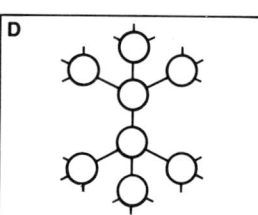

Which *one* of the structures **A** to **D** could be that of
11. chlorine?
12. copper?
13. diamond?
14. sodium chloride?

15 A substance is likely to have a low melting point if it contains
    A small ions.
    B small molecules.
    C large ions.
    D large molecules.

16 Which *one* of the following properties of a metal depends most on the size of its crystal grains?
    A boiling point
    B density
    C reactivity
    D strength

17 Allotropy occurs because the atoms of an element:
    A are arranged differently.
    B form different compounds.
    C have different shapes.
    D have different masses.

18 How many nearest neighbours does each carbon atom have in diamond?
    A 3   B 4   C 6   D 12

Questions 19–24

Complete the following passage by writing down words that would replace the numbers.

The structure of metals can be studied using electron microscopes. These microscopes use a beam of ___(19)___ instead of the beam of ___(20)___ used in an ordinary microscope. Electron microscopes can identify particles as small as ___(21)___.

Metals contain small irregularly shaped areas called ___(22)___. These are crystals of the metal. The crystals contain atoms packed together very closely. The closest possible way of packing the atoms gives a structure that is described as ___(23)___. Structures like metals that are built up from millions and millions of regularly arranged particles are called ___(24)___ structures.

11

Energy and fuels

Energy gets things done; it can move, warm or alter matter. We use it to drive our vehicles, heat our homes and cook our food. Every time we do something, we use energy.

Energy exists in a number of different forms. In the study of chemistry the most important forms of energy are: heat, electricity, light, kinetic (movement) energy and chemical energy. Chemical energy is the energy stored in chemicals. Energy can be converted from one form to another, but it can never be created or destroyed.

Energy changes in chemical reactions

Almost every chemical reaction involves an energy change. The reaction either gives out energy or takes in energy from the surroundings. (The surroundings are the air, the test tube or container, the water in which the chemicals are dissolved, etc.) Usually the energy involved is heat. A reaction that gives out heat is said to be **exothermic**. A reaction that takes in heat from the surroundings is **endothermic** (figure 11.1).

Exothermic reactions are far more common than endothermic ones. The combustion of fuels, the neutralisation of acids and respiration are all exothermic reactions. An example of an endothermic reaction is the thermal decomposition of calcium carbonate.

calcium carbonate →(heat) calcium oxide + carbon dioxide

$CaCO_3(s) \longrightarrow CaO(s) + CO_2(g)$

The amount of energy change: ΔH

The *amount* of energy given out in a chemical reaction can be measured fairly easily. Normally we measure the amount of heat energy (in kilojoules (kJ)) given out or taken in when one mole of a particular chemical reacts. This quantity is called the **heat of reaction** and is given the symbol **ΔH**. For an exothermic reaction the sign of ΔH is *negative*. This is because the chemicals have *lost* energy to the surroundings. For an endothermic reaction the sign of ΔH is positive, because the chemicals *gain* heat from the surroundings.

Examples:
1. When 1 mole (12 g) of carbon burns, 394 kJ of heat is given out. Therefore, we can say that for this reaction, ΔH = −394 kJ/mole:

   $C(s) + O_2(g) \to CO_2(g); \Delta H = -394$ kJ/mole

2. When 1 mole (180 g) of glucose is oxidised during respiration, 2900 kJ of heat is given out. Therefore, we can say that for this reaction, ΔH = −2900 kJ/mole:

   $C_6H_{12}O_6(s) + 6O_2(g) \to 6CO_2(g) + 6H_2O(l);$
   $\Delta H = -2900$ kJ/mole

3. When 1 mole (100 g) of calcium carbonate is decomposed by heating, 178 kJ of heat must be supplied. Therefore, we can say that for this reaction, ΔH = +178 kJ/mole:

   $CaCO_3(s) \to CaO(s) + CO_2(g); \Delta H = +178$ kJ/mole

Measuring ΔH for a reaction

ΔH can be measured quite easily in the laboratory for some reactions. For an exothermic reaction the heat given out can be used to raise the temperature of water.

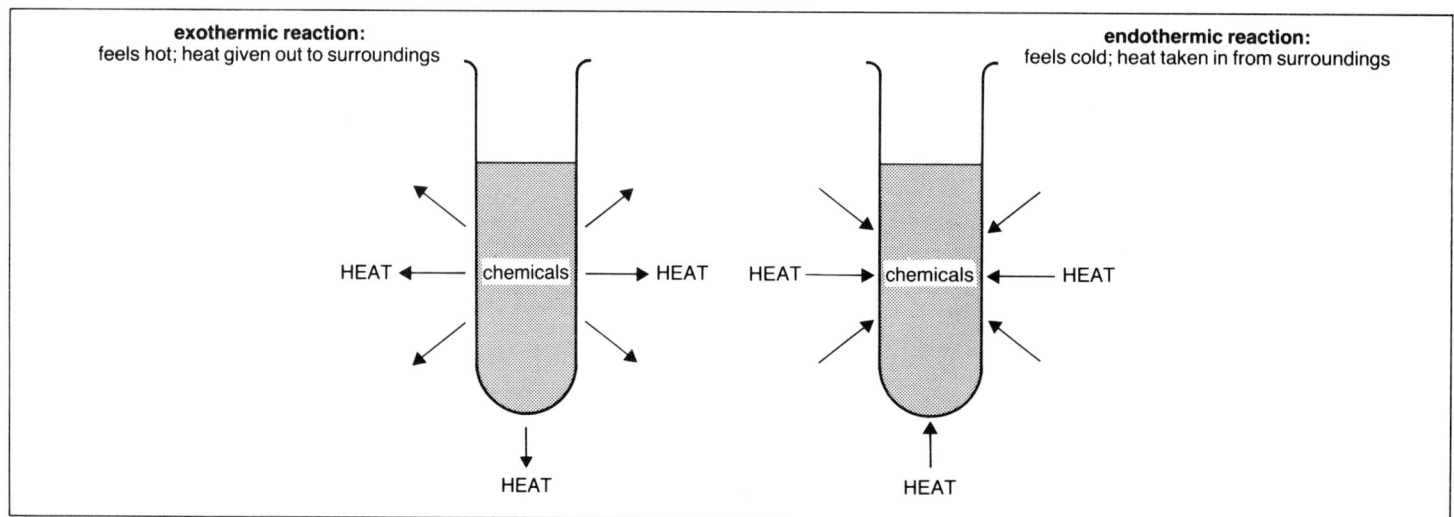

Figure 11.1 *Exothermic and endothermic reactions.*

Where does the energy come from?

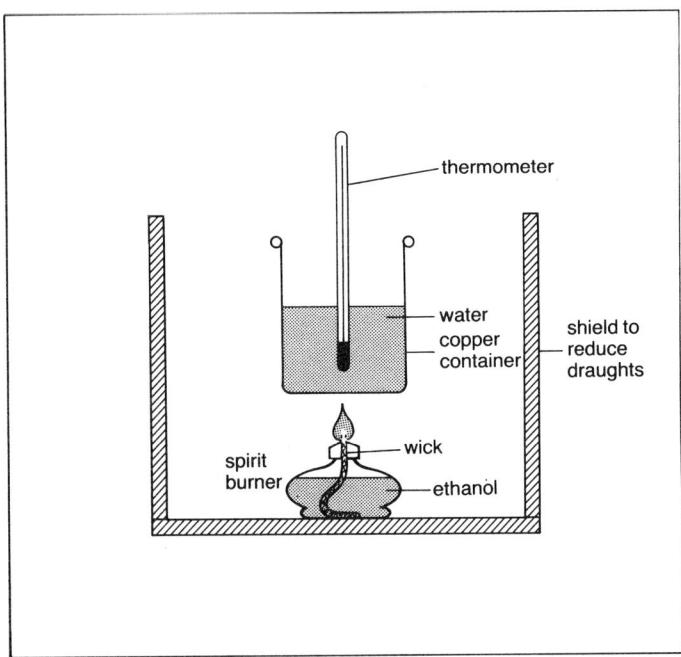

Figure 11.2 *An experiment to find the heat of combustion of ethanol.*

Example – Measuring the heat of combustion of ethanol:
Figure 11.2 shows an experiment that can be used to measure the heat of combustion of ethanol. This is the heat given out when 1 mole of ethanol burns completely in air. ΔH for this reaction will be negative because heat is given out.

A known mass of water is put in a copper container. The temperature of the water is measured.

A spirit burner containing ethanol is weighed. The burner is lit and used to heat the water for a few minutes, while the water is stirred with the thermometer. The burner flame is extinguished, and the final temperature of the water is measured. The spirit burner is weighed again to find how much ethanol has been used up.

Some sample results are given below:
mass of spirit burner at start of experiment = 343.00 g
mass of spirit burner at finish of experiment = 341.50 g
mass of water in copper container = 200 g
temperature of water at start = 18°C
temperature of water at finish = 40°C

Working
mass of ethanol burned = 343.00 − 341.50 = 1.50 g
temperature rise = 40 − 18 = 22°C

heat given out when 1.5 g ethanol burns
= (mass of water) × (specific heat capacity of water) × (temperature rise of water)

= 0.200 kg × 4.2 kJ/°C/kg × 22°C
= 18.48 kJ

mass of 1 mole of ethanol = 46 g
heat given out when 1 mole of ethanol burns
= $18.48 \times \frac{46}{1.5}$ kJ
= 567 kJ
Heat of combustion of ethanol (ΔH_c) = −567 kJ/mole

This value is much lower than the data book value of ΔH_c = −1370 kJ/mole. The inaccuracy is caused by a number of factors, including:
- heat loss due to heat from the flame escaping into the air;
- heat loss from the water;
- incomplete combustion of the ethanol fuel.

Where does the energy come from?

Energy changes in reactions are caused by the making and breaking of chemical bonds.

Breaking chemical bonds takes in energy.
Making chemical bonds releases energy.

In any reaction, bonds in reactant chemicals must first be broken. This requires energy. New bonds are then formed, releasing energy. If the energy released is greater than the energy taken in, the reaction will be exothermic. Figure 11.3 illustrates the idea for the reaction of

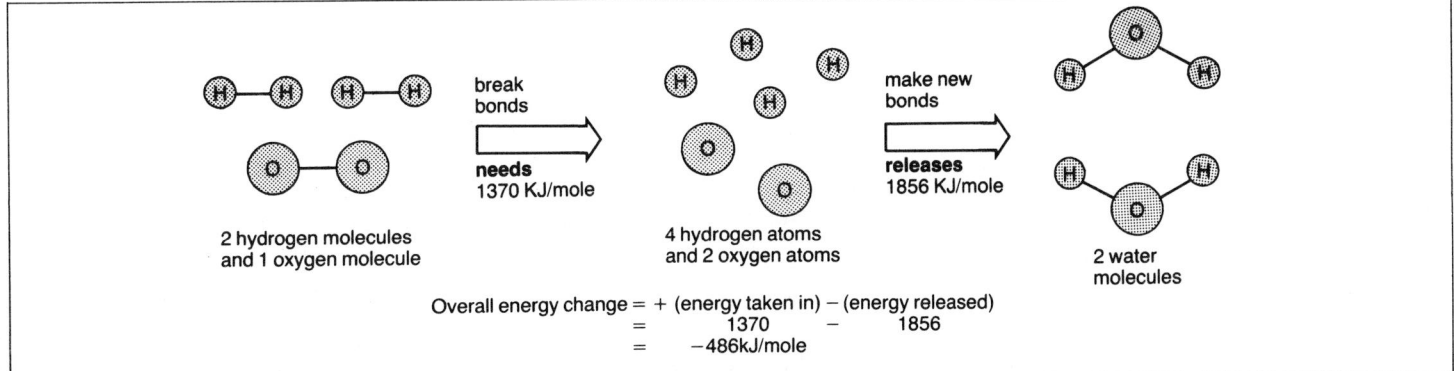

Figure 11.3 *Bond breaking and bond making in the reaction between hydrogen and oxygen.*

hydrogen with oxygen. Note that energy *released* has a negative sign, while energy *taken in* is given a positive sign. This is a standard convention where energy changes are concerned.

It is important to remember that even exothermic reactions need energy to get them started. This energy is needed to break bonds before new bonds can be made. It is called the **activation energy**.

Energy level diagrams

Energy level diagrams are a convenient way to show the energy changes in chemical reactions. Figure 11.4 shows the energy level diagram for an exothermic reaction. Notice that the *reactants* are at a higher energy level than the *products*. The difference between these levels is the energy given out by the reaction.

Figure 11.5 shows the energy level diagram for an endothermic reaction. Notice that the *products* are at a higher level than the *reactants*. The difference between these two levels is the energy taken in by the reaction.

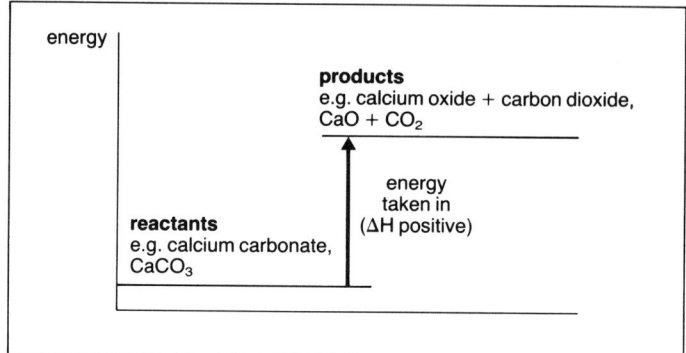

Figure 11.5 *Energy level diagram for an endothermic reaction.*

Fossil fuels

Fossil fuels have been formed as a result of the decay of plants and animals that lived long ago. Table 11.1 compares the three major fossil fuels: coal, oil and natural gas.

All three of these fossil fuels are important sources of chemicals as well as being fuels. You can find out more about crude oil on page 78. Page 8 explains what happens when fuels burn.

Coal can be burned directly as a fuel, without special treatment. Most of the coal mined in Britain is burned in power stations to generate electricity. Coal is also burned on domestic fires in our homes.

Coal can be split up by heating it in the absence of air. This is called **destructive distillation**. The products are shown in figure 11.6.

Comparing fuels

As figure 11.7 shows, most of Britain's energy at present comes from the three fossil fuels.

Different fuels have different advantages and disadvantages. Four important considerations are safety, convenience, pollution and expected lifetimes.

Safety

A good fuel must be easy to ignite, but not so flammable as to cause a fire or explosion risk. Solid fuels are safer than gaseous fuels and volatile liquid fuels like petrol.

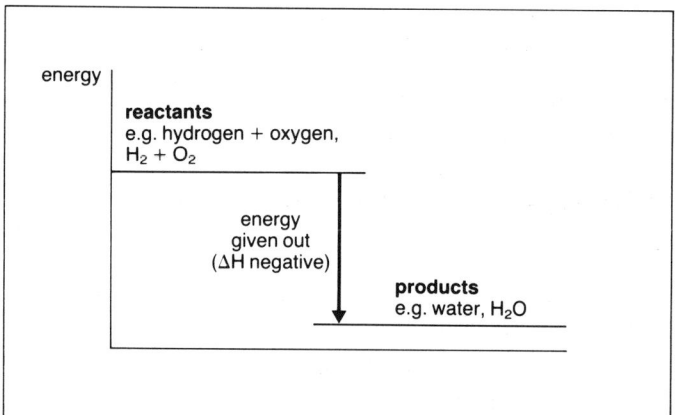

Figure 11.4 *Energy level diagram for an exothermic reaction.*

Fuels

Fuels are substances that can be easily burned in air to release energy. Most fuels contain carbon and hydrogen. The commonest are fossil fuels.

Table 11.1 *Major fossil fuels.*

Fossil fuel	Appearance	What it contains	How it was made
Natural gas	Colourless gas	Mainly methane (CH_4)	By the decay of microscopic animals which lived in ancient seas
Crude oil	Dark brown liquid	A mixture of hydrocarbons, mostly alkanes	As for natural gas
Coal	Black solid	Mainly carbon	By the decay of plants which lived in ancient forests

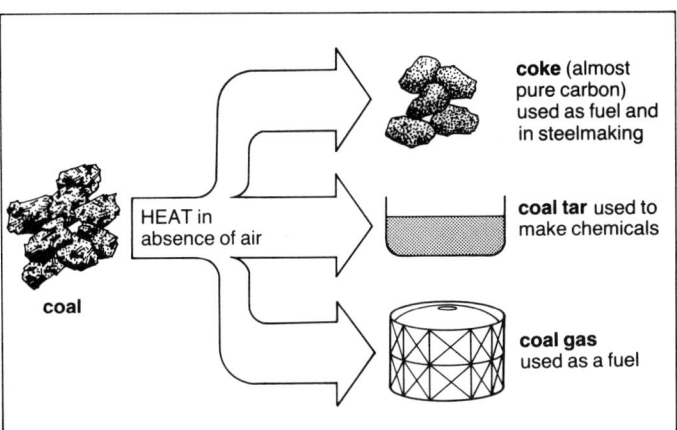

Figure 11.6 *The destructive distillation of coal.*

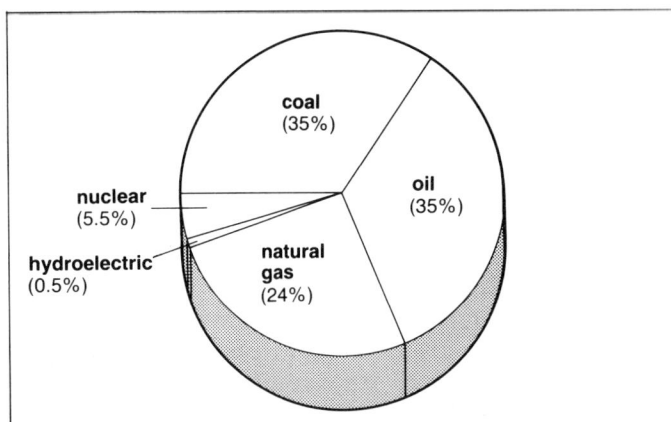

Figure 11.7 *Britain's primary energy sources, 1983. (The figures show how much of Britain's energy came from each source)*

Convenience

Liquid and gaseous fuels tend to be more convenient than solid fuels like coal. They are easier to store and transport, and easier to ignite. Liquid fuels, like petrol and diesel fuel, are particularly convenient for motor vehicles.

Pollution

All fuels cause a certain amount of pollution. However, natural gas causes little pollution because it is almost completely converted to carbon dioxide and water when it burns.

Coal and oil contain sulphur compounds, which form acidic sulphur dioxide when the fuel is burned. This helps to cause acid rain. Oil- and petrol-burning engines also release nitrogen oxides and unburnt hydrocarbons, which can cause more pollution. Some fuels, particularly solid fuels, give off a lot of smoke when they burn. There is more about air pollution on pages 10–11.

Lifetimes

The estimated lifetimes of world supplies of different fuels are compared in figure 11.8 (overleaf). Britain has reserves of all three fossil fuels, but much more coal than gas or oil. It is important to **conserve** these reserves by using them efficiently and saving energy wherever possible.

Alternative energy sources

Eventually, supplies of fossil fuel are bound to run out. Britain will need to find other energy sources, particularly for transport and for generating electricity. Nuclear energy (page 108) is an important possibility, though many people are worried about the safety of nuclear power stations. Besides nuclear power, there are several **alternative sources of energy** that it might be possible to use. They are summarised in table 11.2. Most of these

Table 11.2 *Alternative energy sources.*

Energy source	How it works
Solar power	The Sun's energy is used to heat buildings or water, or to generate electricity using photovoltaic cells
Hydroelectric power	The energy of falling water is used to generate electricity
Tidal power	As the tides come in and go out, water is made to drive turbines and generate electricity
Wind power	Wind is used to drive wind turbines ('windmills') to generate electricity, pump water, etc.
Wave power	The energy of moving water in the waves is used to generate electricity
Biomass	Plant material is grown to provide energy, e.g. firewood, sugar cane for making alcohol fuel
Biogas	A gaseous fuel is collected when waste material is allowed to decompose in the absence of air
Geothermal power	Water is pumped into hot rocks beneath the Earth's surface; this makes steam which is used to drive turbines and generate electricity

70 Energy and Fuels

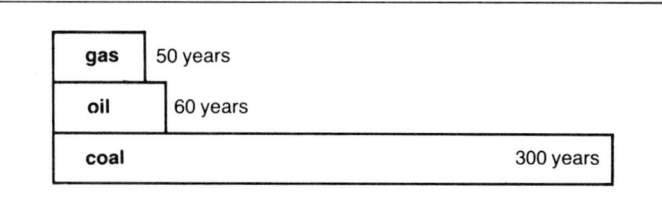

Figure 11.8 *Estimates of how long world supplies of different fossil fuels will last.*

sources are **renewable** – energy can be replaced as it is used up. Fossil fuels are **non-renewable** – once used, they cannot be replaced.

Food as fuel

Like machines, we humans need energy to keep us going. Our energy source is food.

The oxidation of fuels to release energy is called burning, or **combustion**. The oxidation of food to release energy is called **respiration** (page 9). Respiration can be summarised by this equation:

food + oxygen → carbon dioxide + water + energy

For example:

glucose + oxygen → carbon dioxide + water

$C_6H_{12}O_6 + 6O_2 \rightarrow 6CO_2 + 6H_2O + $ energy

The two major classes of energy food are **carbohydrates** and **fats**.

Carbohydrates

Carbohydrates all contain carbon, hydrogen and oxygen, with hydrogen and oxygen atoms in the ratio 2 : 1. One of the simplest carbohydrates is **glucose** ($C_6H_{12}O_6$). Our bodies can quickly use glucose to provide energy through respiration.

Another important carbohydrate is **starch**. Starch molecules consist of chains of glucose molecules linked together as in figure 11.9. The starch molecules are too big to be absorbed into the bloodstream. So when you eat starch it is **hydrolysed** to give separate glucose molecules.

The hydrolysis of starch is normally very slow, but it is speeded up by catalysts (page 85). Starch hydrolysis is catalysed by enzymes (amylase) and by acid.

Table 11.3 gives details of chemical tests that can be used to detect the two carbohydrates, starch and glucose.

Fats

Like carbohydrates, fats contain the elements carbon, hydrogen and oxygen, but they have relatively more C and H and less O. A typical fat has the formula $C_{57}H_{110}O_6$. Like carbohydrates, fats are oxidised in the body to produce carbon dioxide and water, releasing energy. Fats are more concentrated energy sources than carbohydrates, and they are more fattening than carbohydrates.

Photosynthesis

Plants are the source of all our food. Even if we eat animal products we are depending on the plants on which the animal fed.

Plants in turn depend on the Sun to make food. They use the energy of sunlight to drive a series of reactions which convert carbon dioxide and water to carbohydrate and oxygen. This process is called **photosynthesis**. The green material in plants' leaves, **chlorophyll**, is important in photosynthesis because it helps to trap the Sun's energy. Figure 11.10 summarises the process.

Photosynthesis is a complicated series of reactions, but the overall equation is quite simple:

carbon dioxide + water $\xrightarrow{\text{energy from sun}}$ glucose + oxygen

$6CO_2 + 6H_2O \longrightarrow C_6H_{12}O_6 + 6O_2$

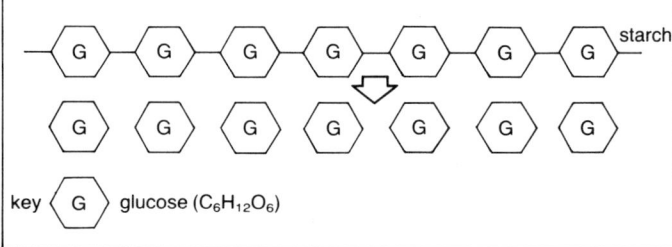

Figure 11.9 *Glucose and starch.*

Table 11.3 *Tests for carbohydrates.*

Test	Method	Results	
		With glucose	With starch
Benedict's test	Add a little Benedict's solution to a solution of the carbohydrate. Warm.	**Positive result:** Turns green, then gives orange-red precipitate	No change
Iodine test	Add a few drops of iodine solution to the carbohydrate solution	No change	**Positive result:** deep blue-black

The Carbon Cycle

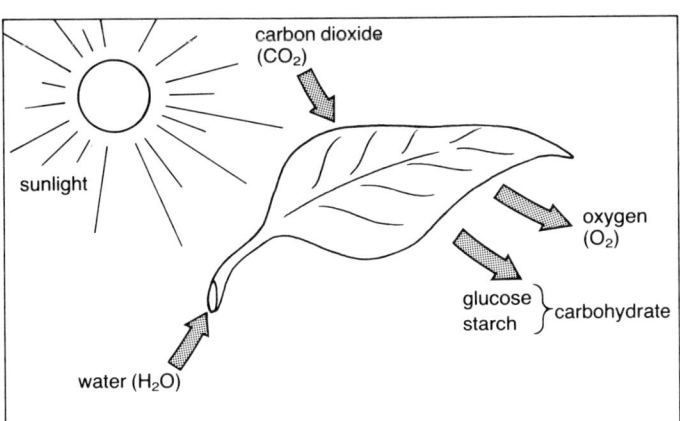

Figure 11.10 *A summary of photosynthesis.*

The glucose formed in photosynthesis can be converted by the plant to starch, cellulose, protein, fat and other useful substances. Material made by photosynthesis is sometimes called **biomass**.

The carbon cycle

If you compare the equations for photosynthesis and respiration, you will see that they are the reverse of each other. Photosynthesis converts carbon dioxide and water to carbohydrate and oxygen, taking in energy. Respiration converts them back again, releasing energy.

Left undisturbed, the processes of photosynthesis and respiration would balance out. Carbon dioxide is used up by photosynthesis as fast as it is produced by respiration. Carbon atoms circulate round and round; this is the **carbon cycle** (figure 11.11).

Notice two things about the carbon cycle in figure 11.11.
- Plants, as well as animals, respire.
- Burning fossil fuels also adds carbon dioxide to the atmosphere. At present, fossil fuels are being burned so fast that carbon dioxide is being added to the atmosphere faster than photosynthesis can remove it. Many scientists are worried that this may have harmful effects, particularly on the weather. The build-up of carbon dioxide may make the Earth hotter. This is called the **greenhouse effect**. The situation is made worse by the fact that many of the Earth's great forests, like the Amazon rain forest, are being cut down. This means there are even less plants to remove carbon dioxide by photosynthesis.

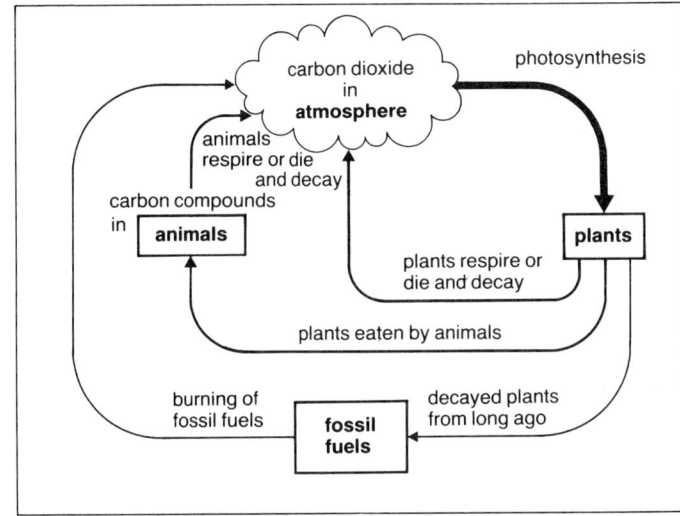

Figure 11.11 *The carbon cycle.*

● Self test

Questions 1–5

Important processes in the carbon cycle are labelled **A** to **E** in the diagram on the right. Choose from **A** to **E** the process that would be labelled

1. burning of fossil fuels.
2. decaying of plants long ago.
3. plants eaten by animals.
4. plants respire or die and decay.
5. photosynthesis by plants.

Questions 6–10

From the list **A** to **E** below:
- **A** biomass
- **B** chlorophyll
- **C** coke
- **D** fat
- **E** natural gas

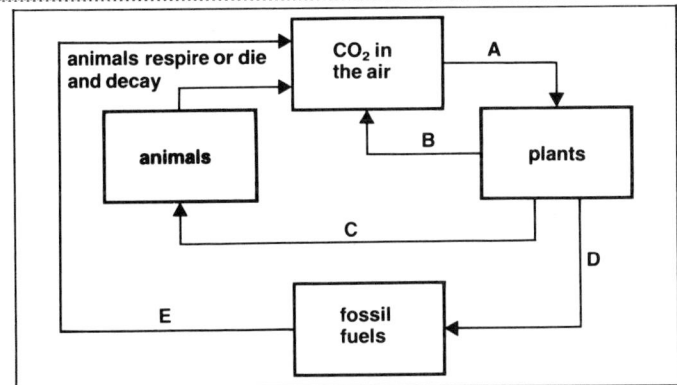

choose the material that
6. helps plants to absorb light energy from the sun.
7. is a fossil fuel.
8. is formed by destructive distillation of coal.
9. is made by photosynthesis.
10. contains only three elements.

Questions 11–13

The pollutants **A** to **E** below can form when coal burns:
- **A** ash
- **B** carbon dioxide
- **C** carbon monoxide
- **D** smoke
- **E** sulphur dioxide

Choose from the list **A** to **E** the pollutant that is mainly responsible for

11 reduction in the amount of sunlight.
12 damage to stone buildings and forests.
13 the 'greenhouse' effect.

14 It is likely that more coal-fired power stations will be built if
- **A** the price of coal falls.
- **B** there is a surplus of oil.
- **C** 'acid rain' problems increase.
- **D** natural gas is plentiful.

15 During an exothermic reaction
- **A** the temperature falls and ΔH is negative.
- **B** the temperature rises and ΔH is negative.
- **C** the temperature falls and ΔH is positive.
- **D** the temperature rises and ΔH is positive.

16 When 0.1 mole of calcium carbonate ($CaCO_3$) is decomposed, 17.8 kJ of heat must be supplied. Therefore ΔH for the reaction, in kJ per mole of $CaCO_3$, is
- **A** +1.78   **B** −1.78   **C** +178   **D** −178

17 A chip-pan fire can be put out by covering the pan with a wet cloth. The main reason why this puts the fire out is that it
- **A** cools the flames.
- **B** conducts heat away.
- **C** stops oil vaporising.
- **D** stops oxygen reaching the flames.

Questions 18–20

The following table shows the reserves of natural gas in five areas of the world.

Area	Reserves in billions of m^3	Estimated time before reserves run out/years	Rate of use in billions of m^3 per year
Africa	6000	150	40
Asia	12000	80	150
Europe	4500	25	180
N. America	10000	50	—
USSR	17000	85	200

18 Which area has the largest reserves of natural gas?
19 Which area will probably be the first to use up its reserves?
20 What is the rate of use of natural gas in North America?

12 Simple carbon compounds

Carbon forms more compounds than all the other elements put together. Many of these are very complex compounds that are often found in living things. **Organic** compounds like this are covered in Chapter 13. In this chapter we are looking at simple compounds of carbon such as carbon monoxide, carbon dioxide and carbonates.

When fuels containing carbon are burned, oxides of carbon are formed. Depending on the amount of oxygen present, the oxide may be carbon monoxide (CO) or carbon dioxide (CO_2).

Carbon monoxide (CO)

Carbon monoxide is a poisonous gas that forms when fuels burn in a limited supply of air. It makes up about 5 per cent of car exhaust gases, which is why these gases are poisonous. Carbon monoxide is also present in cigarette smoke, which is one of the reasons why smoking is unhealthy.

Figure 12.1 summarises the properties of carbon monoxide.

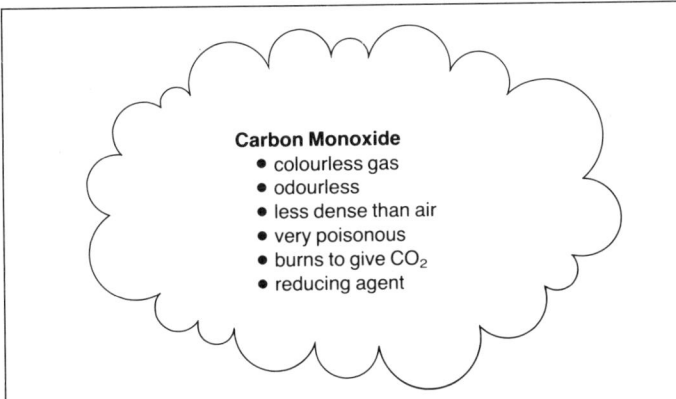

Figure 12.1 *Properties of carbon monoxide.*

Carbon dioxide (CO_2)

Carbon dioxide is one of the most important gases of all. It is formed when fuels burn in a plentiful supply of air. It is also formed during respiration (see page 9), which means we breathe out carbon dioxide.

What are the uses of carbon dioxide?

- **In fizzy drinks.** Fizzy drinks contain dissolved carbon dioxide. When the top is taken off the bottle, the carbon dioxide starts to come out of solution as bubbles.

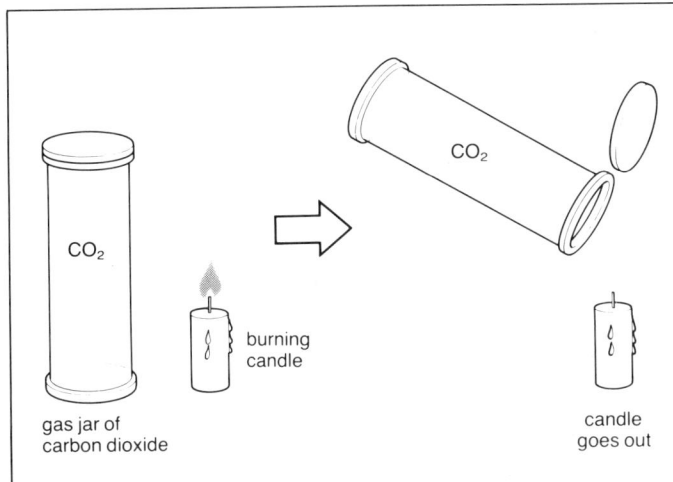

Figure 12.2 *The effect of carbon dioxide on a flame.*

- **In fire extinguishers.** Figure 12.2 shows an experiment to illustrate the effect of carbon dioxide on a flame. Carbon dioxide does not allow things to burn, and does not burn itself. Because of these properties carbon dioxide is used in fire extinguishers. The carbon dioxide forms a kind of 'blanket' over the fire because it is denser than air.
- **To cool things.** When carbon dioxide is cooled below −79°C, it turns directly to a solid (**sublimation**). Solid carbon dioxide is sometimes called 'dry ice'. When the 'dry ice' turns to gas it takes in heat from things around it. So it is a very good refrigerant for cooling things.

Properties of carbon dioxide

Figure 12.3 shows the most important properties of carbon dioxide. Like most non-metal oxides, carbon dioxide

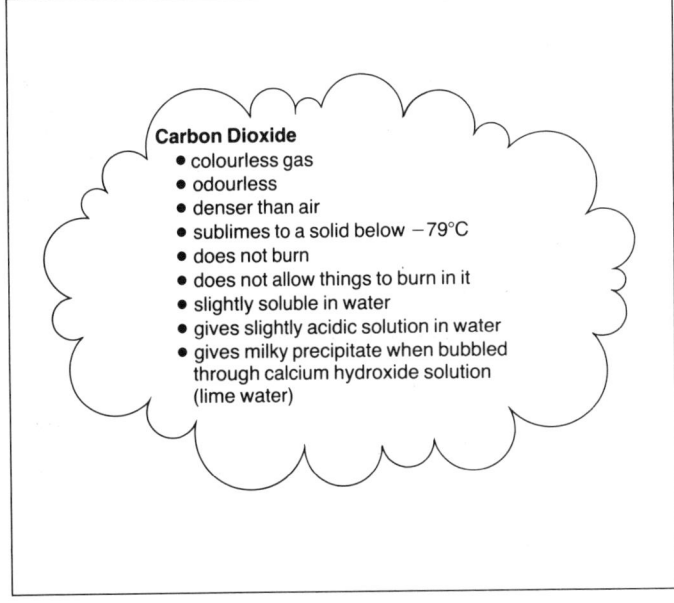

Figure 12.3 *Properties of carbon dioxide.*

is acidic. But it is only weakly acidic. You can taste the slightly sharp acidic taste of carbon dioxide when you drink soda water.

The lime water test for carbon dioxide

When carbon dioxide is bubbled through a solution of calcium hydroxide (**lime water**), a milky-white precipitate is formed. This reaction is a good test for carbon dioxide. The milky-white precipitate is calcium carbonate.

calcium + carbon → calcium + water
hydroxide dioxide   carbonate
(lime water)

$Ca(OH)_2(aq) + CO_2(g) \rightarrow CaCO_3(s) + H_2O(l)$

If carbon dioxide continues to bubble through the milky suspension, the precipitate redissolves to give a clear solution. The insoluble calcium carbonate has been converted to soluble calcium hydrogencarbonate.

calcium + carbon + water → calcium
carbonate dioxide   hydrogencarbonate
insoluble   soluble

$CaCO_3(s) + CO_2(g) + H_2O(l) \rightarrow Ca(HCO_3)_2(aq)$

The same reaction occurs when water containing dissolved carbon dioxide flows over calcium carbonate in limestone rocks. This helps to wear away the rock. It also puts calcium hydrogencarbonate into the water, making it hard (page 76).

If water containing dissolved calcium hydrogencarbonate is heated, the calcium hydrogencarbonate decomposes again. Solid calcium carbonate is reformed. This reaction can cause 'furring' of pipes, boilers and kettles in hard water areas.

Making carbon dioxide

Many chemical reactions produce carbon dioxide. Industrially, carbon dioxide is often produced as a by-product of fermentation (page 83). In the laboratory, it is most conveniently made by the reaction of a carbonate with an acid. Calcium carbonate (marble chips) is usually used; the apparatus is like that shown in figure 12.4.

Carbonates and hydrogencarbonates

Carbonates are compounds containing the CO_3^{2-} ion combined with a metal. Carbonates have two particularly important chemical properties.

- They **decompose when heated**, giving an oxide and carbon dioxide. For example:

copper → copper + carbon
carbonate oxide   dioxide

$CuCO_3(s) \xrightarrow{heat} CuO(s) + CO_2(g)$

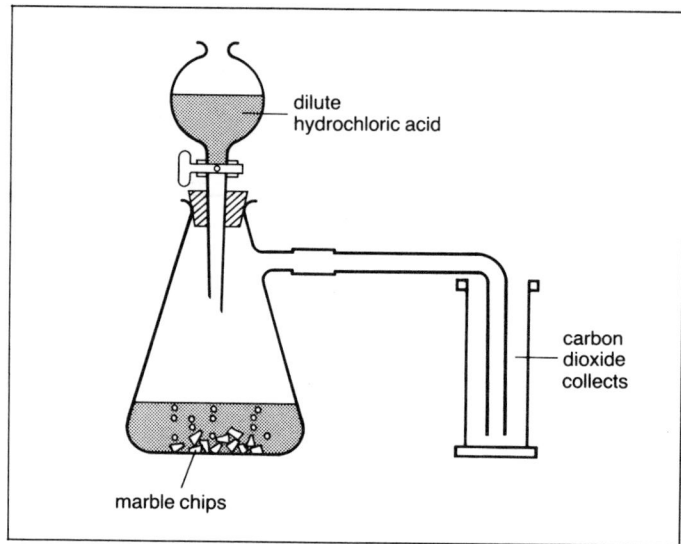

Figure 12.4 *Preparing carbon dioxide in the laboratory.*

The higher the metal is in the reactivity series (page 46), the higher is the temperature needed to make the carbonate decompose.

- They **react with dilute acids**, giving a salt, carbon dioxide and water. For example:

sodium   + hydrochloric → sodium   + carbon + water
carbonate   acid   chloride   dioxide

$Na_2CO_3(s) + 2HCl(aq) \rightarrow 2NaCl(aq) + CO_2(g) + H_2O(l)$

Hydrogencarbonates

Hydrogencarbonates are compounds containing the HCO_3^- ion. An important one is sodium hydrogencarbonate ($NaHCO_3$), which is sometimes called sodium bicarbonate.

Hydrogencarbonates readily decompose when heated. They are much easier to decompose than carbonates. For example, when sodium hydrogencarbonate is heated:

sodium   heat   sodium   + carbon + water
hydrogen-   →   carbonate   dioxide
carbonate

$2NaHCO_3(s) \rightarrow Na_2CO_3(s) + CO_2(g) + H_2O(g)$

Like carbonates, hydrogencarbonates react with acid, giving off carbon dioxide. A mixture of sodium hydrogencarbonate and a weak acid is used to make cakes rise. The mixture is called **baking powder**. The sodium hydrogencarbonate and acid react together to form carbon dioxide. The bubbles of carbon dioxide make the cake rise.

Calcium carbonate

Calcium carbonate ($CaCO_3$) is the commonest and most important carbonate. It occurs as limestone, chalk and marble. Much of the scenery of England is made of calcium carbonate. For example, the Peak District of Derbyshire is limestone, and the Chilterns are chalk.

Uses of calcium carbonate

Huge quantities of calcium carbonate are used each year by industry. The calcium carbonate is usually obtained from quarries as limestone. Unfortunately the best limestone is often found in areas of beautiful scenery. Quarrying the limestone makes an ugly scar on the landscape. We have to weigh our need for limestone against the importance of preserving the countryside.

- **Limestone for making glass.** Glass is made by heating together sodium carbonate, calcium carbonate (limestone) and sand until they melt. The raw materials are cheap, but the energy needed to heat the mixture is expensive. Energy and raw materials can be saved by using glass again instead of throwing it away. Some glass containers like milk bottles can be **reused**. Broken glass can be **recycled** by melting it down to make new glass.
- **Limestone for making cement.** Cement is made by heating together limestone and clay.
- **Limestone for making iron and steel.** Limestone, iron ore and coke are the raw materials that go into a blast furnace for making iron (page 49).
- **Limestone for making lime.** (See 'Reactions of calcium carbonate' below.)
- **Limestone for building.** Limestone is an important building stone. Crushed limestone is used for building motorways and other roads.

Reactions of calcium carbonate

- **Calcium carbonate reacts with dilute acids** to give carbon dioxide and a calcium salt.
- **Calcium carbonate decomposes on heating**, giving calcium oxide (quicklime) and carbon dioxide:

calcium carbonate → calcium oxide (quicklime) + carbon dioxide

$$CaCO_3(s) \xrightarrow{heat} CaO(s) + CO_2(g)$$

This is an important industrial reaction, because calcium oxide has important uses. It can be readily converted to calcium hydroxide, $Ca(OH)_2$ (slaked lime), by adding water.

calcium oxide (quicklime) + water → calcium hydroxide (slaked lime)

$$CaO(s) + H_2O(l) \rightarrow Ca(OH)_2(aq)$$

Calcium hydroxide is a weak alkali. It is cheap and abundant. Farmers put it on their fields to neutralise acidity in the soil.

Figure 12.5 summarises some important reactions involving calcium carbonate, calcium hydrogencarbonate, calcium oxide and calcium hydroxide.

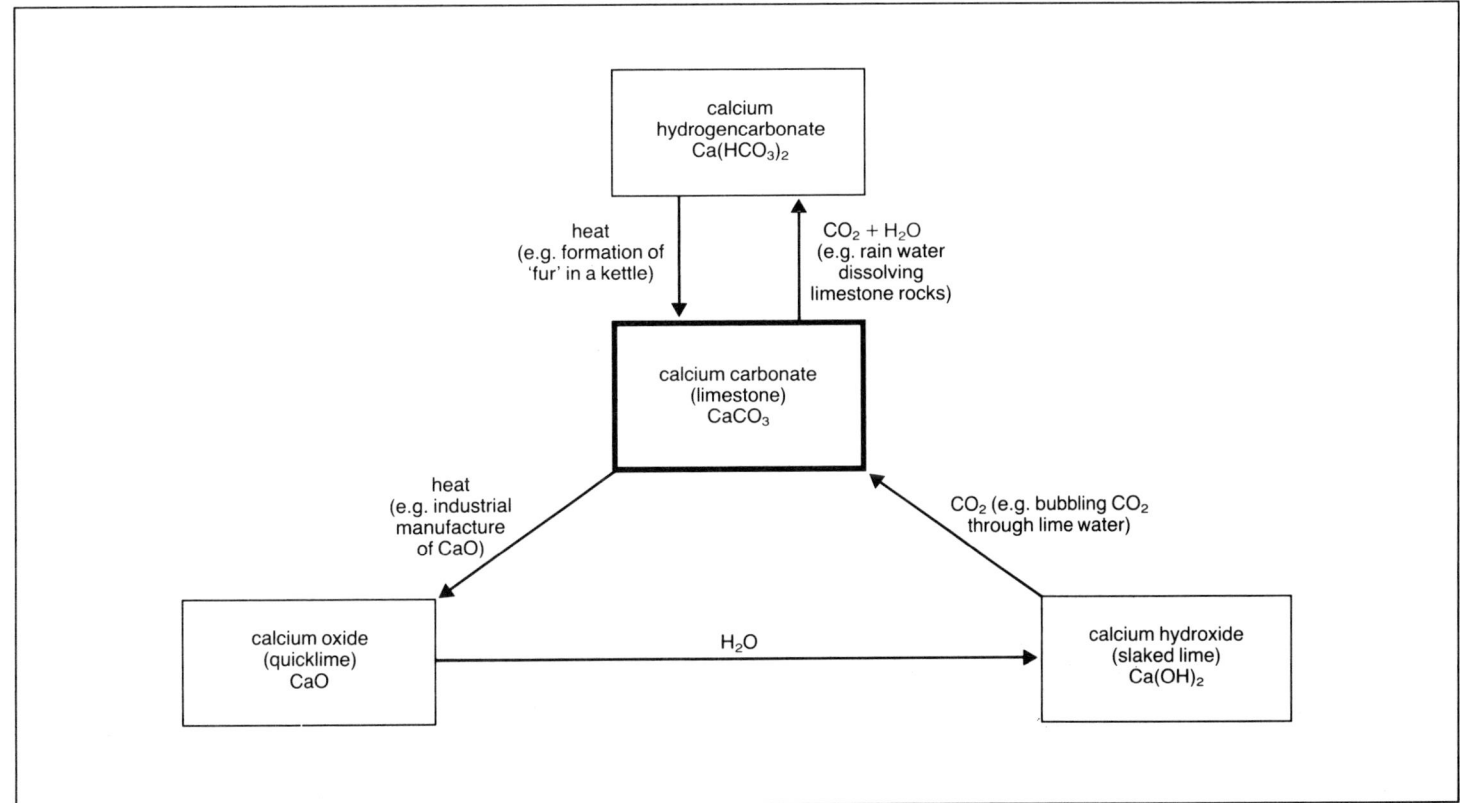

Figure 12.5 *Important reactions of calcium compounds.*

Hardness of water

In limestone areas, the water is hard because it contains dissolved calcium compounds like calcium hydrogencarbonate. It is the Ca^{2+} ions in these compounds that make the water hard. Magnesium ions (Mg^{2+}) also make water hard.

Soap is difficult to lather in hard water. This is because soap reacts with calcium ions to form an insoluble scum. Table 12.1 shows some of the disadvantages and advantages of hard water.

Table 12.1 *Disadvantages and advantages of hard water.*

Disadvantages	Advantages
Makes soap difficult to lather	Often tastes better than soft water
Forms 'scum' with soap	May be better for preventing heart disease than soft water
'Furs up' kettles, pipes and boilers	

Making hard water soft

To make hard water soft, the Ca^{2+} or Mg^{2+} ions must be removed. There are several ways of doing this.

- **Use excess soap** to react with the Ca^{2+} or Mg^{2+} ions until they are removed. This wastes the soap and forms a lot of scum.
- **Distil the water**, leaving the calcium or magnesium ions behind. This needs lot of energy to heat the water, so it is expensive.
- **Add sodium carbonate** to precipitate the Ca^{2+} ions as calcium carbonate:

calcium ions + carbonate ions → insoluble calcium
  in water   from sodium   carbonate
                  carbonate

$$Ca^{2+}(aq) + CO_3^{2-}(aq) \rightarrow CaCO_3(s)$$

- **Use an ion-exchange column.** The water runs through a column containing a special resin (figure 12.6). The resin exchanges sodium ions in the column for calcium ions in the water. Thus, calcium compounds in the water are converted to sodium compounds. These sodium compounds do not form insoluble scum so the water is not hard. Every so often, sodium ions are put back into the column by pouring a strong solution of salt through it. This is the cheapest and most convenient way of softening water once the column has been installed.

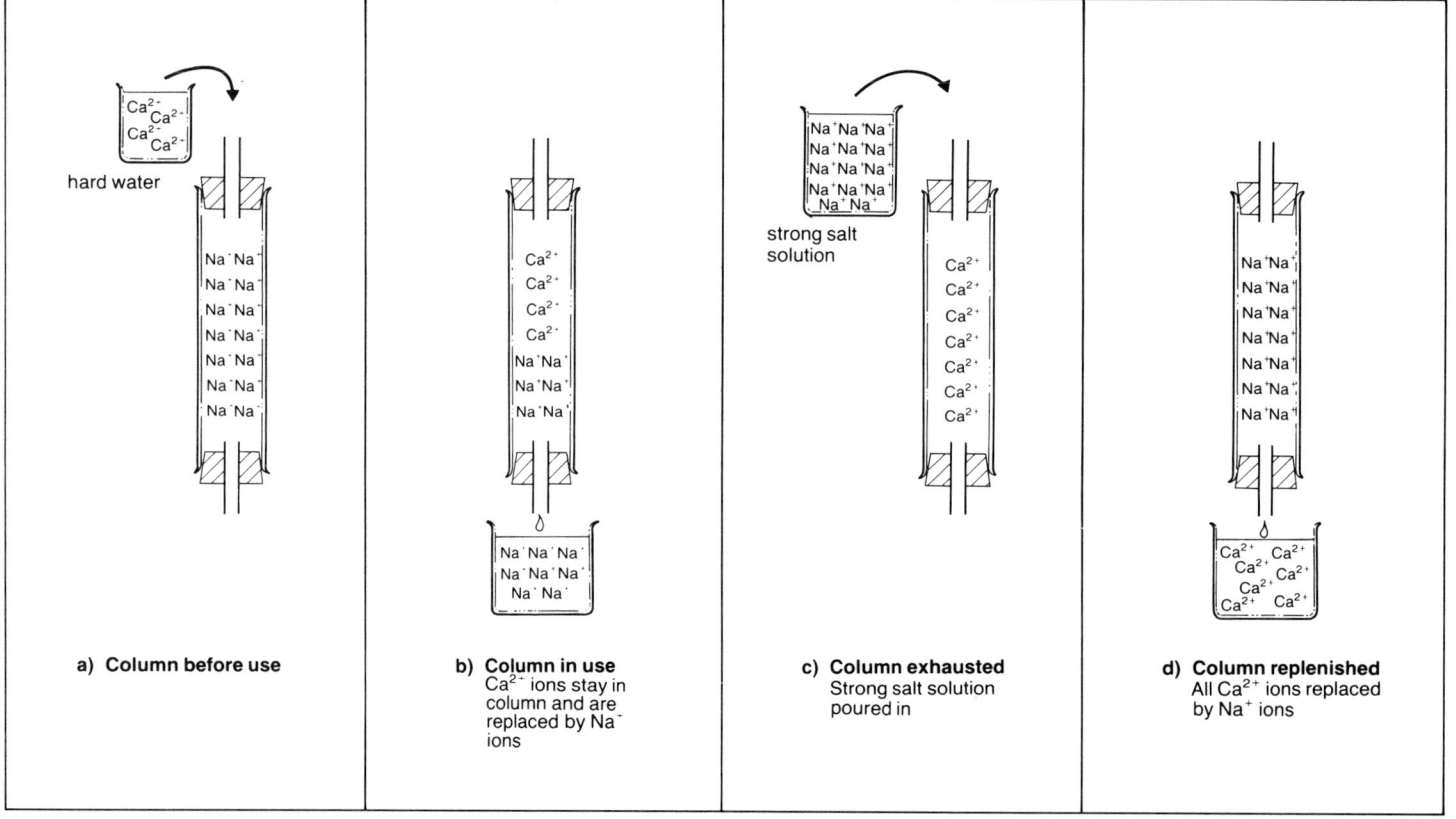

Figure 12.6 *How an ion-exchange column works.*

Hardness of water

Self test

Questions 1–5
The diagram below shows some important reactions of calcium compounds.

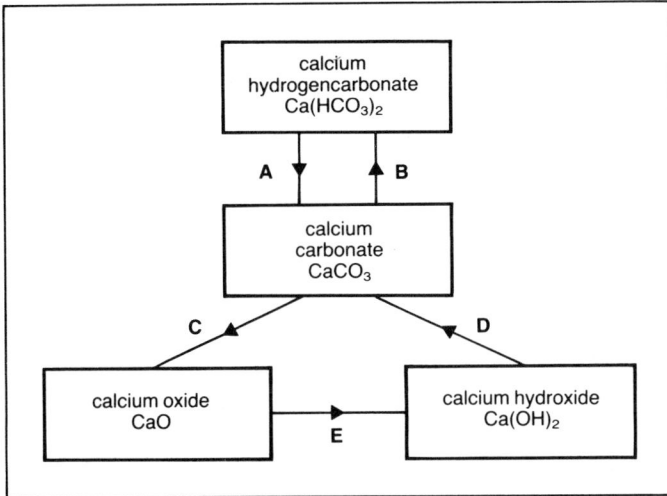

Choose from **A** to **E** the arrow that represents
1. the manufacture of quicklime.
2. the test for carbon dioxide.
3. the formation of slaked lime.
4. the formation of fur in kettles.
5. the dissolving of limestone in rain water.

Questions 6–9
From the list **A** to **D** below
- **A** direct combination of elements
- **B** neutralisation
- **C** precipitation
- **D** thermal decomposition

choose the type of reaction that occurs when
6. carbon dioxide is produced by burning carbon (coke).
7. limestone is heated strongly to make quicklime.
8. slaked lime is used to lime the soil.
9. sodium carbonate is used to soften water.

Questions 10–13
Four methods of softening water are labelled **A** to **D** below
- **A** distillation
- **B** using excess soap
- **C** using ion-exchange resins
- **D** using sodium carbonate

Choose from **A** to **D** the method that
10. makes use of salt solution.
11. precipitates calcium carbonate.
12. produces scum.
13. produces the purest water.

14. Burning petrol produces carbon monoxide when there is
    - **A** too little petrol.
    - **B** too little energy.
    - **C** too little oxygen.
    - **D** too much air.

15. Carbon dioxide and carbon monoxide are both
    - **A** acidic oxides.
    - **B** less dense than air.
    - **C** slightly soluble in water.
    - **D** very poisonous.

16. Solid carbon dioxide is used as a refrigerant because it
    - **A** does not burn.
    - **B** is not poisonous.
    - **C** never liquefies.
    - **D** sublimes easily.

17. An advantage of hard water over soft water is that hard water
    - **A** gives more lather.
    - **B** leads to better health.
    - **C** removes grease better.
    - **D** forms scum quicker.

Questions 18–21
Write down the numbers and symbols that would balance the following equations.

$$Ca(OH)_2 + CO_2 \rightarrow \underline{\quad(18)\quad} + H_2O$$

$$CaCO_3 + CO_2 + \underline{\quad(19)\quad} \rightarrow Ca(HCO_3)_2$$

$$CaCO_3 + \underline{\quad(20)\quad} \rightarrow CaCl_2 + H_2O + \underline{\quad(21)\quad}$$

13 Chemicals from crude oil

This section is about crude oil and the organic chemicals that are made from it. There are millions of different organic chemicals, but all of them are based on the element carbon.

Carbon has two important features which account for its ability to form so many compounds.
- it forms **chains** of carbon atoms linked to one another;
- it always forms four covalent bonds.

Fractional distillation of crude oil

Crude oil (sometimes called petroleum) is a mixture of many different compounds. All these compounds contain carbon and hydrogen, and they are called **hydrocarbons.** Some of these hydrocarbons are volatile (easily vaporised), which makes them useful for petrol engines. Others are less volatile. They are no use in petrol engines, but they can be used in large furnaces.

Crude oil must be separated into **fractions** before it can be useful. Each fraction is a mixture of hydrocarbons with similar properties. The hydrocarbons in a given fraction all have similar boiling points.

The separation of crude oil is done by **fractional distillation**. Figure 13.1 shows a simple laboratory experiment for the fractional distillation of crude oil. As the crude oil is heated, fractions boil off with higher and higher boiling points, and are collected. Table 13.1 shows how the properties of the fractions gradually change.

The change in properties occurs because the number of carbon atoms in the molecules of the hydrocarbons increases. In the first fractions the average number of carbon atoms is small, but the number gradually increases in the later fractions.

Distilling crude oil on an industrial scale

Figure 13.2 shows how crude oil is distilled in an oil refinery. The general principle is the same as for the laboratory experiment, but the scale is much larger.

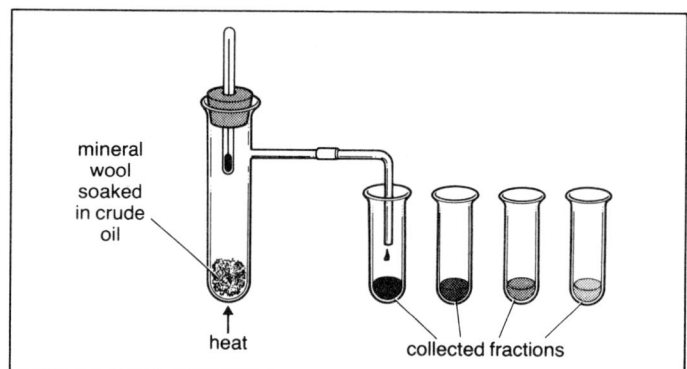

Figure 13.1 *Fractional distillation of crude oil in the laboratory.*

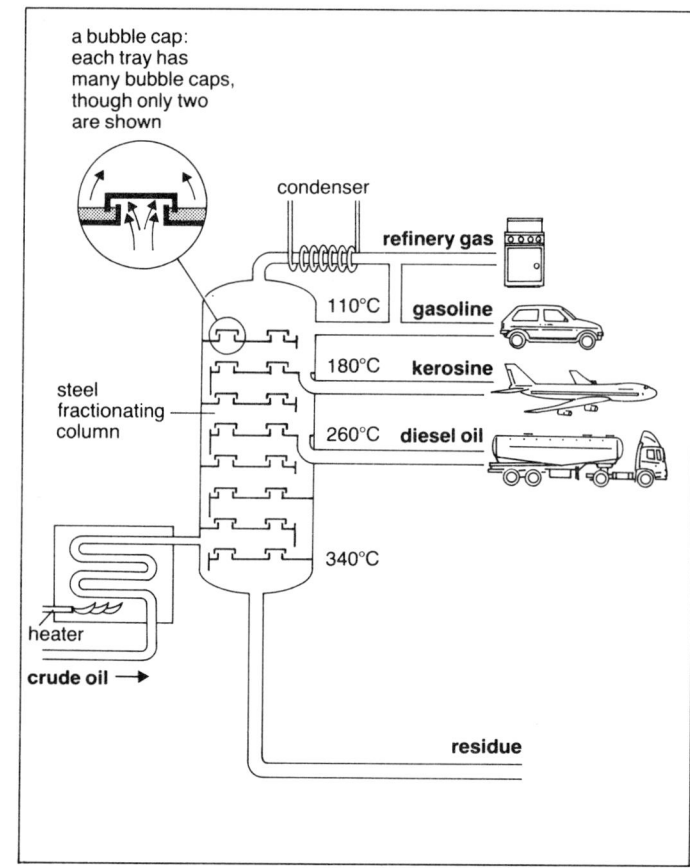

Figure 13.2 *Fractional distillation of crude oil in a refinery.*

Table 13.1 *Changes in the properties of fractions from the distillation of crude oil.*

Order of collecting fraction	1st	2nd	3rd	4th
Boiling point	Low			→ High
Volatility of fraction	Volatile			→ Involatile
Colour	Light yellow			→ Dark brown
Viscosity (stickiness)	Runny			→ Thick and viscous
Ease of burning	Burns easily			→ Burns with difficulty

Table 13.2 *Fractions collected in an oil refinery.*

Fraction	Boiling range	Approximate numbers of carbon atoms in molecules in fraction	Percentage of crude oil	Uses
Refinery gas	Below room temperature	1–4	1–2	Gaseous fuel, chemical manufacture
Gasoline (petrol)	30–160°C	5–10	15–30	Motor car fuel, chemical manufacture
Kerosine (paraffin)	160–250°C	11–12	10–15	Heating fuel, jet fuel
Diesel oil	220–350°C	13–25	15–20	Diesel engine fuel for lorries, trains, etc.
Residue	Above 350°C	Over 25	40–50	Fuel for power stations, ships, etc. Some is distilled further to give lubricating oil, waxes, bitumen, etc.

Table 13.2 shows the fractions that are collected in an oil refinery, and some of their uses.

The uses of the fractions depend on their properties. For example, the gasoline fraction ignites easily, which makes it a good fuel for petrol engines. Higher fractions are thick and sticky; this makes them good lubricants.

The alkanes

Most of the hydrocarbons in crude oil belong to a family called the **alkanes**. A family or **homologous series** is a set of organic compounds with similar formulas and properties. The alkanes are the simplest homologous series. They all contain carbon and hydrogen atoms, joined together by single covalent bonds. Figure 13.3 gives the names and formulas of the first four members of the series.

Notice that each member of the homologous series has one more carbon atom and two more hydrogen atoms than the previous member. The series continues in the same way. The general formula of the alkanes is C_nH_{2n+2}, where n is the number of carbon atoms.

As you go along a homologous series, the properties of the compounds gradually change. For example, the boiling points and melting points of the compounds gradually increase. Thus the first four alkanes are gases, the next fifteen or so are liquids and the rest are solids.

Naming alkanes

All alkanes have names ending in **-ane**. The other part of the name (meth-, eth-, prop-, etc.) tells you the number of carbon atoms in the molecule. For example, any compound whose name begins with **eth-** has two carbon atoms. Any compound beginning with **prop-** has three carbon atoms, and so on.

Isomerism

Look at figure 13.4. It shows that there are two compounds with molecular formula C_4H_{10}. Four carbon atoms and ten hydrogen atoms can be joined together in two different ways. The two compounds are similar, but different. Compounds like this, with the same molecular formula but different structures, are called **isomers**.

name	methane	ethane	propane	butane
molecular formula	CH_4	C_2H_6	C_3H_8	C_4H_{10}
structural formula	H–C(H)(H)–H	H–C(H)(H)–C(H)(H)–H	H–C(H)(H)–C(H)(H)–C(H)(H)–H	H–C(H)(H)–C(H)(H)–C(H)(H)–C(H)(H)–H

Figure 13.3 *The first four alkanes.*

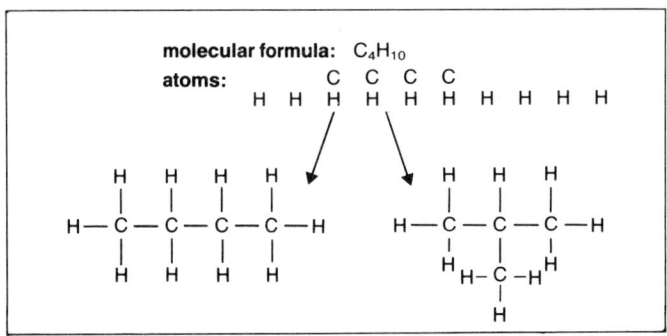

Figure 13.4 *Two different compounds both have the molecular formula C_4H_{10}.*

Isomerism is very common in organic chemistry. It is another reason why there are so many different organic compounds.

Properties of alkanes

Alkanes are rather unreactive compounds. Their most important property is that they burn easily. If the air supply is plentiful, they all burn to give carbon dioxide and water. The most useful fuels are the gaseous alkanes (table 13.3) and the volatile liquids. In fact, the demand for these lighter fractions is greater than the supply from the distillation of crude oil. Fortunately, they can be made from the heavier fractions by a process called **cracking**.

Table 13.3 *Gaseous alkanes as fuels.*

Alkane	Formula	Use as a fuel
Methane	CH_4	Natural gas (North Sea gas) is mainly methane
Propane	C_3H_8	Bottled gas for caravans, boats, etc.
Butane	C_4H_{10}	Lighter gas, camping gas

Cracking

When an alkane is heated with a catalyst, its molecule breaks into two smaller molecules. One of these is a molecule of an alkane. The other molecule has a double bond and is called an **alkene**. For example, undecane, an alkane with eleven carbon atoms, might crack as shown in figure 13.5.

Cracking is very useful. It converts larger molecules from heavier, less useful fractions into smaller molecules that are useful as gasoline. It also produces alkenes, which are very useful for making petrochemicals.

Figure 13.6 shows the simple apparatus that can be used to carry out cracking reactions in the laboratory.

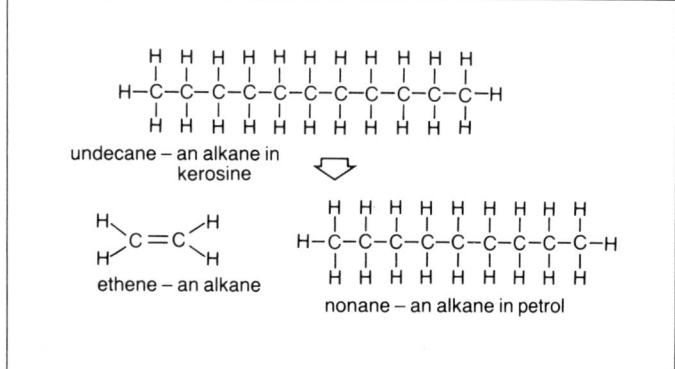

Figure 13.5 *An example of cracking.*

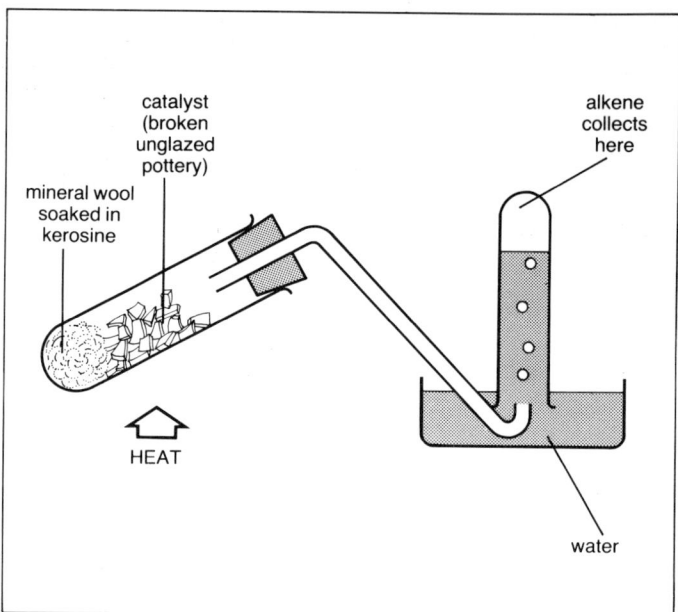

Figure 13.6 *A simple laboratory cracking experiment. The vapour of kerosine is passed over a heated catalyst.*

Alkenes

The alkanes we looked at in the last section have only single bonds in their molecules. They are said to be **saturated**, because no further atoms can be added.

The alkenes are another homologous series. Like alkanes, they are hydrocarbons, but unlike alkanes each alkene has a double bond in its molecule (figure 13.7). All alkenes have names ending in **-ene**.

Alkenes are **unsaturated** compounds, because it is possible to break the double bond and add extra atoms to the molecule.

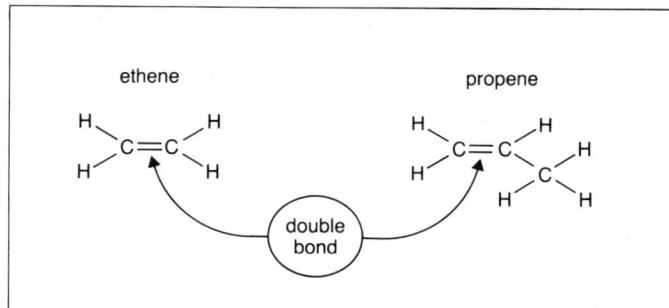

Figure 13.7 *Ethene and propene – the two simplest alkenes.*

Addition reactions

The double bond makes alkenes much more reactive than alkanes; it tends to break open and join on to other atoms. Figure 13.8 shows an example.

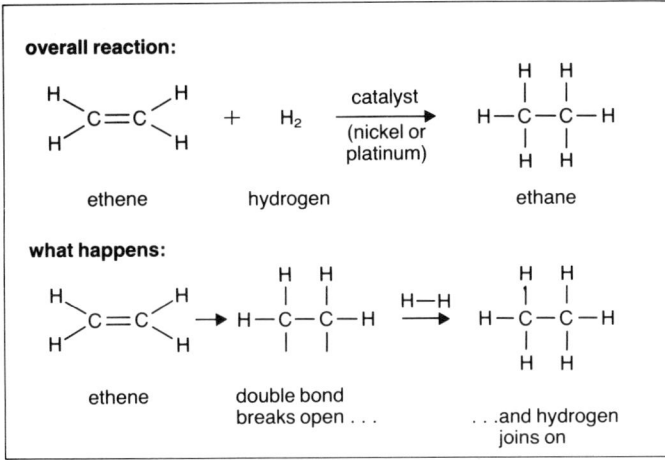

Figure 13.8 *Reaction of ethene with hydrogen in the presence of a catalyst.*

This kind of reaction is called an **addition reaction**. As a result of the reaction the ethene loses its double bond and becomes saturated.

Making margarine

Addition reactions like the one shown in figure 13.8 are used to make margarine from vegetable oil. Vegetable oils are unsaturated, with several double bonds in their molecules. By reacting them with hydrogen and a catalyst, they are made more saturated. This raises the melting point, so the liquid oil becomes a solid fat – margarine.

Many doctors believe that saturated fats are less healthy than unsaturated ones. Because of this, many modern margarines are partially unsaturated – some double bonds are left in the fat molecules.

Addition reactions of ethene

Ethene, with its reactive double bond, is an important 'building block' for making other organic chemicals. The huge amounts of ethene needed by the petrochemical industry are made by cracking alkanes.

Table 13.4 *Important addition reactions of ethene.*

Reaction	Product	Structural formula of product
Ethene reacts with hydrogen and a catalyst	Ethane	H H H—C—C—H H H
Ethene reacts with bromine water	1,2-dibromoethane	H H H—C—C—H Br Br
Ethene reacts with steam and a catalyst	Ethanol	H H H—C—C—O—H H H
Ethene reacts with itself in the presence of a catalyst or on heating	Poly(ethene) (polythene)	H H H H H H -C-C-C-C-C-C- H H H H H H

Table 13.4 shows some important addition reactions of ethene.

The reaction with bromine water is a useful test for any unsaturated compound. Shaking an unsaturated compound with bromine water causes the orange bromine water to turn colourless.

The reaction of ethene with itself is an important example of **polymerisation** (more about this in the next section).

Polymers and plastics

Polymers are organic chemicals with large molecules. They are made by joining together (**polymerising**) many small molecules called **monomers** (figure 13.9).

Polythene is a simple example of a polymer. It is made by polymerising ethene (figure 13.10).

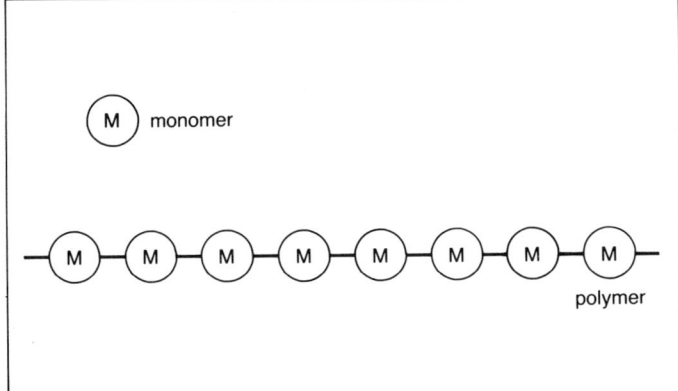

Figure 13.9 *Monomer and polymer.*

Figure 13.10 *Polymerising ethene to give polythene.*

82 Chemicals from Crude Oil

Table 13.5 *Examples of natural and synthetic polymers.*

	Polymer	Monomer
Natural	Starch Cellulose Protein	Glucose Glucose Amino acids
Synthetic	Polythene Polyvinyl chloride (PVC) Polystyrene	Ethene Vinyl chloride (more correctly called chloroethene) Styrene (more correctly called phenylethene)

There are natural and synthetic polymers (table 13.5). All the natural fibres we use are natural polymers. Wool and silk are made from protein, and cotton is made from cellulose.

Plastics and fibres

Plastics, such as polythene and PVC, are synthetic polymers. So are synthetic fibres such as polyester and nylon. The monomers in these synthetic polymers are made by chemists from crude oil.

Plastics and synthetic polymers are gradually replacing traditional materials like wood, metal and natural fibres. Table 13.6 gives some examples. Synthetic polymers often have advantages over traditional materials. They are often cheaper, and they may be lighter and stronger. Unlike natural materials, they do not rot or get broken down by bacteria. In other words they are not **biodegradeable.**

Table 13.6 *Examples of synthetic polymers replacing natural materials.*

Article	Traditionally made from	Synthetic replacement
Bucket	Iron	Polythene
Comb	Bone, wood or ivory	Nylon
Lemonade bottle	Glass	PVC
Blouse	Cotton	Polyester
Tights or stockings	Silk	Nylon
Pullover	Wool	Acrylic

Plastics as pollutants

The fact that plastics do not rot can be a disadvantage as well as a benefit. Once we have finished with them they do not decay, but stay unchanged for years. This makes plastics a serious litter and waste-disposal problem. To get over this problem, chemists are trying to make synthetic polymers that are biodegradeable.

Another problem with plastics is that they usually burn quite easily. This can make them a fire hazard. Some burning plastics give off poisonous fumes, which is an extra danger.

Thermoplastics and thermosets

Some plastics soften when they are heated and harden again when they are cooled. Polythene, PVC and polystyrene are examples. This type of plastic is called a **thermoplastic**. Thermoplastics are easily moulded into useful articles.

Other plastics can be heated and moulded only once. After that they set hard, and will not melt again. Bakelite, melamine and urea-methanal are examples. This type of plastic is called a **thermoset**. Most hard plastics, like those in electric plugs, are thermosets.

Figure 13.11 shows the different molecular structures of thermoplastics and thermosets.

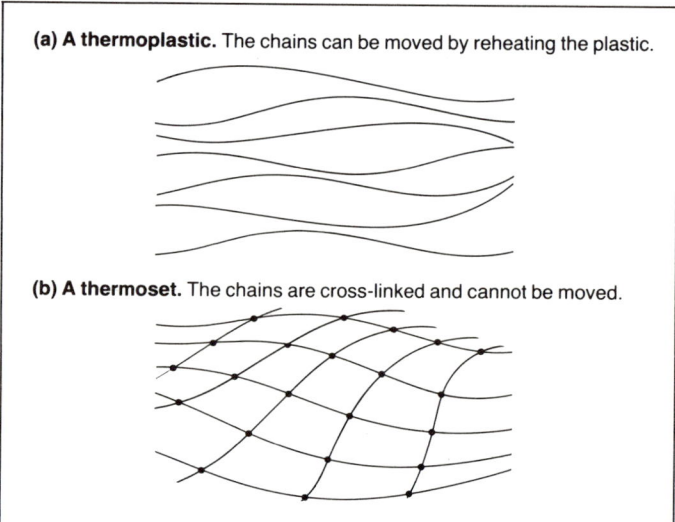

Figure 13.11 *The arrangement of polymer chains in plastics after heating.*

Ethanol – an important alcohol

The **alcohols** are another simple homologous series. All alcohols have an oxygen and a hydrogen atom in their

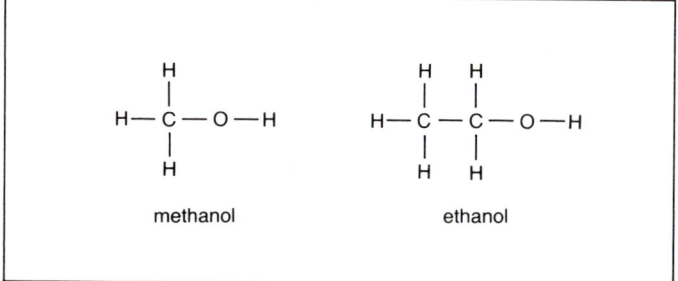

Figure 13.12 *The two simplest alcohols.*

Ethanol – an important alcohol

...her as an –O–H group. Figure 13.12

...the most important alcohol. It is ...ohol'.

Three of the most important uses of ethanol are:

- **As a solvent.** Many things dissolve in ethanol. It is used as a solvent in perfumes to dissolve fragrant oils. Some paints and varnishes also contain ethanol. Many stains (e.g. grass stains) will dissolve in ethanol.

- **As a fuel.** Ethanol burns with a clean, hot flame. It is used as a fuel in spirit burners. Ethanol for this purpose is sold as methylated spirits, or meths. Methylated spirits is ethanol with small amounts of poisonous substances added to it to stop you drinking it. Ethanol can be used to replace petrol as a fuel for motor vehicles. In some countries like Brazil, sugar is plentiful and ethanol fuel can be produced cheaply by fermentation.

- **In alcoholic drinks.** Beer, wine and spirits contain ethanol in varying amounts (table 13.7).

Table 13.7 *Amounts of alcohol in different drinks.*

Drink	Percentage of alcohol in the drink	Amount of drink that contains 1 'alcohol unit'
Beer	4	Half a pint
Wine	10	One wine glass
Sherry	20	One small sherry glass
Spirits (whisky, gin, vodka, etc.)	40	Single measure

Ethanol is a drug. In small quantities it makes people feel happy and sociable. In larger quantities it makes people drunk and unable to do things properly. It is a particularly dangerous drug for people who are driving motor vehicles. People who regularly drink large amounts of alcohol may become addicted to it, and they are then called **alcoholics**. But most doctors agree that drinking moderate amounts of ethanol is safe, provided you are not driving. It may even improve people's health by helping them to relax.

Making ethanol

Ethanol can be made by two methods:

- **From ethene.** (see table 13.4). Most ethanol for industrial use and for fuel is made this way.

- **By fermentation.** Ethanol in drinks is made by fermentation. A microorganism called yeast is added to a solution containing sugar. The yeast uses the sugar to get energy, and in the process the sugar is broken down to give ethanol and carbon dioxide. The process works best at 37°C.

$$\text{sugar solution} \rightarrow \text{ethanol} + \text{carbon dioxide}$$

$$C_6H_{12}O_6(aq) \xrightarrow{yeast} 2C_2H_6O(aq) + 2CO_2(g)$$

Figure 13.13 shows an experiment to carry out fermentation in the laboratory.

Wine is made by fermenting grape juice. Beer is made by fermenting malt. Grape juice and malt both contain plenty of sugar for the yeast to ferment.

Yeast can only produce a solution containing about 10 per cent ethanol. After that, the yeast dies from alcohol poisoning. Drinks with greater than 10 per cent ethanol can be made by **distilling** weaker drinks. This increases the proportion of ethanol in the mixture. For example, brandy is made by distilling wine.

Oxidation of ethanol – the formation of vinegar

If wine or beer is opened and left for a few days, it turns to vinegar. This is because bacteria from the air get into the wine or beer. These bacteria oxidise ethanol, using oxygen from the air. The ethanol is oxidised to a substance called **ethanoic acid** (also called acetic acid). It is this acid that gives vinegar its sharp taste.

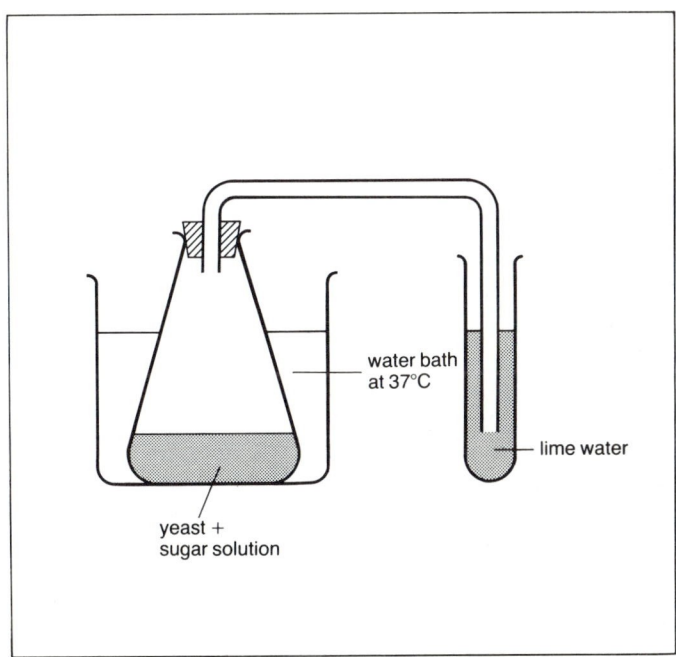

Figure 13.13 *An experiment to illustrate fermentation. What will happen to the lime water? Where will the ethanol be collected?*

84 Chemicals from Crude Oil

• Self test

Questions 1–4

Look at the reaction scheme below.

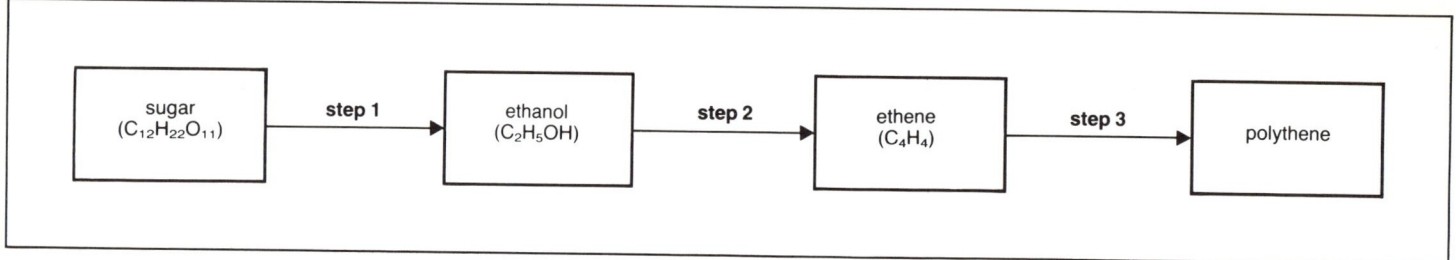

1. Step 1 requires
   A heat B hydrogen C yeast D oxygen

2. Step 2 involves
   A cracking   B dehydration
   C hydration   D synthesis

3. Step 3 involves
   A addition   B decomposition
   C oxidation   D reduction

4. The other product in step 1, besides ethanol, is:
   A carbon dioxide. B hydrogen.
   C oxygen.   D water.

Questions 5–9

From the list **A** to **D** below
   A C_2H_6 B C_3H_6 C C_3H_8 D C_4H_{10}

choose the formula of the compound that
5. is an alkene.
6. is the most volatile.
7. is used in red calor gas cylinders.
8. occurs as isomers.
9. will decolorise bromine water.

Questions 10–15

From the list **A** to **E** below
   A coal
   B crude oil
   C ethanol
   D natural gas
   E petrol

choose the substance that
10. is a pure compound.
11. forms the largest fossil fuel reserves on Earth.
12. is obtained by distillation and cracking.
13. is the major source of paraffin.
14. is composed mainly of methane.
15. is a renewable energy source.

16. The fractions from crude oil
    A are pure alkanes.
    B are equally volatile.
    C contain many hydrocarbons.
    D are all used as fuels.

17. Both alkanes and alkenes
    A are unsaturated compounds.
    B are formed during cracking.
    C form polymers easily.
    D have addition reactions.

18. Which *one* of the following equations involves cracking?
    A butane → ethane + ethene
    B ethanol → ethene + water
    C ethanol + oxygen → ethanoic acid
    D polythene → ethene

19. Which *one* of the following gases is least affected during the reactions in a car engine?
    A carbon monoxide B octane vapour
    C oxygen   D nitrogen

20. Plastics cause a pollution problem because they
    A are not attacked by bacteria.
    B are often coloured with dyes.
    C form giant molecules.
    D are very flammable.

14

Reaction rates and reversible reactions

Different chemical reactions go at different speeds or **rates**. Some, such as explosions, are very, very fast. Others, such as the rusting of iron, are much slower. Table 14.1 gives examples of reactions that go at different rates.

By controlling conditions such as temperature and concentration, it is possible to control the rates of chemical reactions. This is very important in cooking, in the chemical industry and in our own bodies.

Table 14.1 *Examples of reactions that go at different rates.*

Very fast	Medium	Very slow
Explosions, such as the explosion of a petrol–air mixture in a car engine	Burning a solid fuel such as coal or wood	Rusting of iron
Colour change of an indicator	Cooking food, for example boiling an egg or baking a cake	Erosion (wearing away) of limestone by rain water

Factors that affect the rate of chemical reactions

Look at these examples:
- It takes less than ten minutes to fry chips, but about twenty minutes to boil potatoes.
- Peas can be cooked a lot faster than potatoes.
- Badly stained clothes can be cleaned by soaking in a solution of biological detergent.
- Stained clothes are cleaned quicker by using a more concentrated solution of detergent.
- A photographic film is darkened by light. The stronger the light, the quicker it darkens.

These examples illustrate some of the factors that affect the rate of chemical reactions. The factors that we will consider here are:
- temperature
- surface area
- catalysts
- concentration
- light.

Temperature

All reactions go faster at a higher temperature. Temperature has a very noticeable effect. The rate of many reactions is *doubled* by a temperature rise of just 10°C. Temperature is one of the reasons why chips cook faster than boiled potatoes. The fat in which chips are cooked is at a much higher temperature than boiling water.

Surface area

The surface area of a solid means the amount of surface that is exposed. If a solid is cut up into smaller pieces, its surface area gets larger (figure 14.1).

Increasing the surface area of a solid makes it react faster. This is another reason why chips cook faster. They are cut up small, so more surface is exposed to the hot oil. This is also one reason why peas cook faster than potatoes.

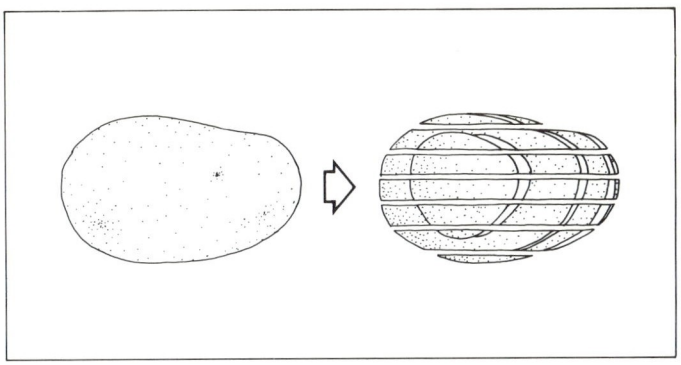

Figure 14.1 *Cutting up a potato into chips. The more finely a solid is divided, the larger is its surface area.*

Catalysts

Catalysts are substances that alter the rate of a chemical reaction without getting used up.

For example, manganese dioxide speeds up the rate of decomposition of hydrogen peroxide (see page 89). At the end of the reaction there is exactly the same amount of manganese dioxide present as at the beginning. Most catalysts *speed up* reactions, like manganese dioxide in this example. But a few catalysts *slow reactions down*. These are called **negative catalysts**.

Catalysts are important in the chemical industry (see pages 91 and 98). They are also vitally important to all living things. These biological catalysts are called **enzymes**. It is the enzymes in biological washing powders that speed up the breakdown of biological stains such as those caused by blood.

Concentration

The **concentration** of a solution means the amount of solute present in a particular volume of solution (figure 14.2 overleaf). The opposite of **concentrated** is **dilute**. Concentration is usually measured in grams per litre (g/l) or moles per litre (mole/l).

Concentrated solutions react faster than dilute ones. This is the reason why a concentrated solution of detergent removes stains faster than a dilute one.

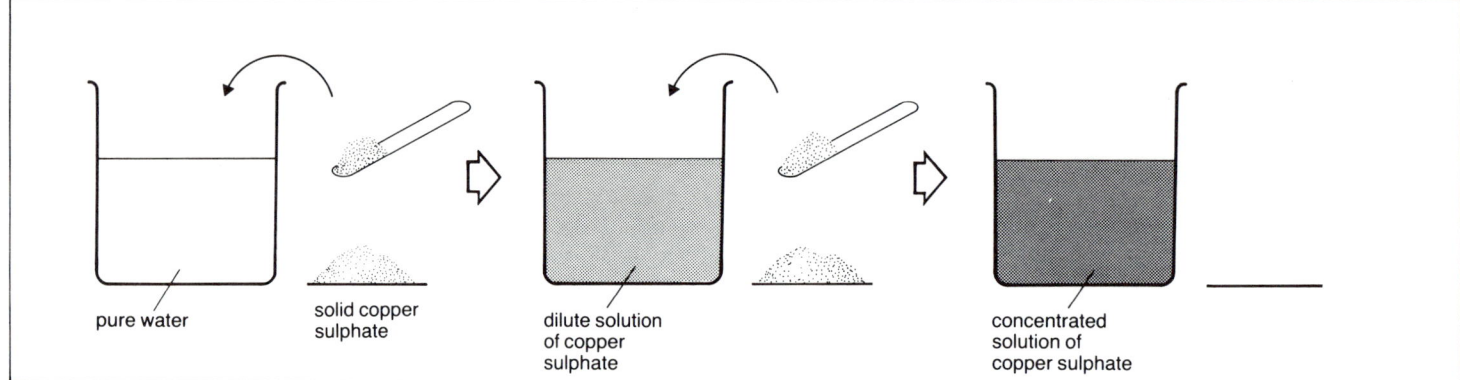

Figure 14.2 *Dilute and concentrated solutions.*

The idea of concentration is normally applied only to solutions. But gases can have their concentration changed too, by changing the pressure. A gas at high pressure is more concentrated than a gas at low pressure (figure 14.3). Gases therefore react faster at higher pressures. This is made use of in a petrol engine. The mixture of petrol vapour and air is compressed before being ignited by the sparking plug.

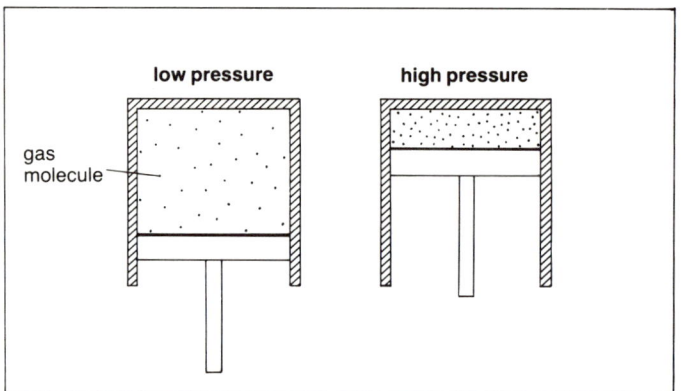

Figure 14.3 *A gas at high pressure is more concentrated than a gas at low pressure.*

Light

A few chemical reactions are speeded up by light. Two important examples are photosynthesis (page 70) and photography. Photography uses light to decompose silver compounds on a photographic film.

Investigating reaction rates in the laboratory

In this section we will look at some experiments to investigate reaction rates in the laboratory.

To investigate the rate of a reaction, we need to follow the changes in some property of one of the chemicals involved. This property might be the colour of a solution, the volume of a gas evolved or the amount of a precipitate. Changes in the property are recorded at different times. From these measurements, we can work out how the amount of the substance present is changing with time. The rate of the reaction is given by the expression:

$$\text{reaction rate} = \frac{\text{change in amount of a substance}}{\text{time taken}}$$

For example, take the reaction:

zinc + hydrochloric acid → zinc chloride + hydrogen

Suppose that in 10 minutes 1 gram of zinc is used up. In the same time, 370 cm^3 of hydrogen is given off. We could then say:

$$\text{reaction rate} = \frac{\text{change in amount of substance}}{\text{time taken}}$$

$$= \frac{1 \text{ g zinc}}{10 \text{ min}}$$

$$= 0.01 \text{ g zinc per min}$$

or:

$$\text{reaction rate} = \frac{370 \text{ cm}^3 \text{ hydrogen}}{10 \text{ min}}$$

$$= 37 \text{ cm}^3 \text{ hydrogen per min}$$

In the study of reaction rates, we often do not work out the actual rate. Instead, we plot graphs of amount of substance at different times, and work out the rate from them.

Investigating the effect of temperature: the reaction between sodium thiosulphate and acid

A solution of sodium thiosulphate ($Na_2S_2O_3$ (aq)) reacts with dilute hydrochloric acid to give a precipitate of sulphur:

sodium thiosulphate + hydrochloric acid → sodium chloride + sulphur + sulphur dioxide + water

$Na_2S_2O_3(aq) + 2HCl(aq) \rightarrow 2NaCl(aq) + S(s) + SO_2(aq) + H_2O(l)$

Investigating reaction rates in the laboratory 87

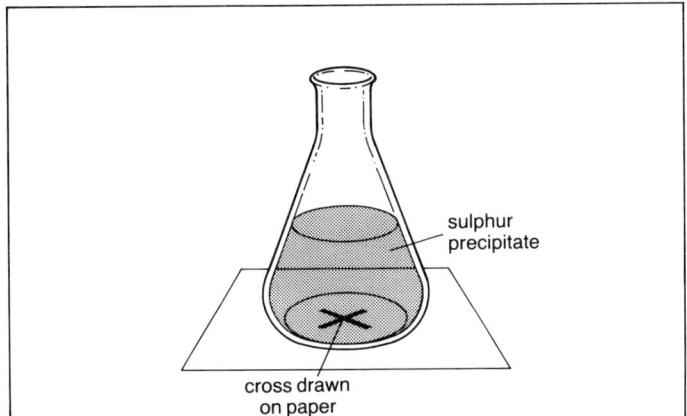

Figure 14.4 *Following the reaction between sodium thiosulphate and dilute hydrochloric acid.*

The precipitate of sulphur makes the solution go cloudy (see figure 14.4). As the solution gets cloudier, a cross drawn on a piece of paper under the flask slowly disappears from view. We can find the reaction rate by measuring the time it takes for the cross to disappear completely. The faster the reaction, the less time it takes for the cross to disappear.

Table 14.2 *Results of an experiment to study the rate of the reaction between sodium thiosulphate solution and hydrochloric acid at different temperatures.*

Temperature /°C	Time for cross to disappear/s
25	110
30	80
35	60
40	46
45	37
50	29

Table 14.2 shows some typical results for this reaction. The results are plotted on the graph in figure 14.5.

Look carefully at the graph in figure 14.5 and notice these points:
- The higher the temperature, the less time it takes for the cross to disappear – in other words, the faster the rate.
- For a 10°C temperature rise (e.g. 30°C to 40°C), the time for the cross to disappear roughly halves. In other words, the rate is twice as fast.

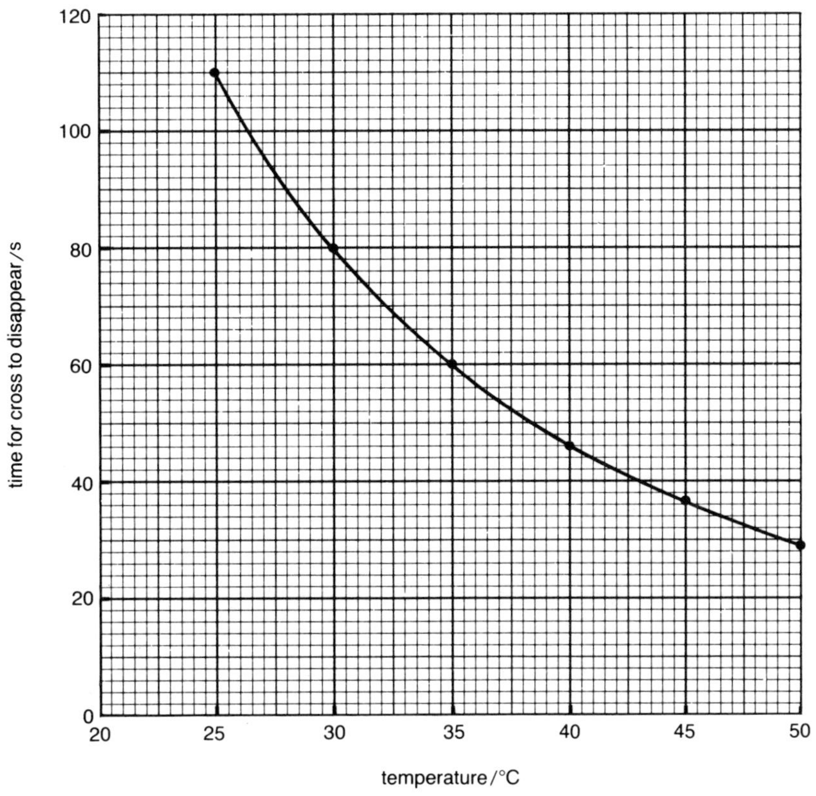

Figure 14.5 *A graph showing the time for the cross to disappear at different temperatures.*

Investigating the effect of surface area: the reaction between marble chips and acid

Marble chips are calcium carbonate ($CaCO_3(s)$). Like all carbonates, marble chips react with dilute acid, giving off carbon dioxide. Thus:

calcium + hydrochloric → calcium + carbon + water
carbonate   acid   chloride   dioxide
(marble chips)
$CaCO_3(s) + 2HCl(aq) \rightarrow CaCl_2(aq) + CO_2(g) + H_2O(l)$

If the reaction is carried out in an open container, the carbon dioxide escapes into the air (figure 14.6). This causes the mass of the reaction system to fall. We can follow the reaction by seeing how the mass of the apparatus changes with time.

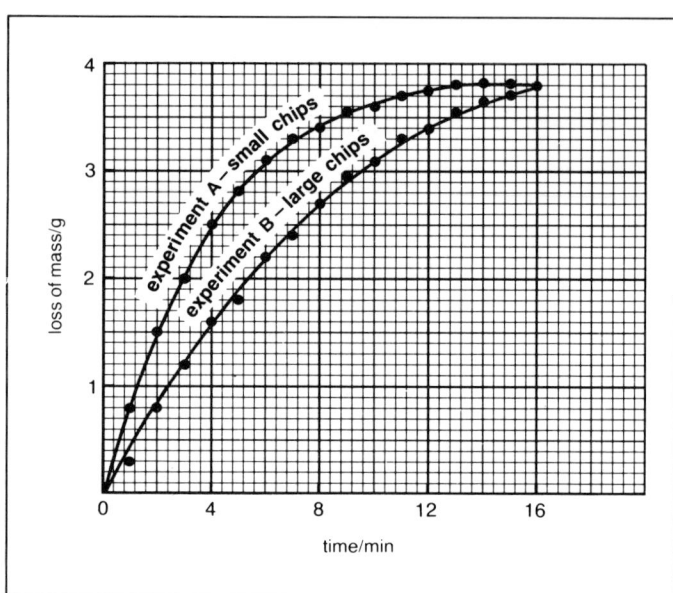

Figure 14.7 *Results of an investigation of the rate of reaction between marble chips and hydrochloric acid.*

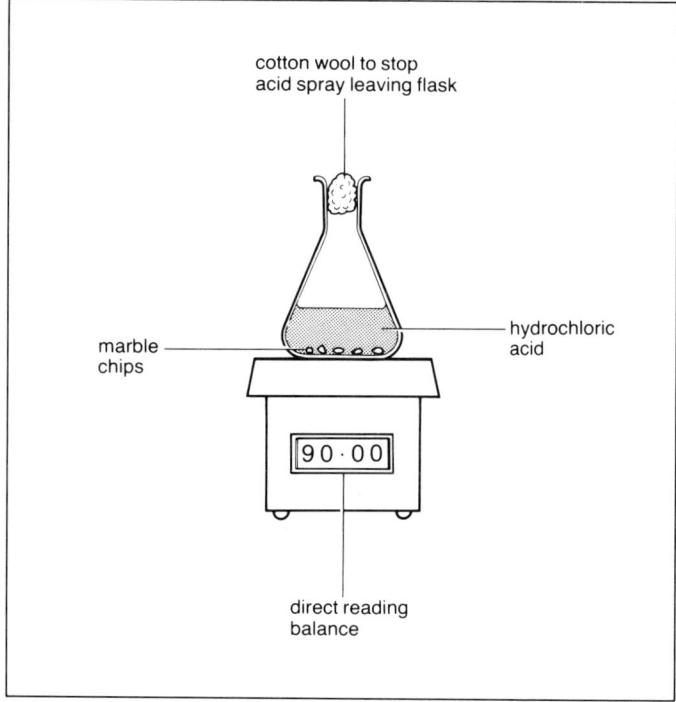

Figure 14.6 *An experiment to investigate the rate of the reaction between marble chips and hydrochloric acid.*

Some typical results are plotted in the graph in figure 14.7. In experiment A, 10 g of *small* marble chips were reacted with 100 cm³ of dilute hydrochloric acid. In experiment B, the quantities were the same, but *large* chips were used instead of small. The total surface area of these large chips is less than for the small chips in experiment A.

Look at the graphs in figure 14.7 and note the following points.
- The steeper the graph, the faster is the reaction.
- Both reactions start off fast (steep graphs), then slow down and stop (graphs level off).
- Experiment A, with small chips and a large surface area, starts off faster than experiment B, with large chips.

- Both graphs level off at the same value. This is because the same quantities of marble chips and hydrochloric acid were used in both reactions. The final loss of mass is the same.

Investigating the effect of concentration: the reaction between magnesium and acid

Magnesium reacts rapidly with cold dilute hydrochloric acid, forming magnesium chloride and hydrogen:

magnesium + hydrochloric → magnesium + hydrogen
                acid   chloride
$Mg(s) + 2HCl(aq) \rightarrow MgCl_2(aq) + H_2(g)$

The reaction can be followed by measuring the volume of hydrogen given off at different times. The apparatus used is shown in figure 14.8.

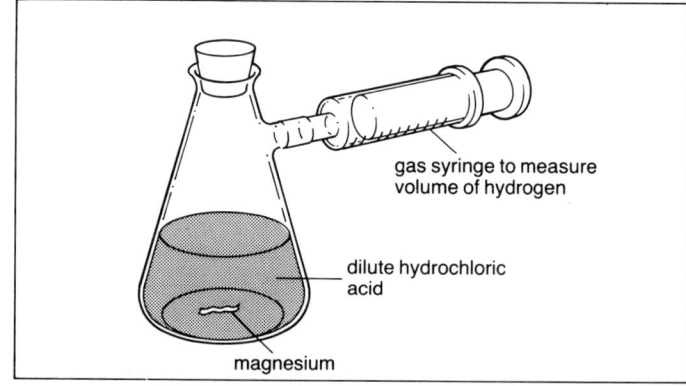

Figure 14.8 *An experiment to investigate the rate of reaction between zinc and hydrochloric acid*

Some typical results are plotted on the graph in figure 14.9. In both experiment X and experiment Y, 0.06 g of magnesium and 50 cm³ of hydrochloric acid were used. But in experiment X the concentration of the acid was 2 mol/l, while in experiment Y it was 1 mol/l (half as concentrated).

Look at the graphs in figure 14.9 and note these points.
- The graph in experiment X starts off twice as steep as the graph in experiment Y. This means that the reaction starts off twice as fast. In other words, doubling the concentration of the acid doubles the rate.
- In both experiments the reaction starts off fast, with a steep graph. The reaction then slows down and the graph becomes less steep. This is because the hydrochloric acid and magnesium are getting used up.
- Both graphs level off at the same value. This is because in both cases the hydrochloric acid is in excess. There is more than enough of it to react with the magnesium. Therefore, the reaction stops when the magnesium is all used up. Since the same amount of magnesium (0.06 g) is used in both reactions, both reactions stop at the same point.

Investigating the effect of catalysts: the decomposition of hydrogen peroxide

Hydrogen peroxide (H_2O_2) decomposes to give water and oxygen:

hydrogen peroxide → water + oxygen

$$2H_2O_2(aq) \rightarrow 2H_2O(l) + O_2(g)$$

Under normal conditions the reaction is very slow. But if a little powdered manganese(IV) oxide is added, the hydrogen peroxide fizzes rapidly, showing that the rate of the reaction has been greatly speeded up. Other catalysts, such as platinum, also speed up the decomposition of hydrogen peroxide.

Many living things contain an enzyme, called catalase, which is a very effective catalyst for this reaction. Liver contains lots of catalase, and a piece of liver causes hydrogen peroxide solution to decompose very fast indeed.

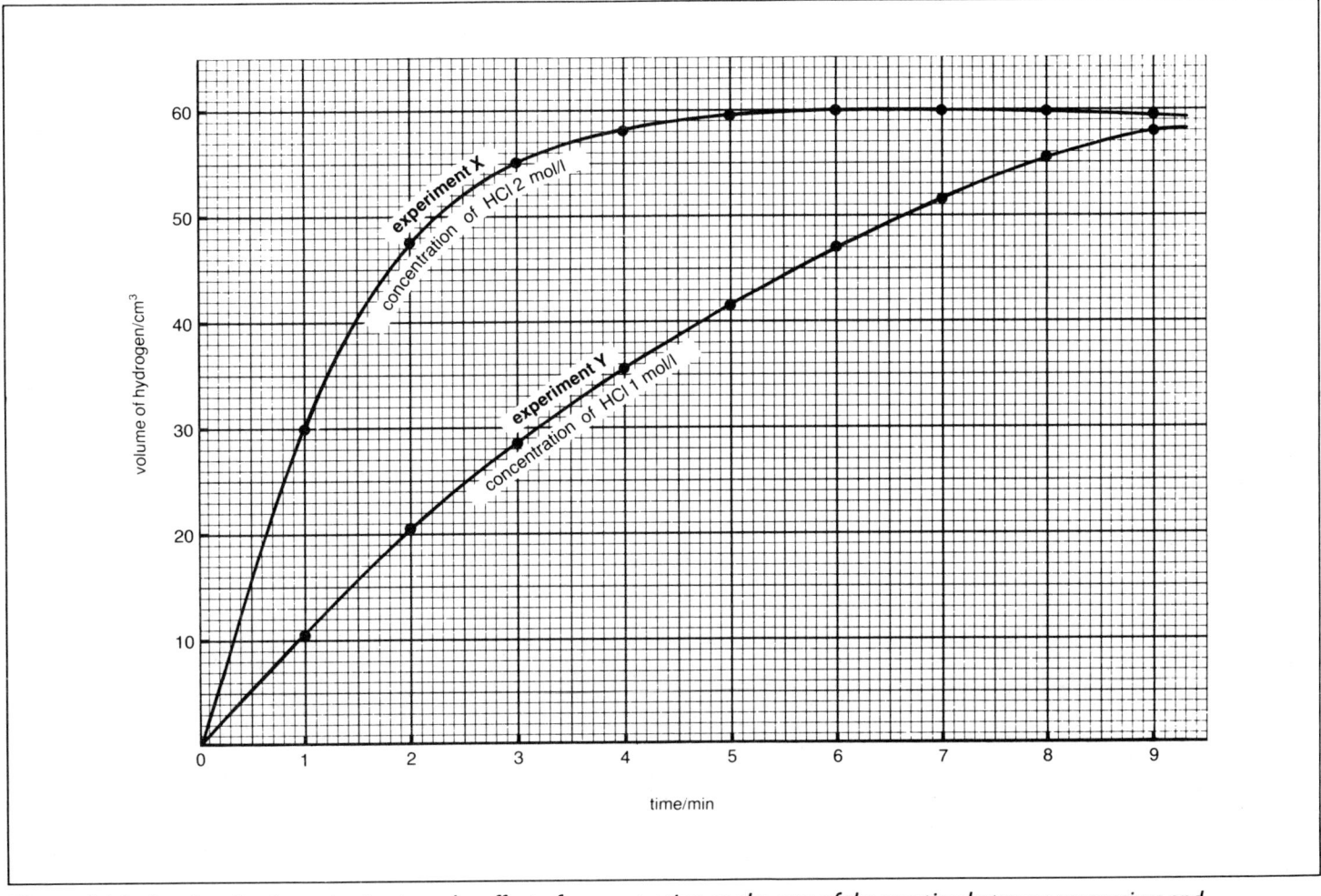

Figure 14.9 *Results of an investigation into the effect of concentration on the rate of the reaction between magnesium and hydrochloric acid.*

Investigating the effect of light: the decomposition of silver chloride

Figure 14.10 shows an experiment with silver chloride. Tubes A and B both contain a suspension of silver chloride. This can be made by mixing a silver nitrate solution with a sodium chloride solution. Tube B is exposed to light; it darkens. Tube A is protected from light; it remains white. Light has the effect of decomposing silver chloride.

$$\text{silver chloride} \xrightarrow{\text{light}} \text{silver} + \text{chlorine}$$
$$2AgCl(s) \rightarrow 2Ag(s) + Cl_2(g)$$

The precipitate of silver makes the suspension dark. Without light, the decomposition is so slow it is unnoticeable.

Explaining the factors affecting reaction rates: the collision theory

We can use the **collision theory of reactions** to explain why reaction rates vary. The collision theory says that

chemical reactions occur when particles of the reactants collide. They must collide with a certain minimum speed, otherwise they just bounce off one another.

For example, in the reaction between hydrogen and oxygen, a hydrogen molecule has to collide with an oxygen molecule before a reaction occurs. Furthermore,

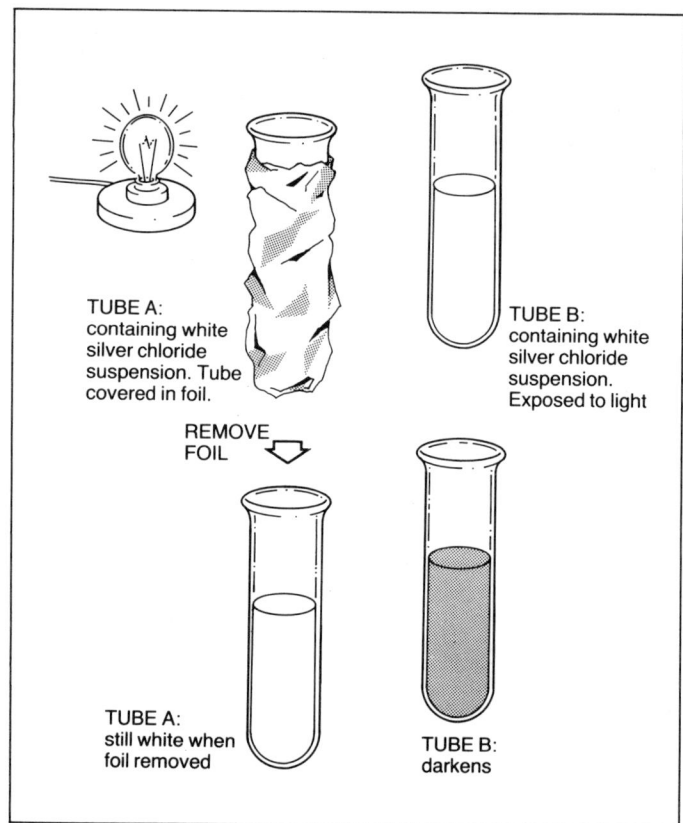

Figure 14.10 *The effect of light on the decomposition of silver chloride.*

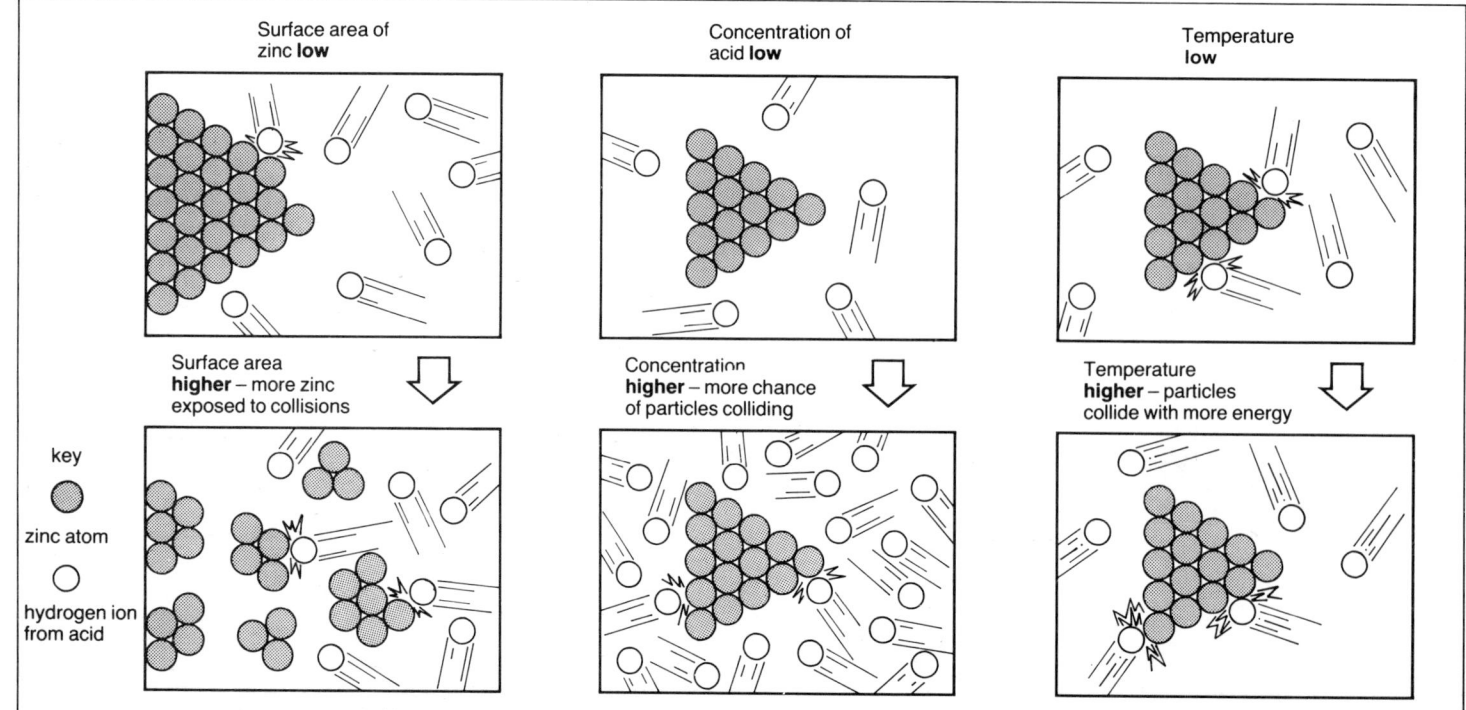

Figure 14.11 *Using the collision theory to explain the factors affecting the rate of reaction between zinc and hydrochloric acid.*

the molecules must collide at a certain minimum speed. This is why hydrogen and oxygen do not react at room temperature. To make them react, they must be heated so that the molecules move faster.

Figure 14.11 uses the collision theory to explain the effect of surface area, concentration and temperature on the rate of a reaction.

Reversible reactions

Many of the reactions we meet every day go in one direction only. It is impossible to make the products turn back into the reactants.

For example, when you burn toast, a chemical reaction occurs:

$$\text{bread} \xrightarrow{\text{heat}} \text{burnt toast}$$

This is a one-way reaction – you cannot turn the burnt toast back to unburnt bread.

Another example is the burning of natural gas (methane):

methane + oxygen → carbon dioxide + water

$$CH_4(g) + 2O_2(g) \rightarrow CO_2(g) + 2H_2O(l)$$

You cannot turn the carbon dioxide and water back into methane and oxygen.

These one-way reactions are called **irreversible reactions**. However, some reactions *can* be made to go backwards. They are called **reversible reactions**.

For example, if you heat blue, hydrated copper sulphate crystals, they turn to a white powder. The copper sulphate loses its water of crystallisation and becomes anhydrous.

hydrated copper sulphate (blue) $\xrightarrow{\text{heat}}$ anhydrous copper sulphate (white) + water

$$CuSO_4.5H_2O(s) \rightarrow CuSO_4(s) + 5H_2O(g)$$

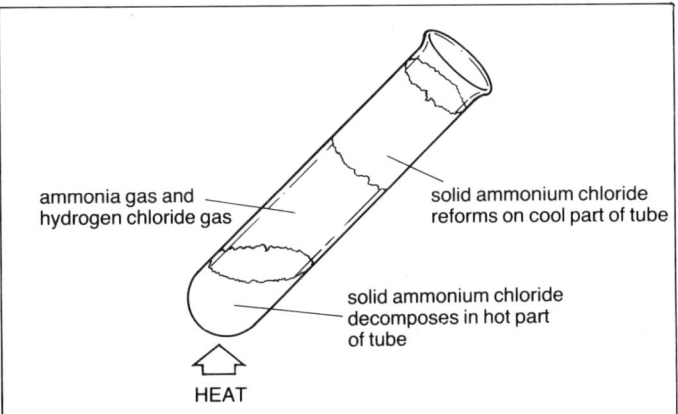

Figure 14.12 *Decomposition of ammonium chloride – a reversible reaction.*

If you add water to the white powder it goes blue again. The reaction has been reversed, and hydrated copper sulphate reforms.

anhydrous copper sulphate + water → hydrated copper sulphate

$$CuSO_4(s) + 5H_2O(l) \rightarrow CuSO_4.5H_2O(s)$$

We can show that the reaction is reversible by using a two-way arrow ⇌ in the equation:

$$CuSO_4.5H_2O(s) \rightleftharpoons CuSO_4(s) + 5H_2O(l)$$

Another reversible reaction occurs with ammonium chloride (figure 14.12). Heating solid ammonium chloride causes it to decompose. The products are two gases: ammonia and hydrogen chloride. When these gases cool, they recombine to form ammonium chloride. It is a reversible reaction.

ammonium chloride $\underset{\text{cool}}{\overset{\text{heat}}{\rightleftharpoons}}$ ammonia + hydrogen chloride

$$NH_4Cl(s) \rightleftharpoons NH_3(g) + HCl(g)$$

Important industrial processes: the Haber process

In this section and the next we will be looking at the industrial processes used to make two important chemicals – ammonia and sulphuric acid. In both cases we will see how chemical engineers have chosen reaction conditions in order to get as much of the product as possible, as fast as possible.

Making ammonia in the Haber process

Ammonia is a very important industrial chemical. It is used to make nitric acid, fertilizers and explosives (page 96).

The method used to make ammonia is called the **Haber process**. It is very cheap to run, and can make ammonia in huge quantities. The process involves a reversible reaction between nitrogen and hydrogen.

nitrogen + hydrogen ⇌ ammonia

$$N_2(g) + 3H_2(g) \rightleftharpoons 2NH_3(g)$$

The nitrogen for this process is extracted from air. The hydrogen is made by a reaction between natural gas and water.

Under normal conditions, the reaction between nitrogen and hydrogen is very slow. To speed it up, it is carried out:
- at high temperature
- at high pressure
- with a catalyst (made of iron).

Unfortunately, the reaction is a reversible one. Ammonia tends to decompose again and reform nitrogen and hydrogen. This happens more at higher temperatures. To avoid the ammonia decomposing, an intermediate

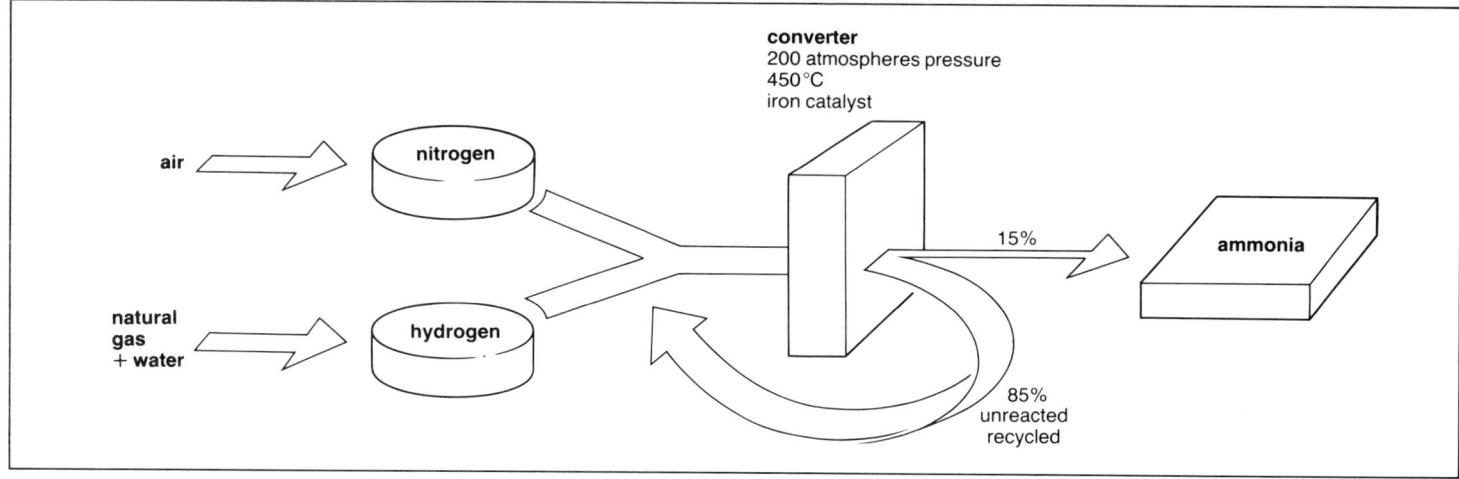

Figure 14.13 *An outline of the Haber process for the manufacture of ammonia.*

temperature (450°C) is used. This is high enough to make the reaction go quickly, but low enough to prevent too much ammonia decomposing. Even so, only about 15 per cent of the nitrogen and hydrogen is converted to ammonia. The remaining 85 per cent must be separated from the ammonia product and recycled (used again). This is shown in figure 14.13.

Important industrial processes: the Contact process for making sulphuric acid

Sulphuric acid (H_2SO_4) is one of the most important industrial chemicals. The chemical industry uses sulphuric acid in huge quantities. The most important uses are shown in figure 14.14.

To meet this need, the **Contact process** makes cheap sulphuric acid in large quantities. The process is outlined in figure 14.15.

First sulphur is burned in air in a furnace, to give sulphur dioxide:

sulphur + oxygen → sulphur dioxide

$S(s) + O_2(g) → SO_2(g)$

This is an exothermic process. The sulphur dioxide is cooled in a heat exchanger. The heat given out can be put to good use, for example to heat the catalyst in the next stage.

Next, the sulphur dioxide (SO_2) is converted to sulphur trioxide (SO_3) by reacting it with oxygen in the air:

sulphur + oxygen → sulphur
dioxide   trioxide

$2SO_2(g) + O_2(g) → 2SO_3(g)$

This is the most difficult part of the process. It is a slow reaction, and to speed it up it is carried out:
- with a catalyst (vanadium pentoxide, V_2O_5)
- at high temperature (450°C).

However, the reaction is reversible. At very high temperatures the sulphur trioxide breaks down to give sulphur dioxide again. This means that very high temperatures (above 500°C) cannot be used because they would make the sulphur trioxide decompose. This must be avoided because it could release sulphur dioxide, polluting the atmosphere.

Finally, the sulphur trioxide is absorbed in water to give sulphuric acid:

water + sulphur → sulphuric
        trioxide   acid

$H_2O(l) + SO_3(g) → H_2SO_4(aq)$

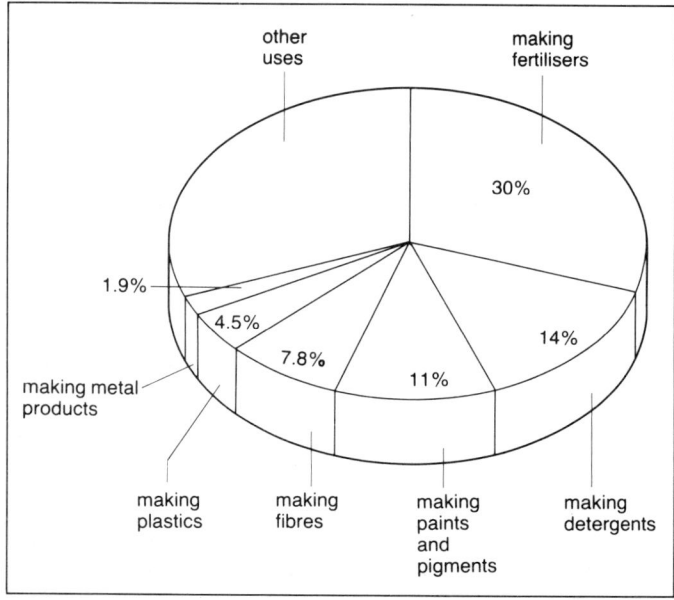

Figure 14.14 *Uses of sulphuric acid.*

Important industrial processes: the Contract process for making sulphuric acid

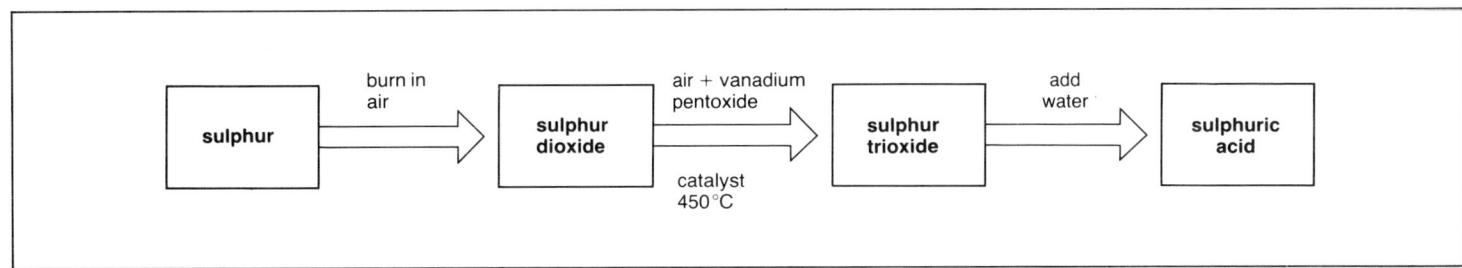

Figure 14.15 *An outline of the Contact process for making sulphuric acid.*

In fact this is difficult to do because sulphur dioxide reacts so readily with water that a fine mist of sulphuric acid droplets is formed. To avoid this problem, the sulphur trioxide is absorbed in 98 per cent sulphuric acid. This gives 99.5 per cent sulphuric acid, which is watered down to give 98 per cent acid again. The process goes on continuously.

Self test

Questions 1–5

The flow diagram below shows the main steps in the manufacture of sulphuric acid.

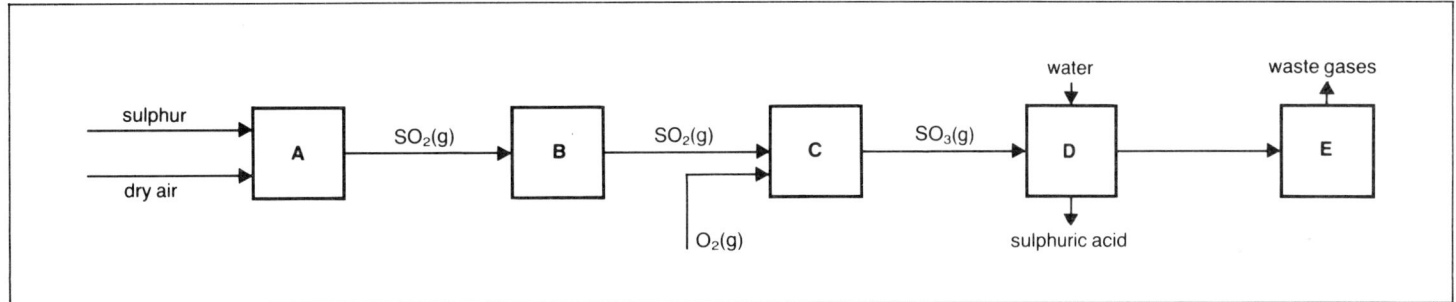

Choose from **A** to **E** the box that would be labelled
1. absorber
2. catalytic converter
3. chimney
4. furnace
5. heat exchanger

Questions 6–9

Factors that affect the rate of a reaction include
   A catalysts
   B concentration
   C light
   D surface area
   E temperature

Choose the factor from **A** to **E** that explains why
6. carrots cook faster when they are sliced.
7. stained clothes can be cleaned by soaking in biological detergent.
8. indoor photographs require the use of a flash.
9. vegetables cook faster in a pressure cooker.

Questions 10-13

An experiment was carried out to investigate the decomposition of hydrogen peroxide by the enzyme catalase. A graph was plotted to show the volume of gas produced against time.

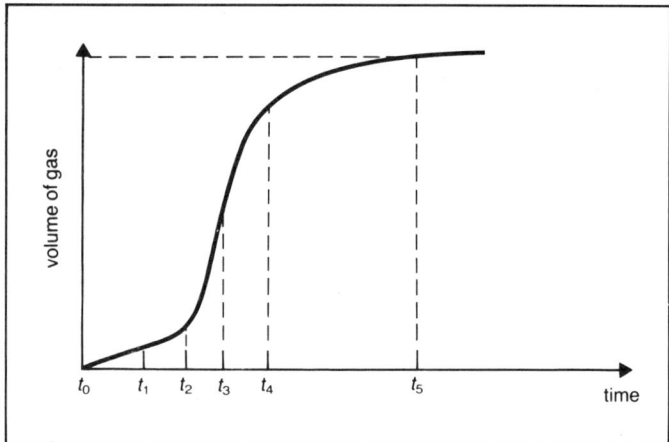

10 At which time was gas being produced at the fastest rate?
    A t_0 B t_1 C t_2 D t_3

11 How long did it take for half the hydrogen peroxide to react?
    A t_1 B t_2 C t_3 D t_4

12 What gas is produced?
    A carbon dioxide   B hydrogen
    C nitrogen   D oxygen

13 The reaction eventually stops because
    A the enzyme is used up.
    B the hydrogen peroxide is used up.
    C the gas poisons the catalase.
    D the reaction is reversible.

14 One reason for using catalysts in industry is that they increase
    A the yield of products.
    B the temperature of reactants.
    C the rate of reaction.
    D the concentration of reactants.

15 Iron will rust fastest on a
    A warm, dry day.
    B warm, wet day.
    C cold, dry day.
    D cold, wet day.

16 Increasing concentration increases the rate of a reaction because the particles
    A collide more often.
    B collide with more force.
    C have more energy.
    D move faster.

Questions 17-20

The figure below shows the percentage of ammonia produced in the Haber process at different temperatures and pressures.

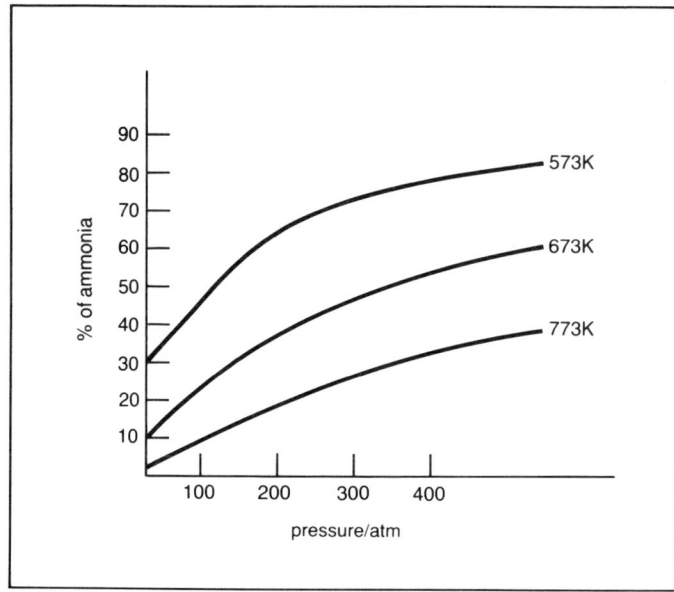

17 What percentage of ammonia is produced at 573K and 200 atm.?

18 At what pressure is 30 per cent ammonia produced at 673K?

19 How is the percentage of ammonia affected by increase in pressure?

20 How is the percentage of ammonia affected by increase in temperature?

15 Nitrogen and fertilisers

The graph in figure 15.1 shows how the world's population has grown since the year 1900. In spite of this tremendous increase, the world's farmers can grow enough food for everyone. Of course, there are parts of the world where there is not enough food. But in other parts of the world there is too much. We can grow enough food, but we still need to solve the problem of getting it to where it is needed. And it has to be at a price that the poorer countries can afford.

How have farmers kept up with the tremendous increase in the number of mouths to feed? Fertilisers provide one of the answers to this question.

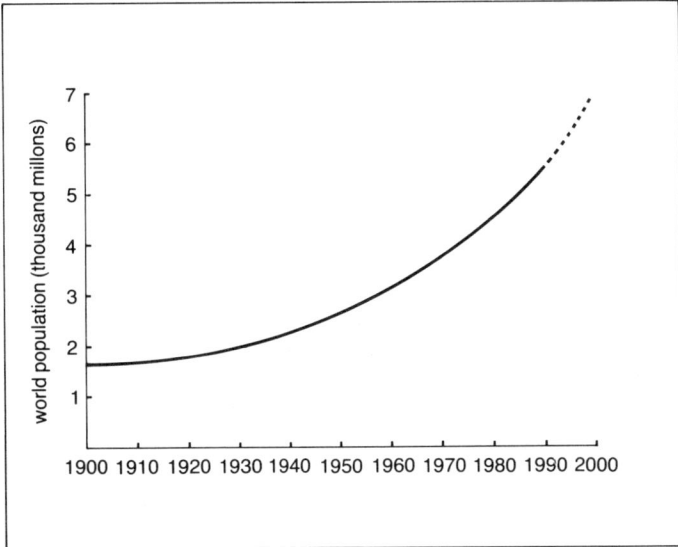

Figure 15.1 Growth of the world's population since 1900.

Fertilisers and food

Plants need to get certain elements from the soil in order to grow well. Three elements are needed in large quantities. They are nitrogen (N), phosphorus (P) and potassium (K). Under natural conditions, plants can get enough of these vital elements from the soil. The elements occur in the soil as compounds like nitrates and phosphates. Plants can absorb these soluble compounds through their roots. As the plants die and decay, they return the elements to the soil.

Under the less natural conditions of a farm, the vital elements are not returned to the soil. They are removed when the crops are harvested. So farmers use artificial fertilisers to put the elements back. By using the right amount of fertilisers, big crops can be grown.

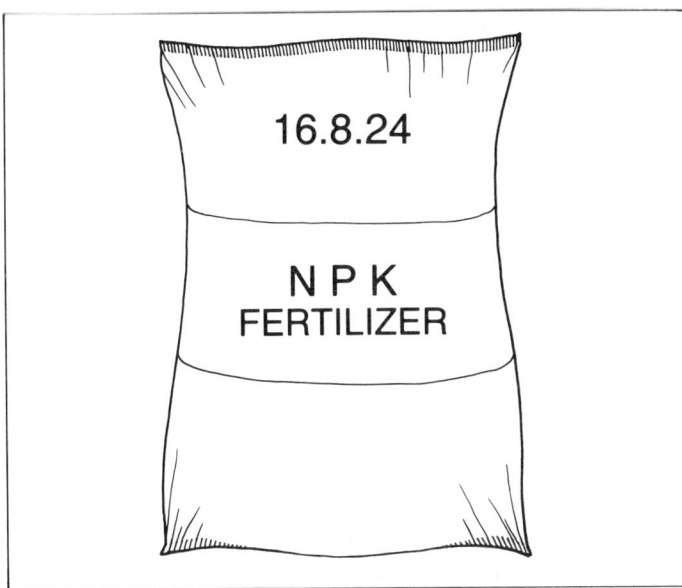

Figure 15.2 A sack of NPK fertiliser, showing the proportions of the different elements present. This sack contains a mixture with 16% nitrogen, 8% phosphorus and 24% potassium.

Nitrogen is the most important of the three elements, because plants use it to make proteins (page 96). This chapter is mostly about **nitrogenous fertilisers**. But many fertilisers contain phosphorus and potassium compounds as well as nitrogen compounds. These mixed fertilisers are called **'NPK'** fertilisers. Farmers can buy NPK fertilisers containing different proportions of the three elements. Numbers written on the fertiliser bag show the proportions (figure 15.2). The farmer chooses the fertiliser to suit the soil and the crop being grown.

The nitrogen cycle

Proteins

Proteins are vital to all living things. They are the material from which much of our bodies is built. Hair, skin and muscle are all made from protein. Without proteins we cannot grow, or keep our bodies in good condition.

We get proteins from the food we eat. Meat, eggs, fish, milk, nuts, peas and beans are all high-protein foods. Plants are the original source of all our protein. This is because cows, chickens, fish and other animals get their protein from the plants they eat.

Proteins are polymers (pages 81–2). All proteins contain the elements carbon, hydrogen, oxygen and nitrogen. To make proteins, plants need a supply of all these elements. Figure 15.3 (overleaf) shows where they get them from.

Plants get their nitrogen by absorbing compounds from the soil. They can absorb only soluble compounds like nitrates (containing NO_3^- ions) and ammonium compounds (containing NH_4^+ ions). Nitrogen gas in the air is no use to plants because it is insoluble and cannot be absorbed. To make nitrogen gas useful to plants it has to

96 Nitrogen and fertilisers

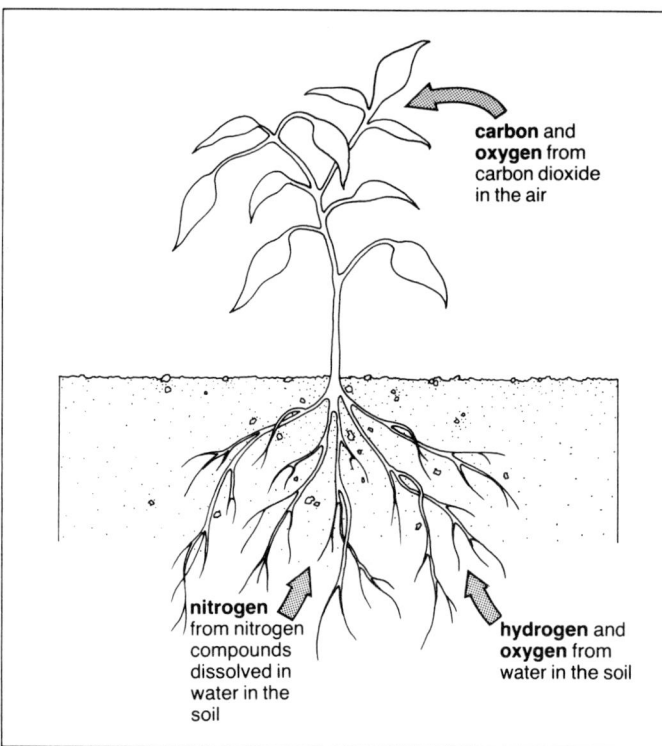

Figure 15.3 *How a plant obtains the carbon, hydrogen oxygen and nitrogen it needs.*

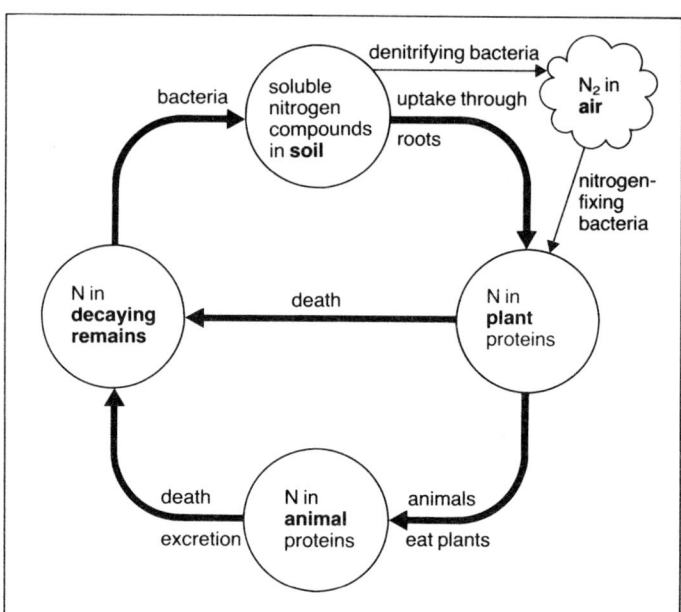

Figure 15.4 *The nitrogen cycle.*

be made into a soluble compound. This is called **nitrogen fixation**. Fixed nitrogen gets into the soil either from decaying plants and animals or from fertilisers.

The nitrogen cycle

Figure 15.4 represents the **nitrogen cycle** that occurs under natural conditions. It shows how nitrogen is removed from the soil and returned to it. Look at the cycle, and notice the following points.

- Plants put fixed nitrogen compounds back into the soil when they die and decay.
- Animals eat plants, and put fixed nitrogen back into the soil when they die. In addition, animals excrete fixed nitrogen in their faeces and urine. This also returns fixed nitrogen compounds to the soil.
- Fixed nitrogen compounds are removed from the soil by plants. Plants absorb these compounds through their roots.
- Fixed nitrogen is also removed by denitrifying bacteria. These bacteria turn the fixed nitrogen compounds in the soil into useless nitrogen gas.
- Other bacteria can help plants to turn nitrogen gas into proteins. They are called nitrogen-fixing bacteria. They are found in bumpy nodules on the roots of plants in the pea and bean family.
- One important way of adding extra fixed nitrogen to the soil is not shown on the diagram. It is by the use of nitrogenous fertilisers.

Before looking at the manufacture of nitrogenous fertilisers, we need to know about the compound they are made from. This is ammonia.

Ammonia

Figure 15.5 shows some of the important properties of ammonia.

Ammonia has many uses. Three important uses are:
- **As a nitrogenous fertiliser.** Sometimes liquid ammonia is applied directly to the ground. More often, it is converted to ammonium salts for use as fertilisers (page 98).

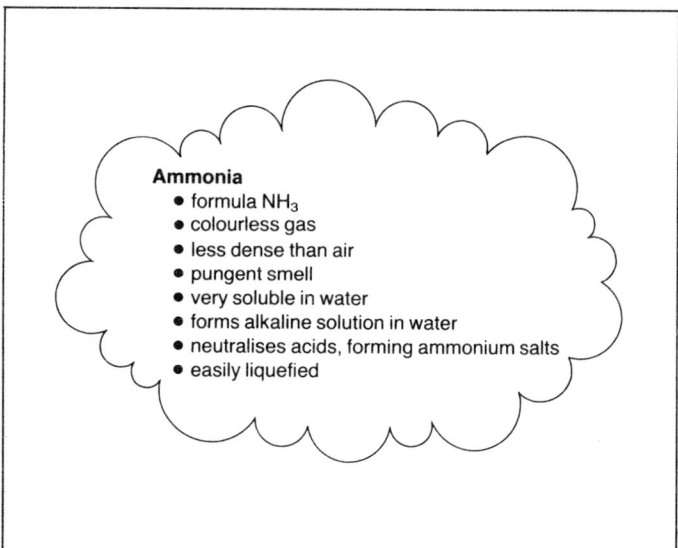

Figure 15.5 *Some important properties of ammonia.*

- **For making nitric acid** (page 98).
- **As a household cleaner.** Ammonia solution is alkaline. This enables it to break down grease. Because of this, it is particularly useful for cleaning ovens and cookers.

Ammonia as a base

A base is a substance that neutralises acids to form salts (page 54). Ammonia neutralises acids to form **ammonium salts**. The ammonia combines with an H^+ ion from the acid, forming the **ammonium ion (NH_4^+)**.

For example, when ammonia neutralises hydrochloric acid, ammonium chloride is formed:

ammonia + hydrochloric → ammonium
             acid   chloride

$NH_3(aq) + HCl(aq) \rightarrow NH_4Cl(aq)$

With sulphuric acid, ammonium sulphate is formed:

ammonia + sulphuric → ammonium
          acid   sulphate

$2NH_3(aq) + H_2SO_4(aq) \rightarrow (NH_4)_2SO_4(aq)$

With nitric acid, ammonium nitrate is formed:

ammonia + nitric → ammonium
          acid   nitrate

$NH_3(aq) + HNO_3(aq) \rightarrow NH_4NO_3(aq)$

Making ammonium salts in the laboratory

Ammonium salts are manufactured in huge quantities for use as fertilisers (page 98). You can make ammonium sulphate on a small scale in the laboratory. The method involves adding ammonia solution to sulphuric acid until it is just neutral. This gives a *solution* of ammonium sulphate. You can get ammonium sulphate *crystals* by heating the solution until it begins to crystallise. The solution is then left for a few days to allow the crystals to grow. The method is summarised in figure 15.6.

The reaction of ammonia with water

Ammonia is very soluble in water. It dissolves to form an alkaline solution. The solution in water is alkaline because some of the ammonia reacts with water to form ammonium hydroxide.

ammonia + water → ammonium hydroxide

$NH_3(g) + H_2O(l) \rightarrow NH_4OH(aq)$

Ammonium hydroxide ionises to form NH_4^+ and OH^- ions. It is the OH^- ions that make the solution alkaline.

Turning ammonium salts back to ammonia

If an ammonium salt is heated with an alkali, ammonia is formed. The alkali removes an H^+ ion from the ammonium ion, leaving ammonia.

ammonium + hydroxide → ammonia + water
  ion   ions
         from alkali

$NH_4^+ + OH^- \rightarrow NH_3 + H_2O$

This reaction provides a good way of preparing small amounts of ammonia in the laboratory. Figure 15.7 (overleaf) shows how this can be done using ammonium chloride and calcium hydroxide.

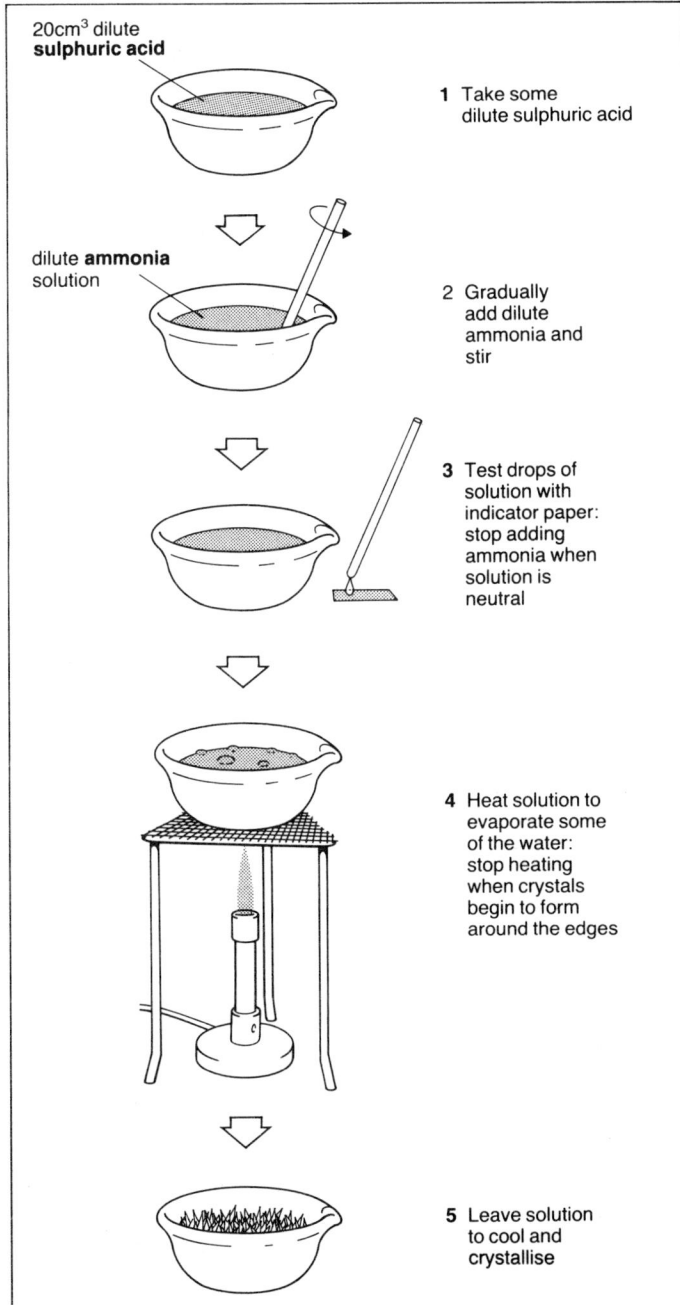

Figure 15.6 *Making ammonium sulphate crystals in the laboratory.*

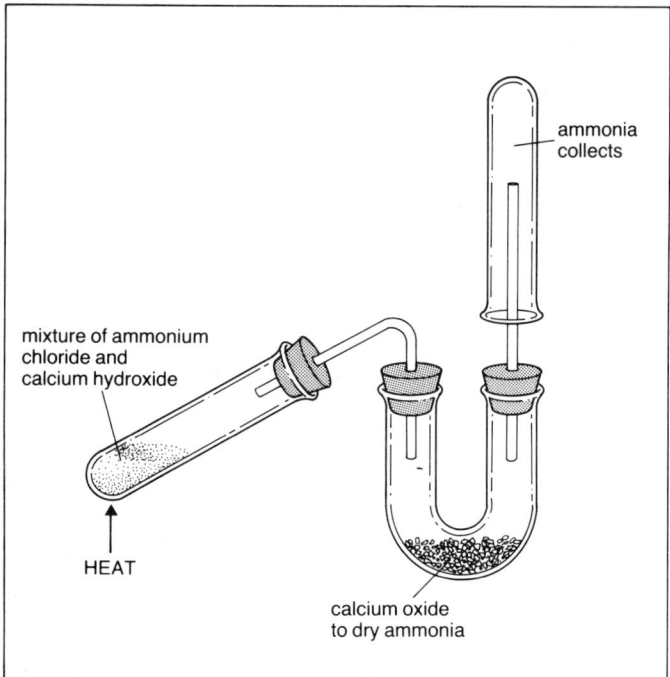

Figure 15.7 *Preparing and collecting ammonia in the laboratory.*

Manufacturing fertilisers

The fertiliser industry is based on ammonia. The manufacture of ammonia is covered on page 91.

Most nitrogenous fertilisers contain ammonium compounds. The commonest ammonium compound in fertilisers is ammonium nitrate (NH_4NO_3). This contains a 'double dose' of nitrogen.

To make ammonium nitrate, you need ammonia and nitric acid (HNO_3). Nitric acid is itself made from ammonia.

The manufacture of nitric acid

Figure 15.8 summarises the manufacture of nitric acid from ammonia. There are three major steps.

Step 1. Ammonia is oxidised to nitrogen monoxide (NO).

ammonia + oxygen $\xrightarrow{\text{platinum catalyst}}$ nitrogen monoxide + water

$4NH_3(g) + 5O_2(g) \longrightarrow 4NO(g) + 6H_2O(g)$

This reaction is exothermic and the gases get hot.

Step 2. Nitrogen monoxide reacts with more oxygen to form nitrogen dioxide (NO_2). This reaction happens of its own accord when the gases are cooled.

nitrogen monoxide + oxygen → nitrogen dioxide

$2NO(g) + O_2(g) \rightarrow 2NO_2(g)$

Step 3. Nitrogen dioxide and yet more oxygen react with water to form nitric acid.

nitrogen dioxide + oxygen + water → nitric acid

$4NO_2(g) + O_2(g) + 2H_2O(l) \rightarrow 4HNO_3(aq)$

Different fertilisers for different jobs

- **Straight-N fertilisers.** These contain just nitrogen compounds. The commonest is ammonium nitrate, sometimes sold as 'NITRAM'. It is made by neutralising nitric acid with ammonia.
- **NPK fertilisers.** NPK fertilisers contain phosphorus compounds and potassium compounds as well as nitrogen compounds. The potassium compound is usually potassium chloride, which is mined as the mineral potash. The phosphorus compound is usually ammonium phosphate. This is made from ammonia, sulphuric acid and imported phosphate rock.

Siting a fertiliser works

All these different fertilisers are usually made on one large site. The site is chosen so that all the necessary raw materials can be brought together easily. There is a major fertiliser plant at Billingham on Teesside. Figure 15.9 shows why this is a particularly good site for a fertiliser plant.

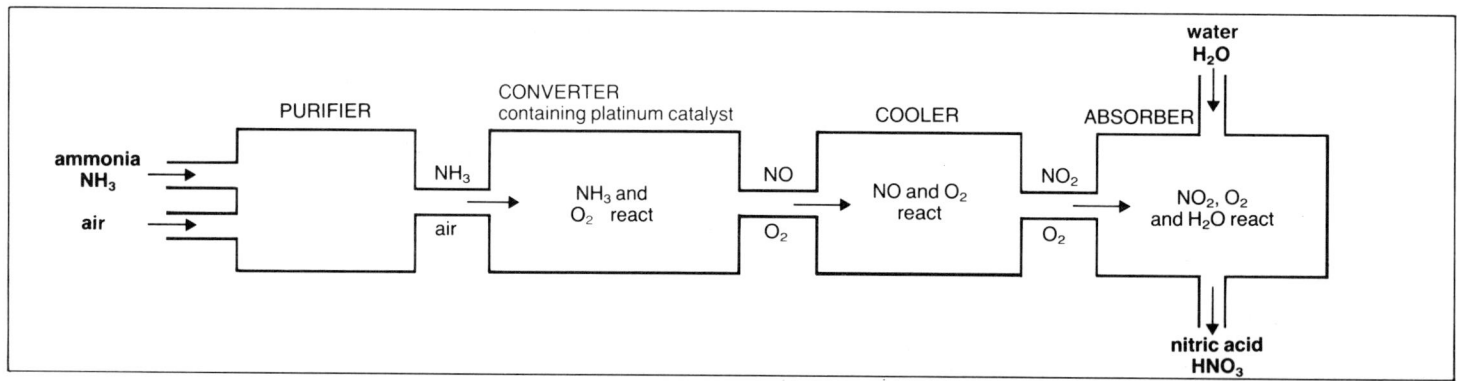

Figure 15.8 *A summary of the manufacture of nitric acid from ammonia.*

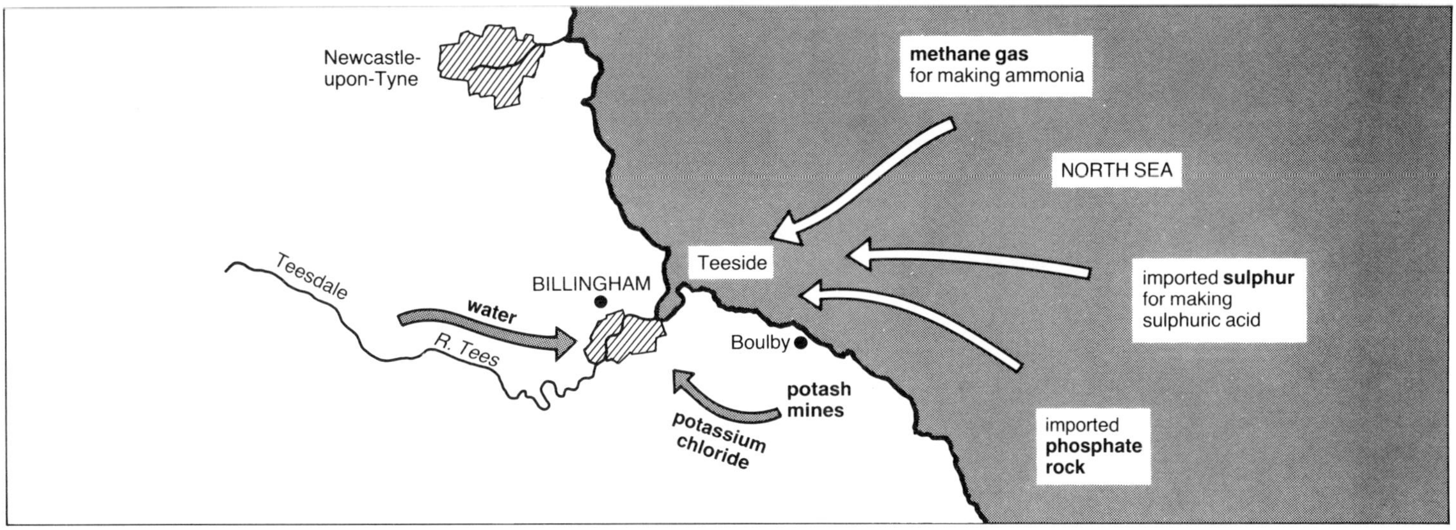

Figure 15.9 *A map showing the position of Billingham, where there is a major fertiliser works.*

Fertilisers – good and bad news

Fertilisers can double the yield that a farmer gets from a crop. They have played an important part in helping to produce enough food for the world's rapidly growing population.

But problems arise if farmers rely on fertilisers too much. The raw materials from which fertilisers are made – air, water, phosphate rock, potassium chloride – are abundant. They should last a long time. But making fertilisers uses a lot of energy. Manufacturing a half-tonne bag of fertiliser uses up the energy equivalent of 300 litres of petrol. This energy is supplied by fossil fuels, particularly natural gas. To conserve our reserves of fossil fuels, we need to avoid over-use of fertilisers.

Fertilisers can also cause pollution problems. The nitrogen compounds in fertilisers are all very soluble. They can be carried off by rain water as it drains from farmland. As a result nitrogen compounds, particularly nitrates, build up in underground water supplies. Traces of these nitrogen compounds are already beginning to appear in our drinking water. No one knows just what effects these nitrogen compounds may have on our health. But, in years to come, water authorities may have to spend a lot of money removing them from drinking water.

Pesticides

Pesticides are chemicals that control animal pests, diseases and weeds (figure 15.10).

Like fertilisers, pesticides have helped farmers to increase the yields they can get from their crops. But over-using pesticides also brings problems. Pesticides are designed to kill living things. They are poisons. Inevitably, traces of the pesticides used by farmers get into our food.

All pesticides are tested very carefully before they are allowed to be sold. Even so, many people are worried. They are concerned about the effects on our health of the traces of pesticides in our food.

Pesticides can also be dangerous to harmless wildlife. Some pesticides are particularly dangerous because they remain in the soil a long time without breaking down. They stay in the environment and may get eaten by wildlife. The pesticide moves along the food chain from one organism to another. As it does so it becomes more and more concentrated. Eventually, it may be concentrated enough to affect seriously the organisms at the end of the food chain. This happened with the insecticide DDT, which caused a dramatic reduction in the numbers of birds of prey in the 1960s.

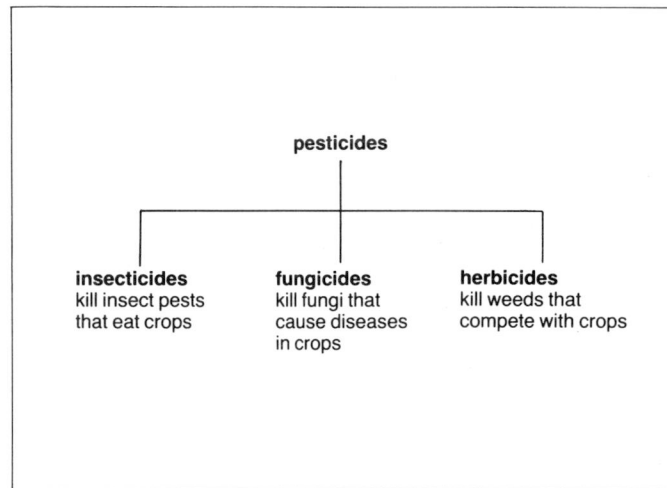

Figure 15.10 *Different kinds of pesticides.*

100 Nitrogen and fertilisers

● Self test

Questions 1–5
The nitrogen cycle is shown below.

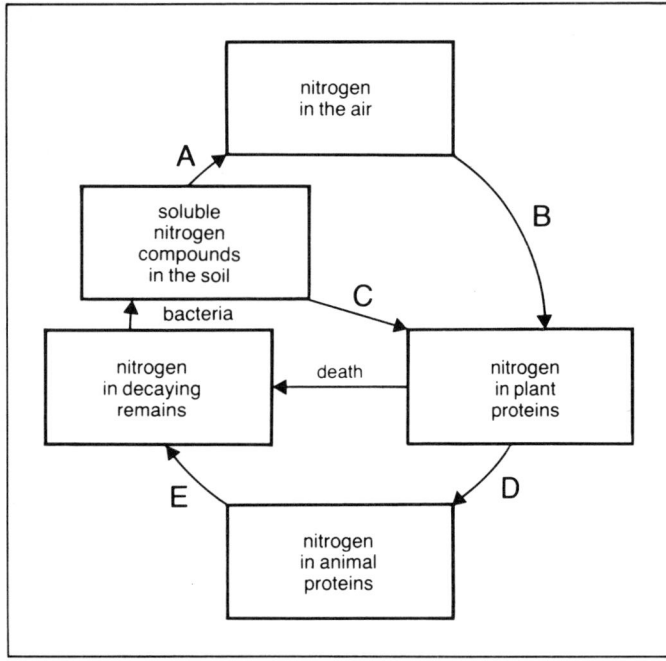

Choose from **A** to **E** the arrow that would be labelled
1. absorption through roots.
2. death or excretion.
3. denitrifying bacteria.
4. feeding.
5. nitrogen-fixing bacteria.

Questions 6–8
Choose from **A** to **E**
   A ammonium sulphate
   B calcium carbonate
   C calcium phosphate
   D compost
   E potassium chloride
the substance that increases soil fertility by
6. making nitrogen rapidly available to plants.
7. slowly releasing nitrogen-containing compounds under the action of bacteria in the soil.
8. increasing the pH of soil.

Questions 9–13
The manufacture of nitric acid is summarised in the flow diagram below.

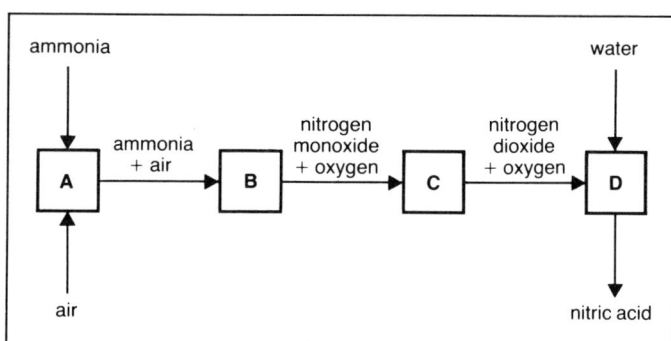

Choose from **A** to **D** the box
9. that would be labelled absorber.
10. that would be labelled cooler.
11. that would be labelled purifier.
12. in which catalysis occurs.
13. in which no chemical reaction occurs.

14. The soil in a particular field contains plenty of potassium and phosphorus, but not enough nitrogen. The best fertiliser to add to the soil would be
    A ammonium nitrate   **B** ammonium phosphate
    C ammonium sulphate   **D** potassium nitrate

15. A good fertiliser should be
    A fertile **B** soluble **C** toxic **D** volatile

16. Ammonium sulphate can be prepared by adding a slight excess of ammonia solution to sulphuric acid and then
    A distilling off the ammonium sulphate.
    B evaporating until crystals begin to form.
    C filtering off the ammonium sulphate.
    D neutralising the solution.

17. In NPK fertiliser, the P is present as
    A phosphate.   **B** phosphorus.
    C potash.   **D** potassium.

18. Fertilisers can cause problems because they
    A are not biodegradeable.
    B are soluble in water.
    C can get into drinking water.
    D can poison growing plants.

16 Atomic structure

Inside atoms

Less than a hundred years ago, scientists believed that atoms were solid particles like tiny snooker balls. Since then, experiments have shown that all atoms are made up from three particles – protons, neutrons and electrons (table 16.1).

Table 16.1 *The relative masses, relative charges and positions of protons, neutrons and electrons.*

Particle	Position in the atom	Mass (relative to a proton)	Charge (relative to that on a proton)
Proton	Nucleus	1	+1
Neutron	Nucleus	1	0
Electron	Shells	$\frac{1}{1840}$	−1

The centre of an atom is called the **nucleus**. The nucleus contains **protons** and **neutrons**. Protons and neutrons have the same mass. Protons are positively charged but neutrons have no charge. The nucleus occupies only a very small volume of the atom.

The rest of the space is occupied by **electrons**, which are negatively charged. The electrons move around very fast in layers, or **shells**, at different distances from the nucleus. The mass of an electron is 1840 times less than that of a proton or neutron. You can imagine an atom as a small, heavy, positive nucleus surrounded by a negative cloud of electrons.

Building up atoms from protons, neutrons and electrons

Protons, neutrons and electrons are the building blocks for atoms. Different atoms have different numbers of the three particles. Hydrogen atoms are the simplest. They have one proton, no neutrons and one electron (figure 16.1). The next simplest are helium atoms with two protons, two neutrons and two electrons. Next come lithium atoms with three protons, four neutrons and three electrons.

Notice that atoms always have equal numbers of protons and electrons. This means that the positive charges (on the protons) balance the negative charges (on the electrons). Notice also that hydrogen, the first element in the periodic table, has one proton. Helium, the second element in the periodic table, has two protons. Lithium, the third element in the periodic table, has three protons, and so on.

Atomic number and mass number

Hydrogen atoms are the only atoms with one proton. Helium atoms are the only atoms with two protons. Lithium atoms are the only atoms with three protons, and so on. Each element has its own, unique number of protons. Because of this, scientists have a special name for the number of protons in the nucleus of an atom; they call it the **atomic number**.

Atomic number = number of protons.

So, hydrogen has an atomic number of 1, helium has an atomic number of 2, lithium has an atomic number of 3, and so on. Aluminium, the thirteenth element in the periodic table with thirteen protons and thirteen electrons, has an atomic number of 13.

The mass of an atom is made up from protons and neutrons. (The mass of electrons is so small that it can usually be ignored in working out the total mass of an atom.) Thus, the mass of an atom depends upon the number of protons and the number of neutrons added together. This number is called the **mass number** of the atom.

Mass number = number of protons + number of neutrons.

Thus, hydrogen atoms (with one proton and no neutrons) have a mass number of 1. Helium atoms (two protons and two neutrons) have a mass number of 4 and lithium atoms (three protons and four neutrons) have a mass number of 7. Figure 16.2 shows how we can represent the mass number and the atomic number of an atom with its symbol. A lithium ion would be written as $^{7}_{3}Li^+$, and an electron (mass almost zero, charge −1) is shown as $^{0}_{-1}e^-$. In the periodic table, elements are arranged in order of atomic number. This makes it easy to work out the atomic number of an element. For example, chlorine is the seventeenth element in the periodic table, so its atomic number is 17.

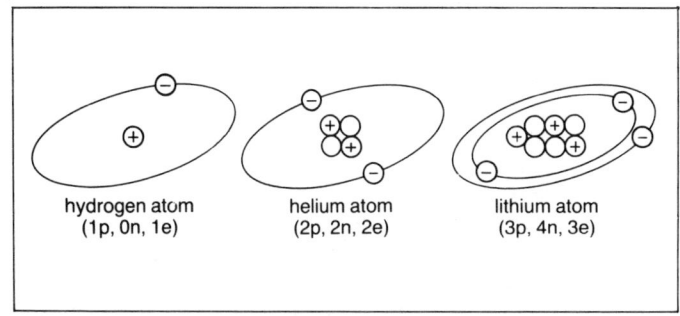

Figure 16.1 *Protons, neutrons and electrons in hydrogen, helium and lithium atoms:* $\oplus \equiv$ *proton,* $\bigcirc \equiv$ *neutron,* $\ominus \equiv$ *electron.*

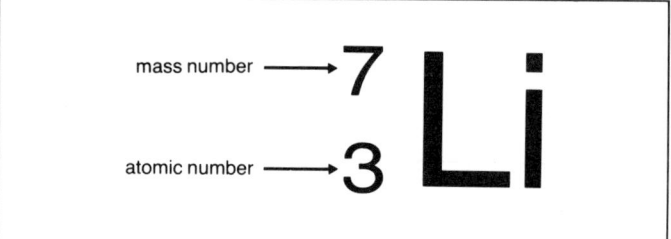

Figure 16.2 *Representing the mass number and atomic number with the symbol of an atom.*

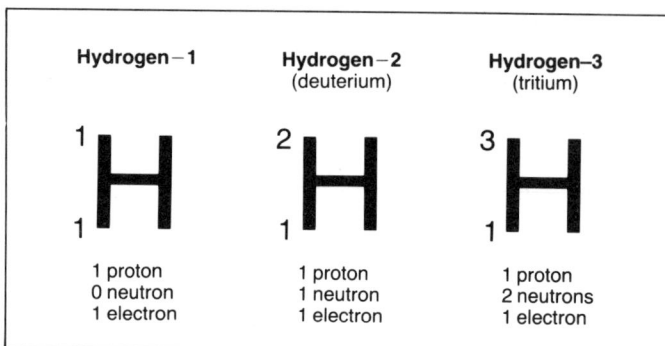

Figure 16.4 *The isotopes of hydrogen.*

Isotopes

In 1919, F. W. Aston built the first mass spectrometer (figure 16.3). This enabled scientists to compare the relative masses of atoms much more accurately than before. Using his mass spectrometer, Aston discovered that some elements contained atoms with different masses. When atoms of these elements were ionised and passed through a mass spectrometer, the beam of ions separated into two or more paths. This showed that one element could have atoms with different masses. These atoms of the same element with different masses are called **isotopes.**

All the isotopes of one particular element have the same number of protons. Therefore, they have the same atomic number. But they have different masses because they contain different numbers of neutrons. So:

Isotopes have the same atomic number, but different mass numbers.

For example, hydrogen has three isotopes. Each isotope has an atomic number of 1, but their mass numbers are 1, 2 and 3 (figure 16.4). The isotopes are named hydrogen-1, hydrogen-2, and hydrogen-3 to show their different mass numbers.

Notice that isotopes have the same number of electrons. This gives them the same chemical properties because chemical properties depend on the transfer and sharing of electrons. Isotopes do, however, have different numbers of neutrons and therefore different masses. This means that they have slightly different physical properties such as different densities, different melting points and different boiling points.

Relative atomic masses

Most elements contain a mixture of isotopes. This explains why their relative atomic masses are *not* whole numbers. The **relative atomic mass** of an element is the 'average' relative mass of one atom, taking into account the different isotopes and their proportions. For example, chlorine consists of two isotopes with mass numbers of 35 and 37. The symbols for these isotopes are $^{35}_{17}Cl$ and $^{37}_{17}Cl$. If chlorine were 100 per cent $^{35}_{17}Cl$, its relative atomic mass would be 35 (table 16.2). If it were 100 per cent $^{37}_{17}Cl$, its relative atomic mass would be 37. A 50 : 50 mixture of $^{35}_{17}Cl$ and $^{37}_{17}Cl$ would have a relative atomic mass of 36. Naturally occuring chlorine actually has 75 per cent $^{35}_{17}Cl$ and 25 per cent $^{37}_{17}Cl$. This gives a relative atomic mass of 35.5 (table 16.2).

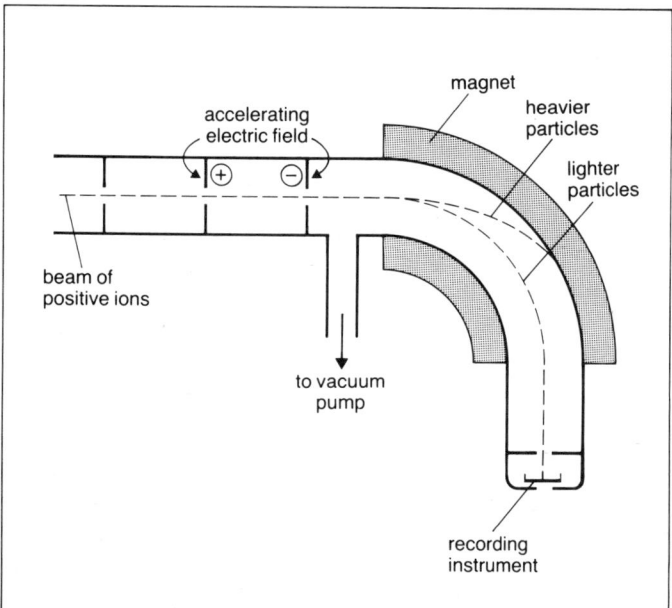

Figure 16.3 *A mass spectrometer. A beam of positive ions is accelerated by an electric field and then deflected by a magnetic field. The amount of deflection depends on the mass of the particles. Lighter particles are deflected more than heavier particles. As the strength of the magnetic field increases, particles are deflected more and so heavier particles are detected on the recording instrument.*

Table 16.2 *The relative atomic mass of chlorine.*

Percentage of $^{35}_{17}Cl$	100	**75**	50	25	0
Percentage of $^{37}_{17}Cl$	0	**25**	50	75	100
Relative atomic mass	35	**35.5**	36	36.5	37

Electron structures

During chemical reactions, electrons are transferred or shared out between atoms. Once this movement of electrons has taken place, the atoms become stable and unreactive. Noble gases such as helium, neon and argon are very unreactive. Chemists suggested that this was because they have atoms with very stable electron structures. This means that atoms and ions will have stable electron structures if they have two electrons (like helium), ten electrons (like neon), eighteen electrons (like argon) and so on.

Chemists now believe that the first shell of electrons is full and stable when it contains two electrons like helium. The second shell is stable when it contains eight electrons. So, neon with ten electrons has two electrons in the first shell and eight electrons in the second shell. Its electron structure is written as 2,8 (figure 16.5). Argon is unreactive because its first, second and third shells are all full and stable with two, eight and eight electrons respectively. Its electron structure is 2,8,8.

Figure 16.6 shows the first 20 elements in the periodic table. The electron structure of each element is written below its symbol. When the first shell is full at helium, electrons go into the second shell. So, the electron structure of lithium is 2,1; beryllium is 2,2; boron is 2,3 and so on. When the second shell is full at neon, electrons start to fill the third shell. The electron structure of sodium is therefore 2,8,1.

Using electron structures, it is easy to see why elements in the same group of the periodic table have similar properties. Look at the alkali metals (lithium, sodium and potassium) in the first column of figure 16.6. Each alkali metal has one electron in its outer shell. By losing this outer electron, the alkali metals form positive ions (Li$^+$, Na$^+$, K$^+$). Each of these positive ions has a stable electron structure, like a noble gas. So all the alkali metals are very reactive because they lose the electron in the outer shell easily. They form compounds with similar formulas because they all form positive ions with one charge.

Now look at the halogens (fluorine and chlorine) in figure 16.6. These elements each have seven electrons in

period 1	H 1							He 2
period 2	Li 2,1	Be 2,2	B 2,3	C 2,4	N 2,5	O 2,6	F 2,7	Ne 2,8
period 3	Na 2,8,1	Mg 2,8,2	Al 2,8,3	Si 2,8,4	P 2,8,5	S 2,8,6	Cl 2,8,7	Ar 2,8,8
period 4	K 2,8,8,1	Ca 2,8,8,2						

Figure 16.6 *Electron structures of the first twenty elements in the periodic table.*

their outer shell. By gaining one electron, the halogens form negative ions (F$^-$, Cl$^-$, Br$^-$). Each of these negative ions has a stable electron structure, like the next noble gas.

Thus, all the halogens are reactive because they gain the extra electron very readily. They form compounds with similar formulae because they all form negative ions with one charge.

Forming compounds

Figure 16.7 shows the electron structures of the atoms and ions formed by elements in the third period.

The first three elements in the period (Na, Mg and Al) lose the electrons in their outer shell to form positive ions (Na$^+$, Mg^{2+} and Al^{3+}). These ions have an electron structure like the noble gas that precedes them in the periodic table, neon (2,8). The sixth and seventh elements in the period (S and Cl) gain electrons to form negatively charged ions (S^{2-} and Cl$^-$). These ions have an electron structure like argon (2,8,8), the noble gas that follows them in the table.

Elements in the middle of a period, such as silicon and phosphorus, do not usually form ions in their compounds. This is because they would have to lose or gain too many electrons in order to achieve a noble gas structure. But how *do* elements in the middle of the periodic table achieve stable electronic structures in their compounds? They do it by sharing electrons. This sharing of electrons results in covalent bonds between atoms.

When elements form compounds, they lose, gain or share electrons in order to get a stable electron structure like a noble gas.

This idea is the basis of the electronic theory of chemical bonding.

noble gases
He 2
Ne 2, 8
Ar 2, 8, 8

Figure 16.5 *Electron structures of the first three noble gases.*

104 Atomic structure

element	Na	Mg	Al	Si	P	S	Cl	Ar
electron structure of atom	2,8,1	2,8,2	2,8,3	2,8,4	2,8,5	2,8,6	2,8,7	2,8,8
ion	Na⁺	Mg²⁺	Al³⁺	—	—	S²⁻	Cl⁻	—
electron structure of ion	2,8	2,8	2,8	—	—	2,8,8	2,8,8	—

Figure 16.7 *The electron structures of atoms and ions formed by elements in the third period.*

Ionic bonds – transfer of electrons

Ionic bonds are formed when metals react with non-metals. Figure 16.8 shows the transfer of electrons when sodium and chlorine react to form sodium chloride. The electrons in the outer shells of the two atoms are shown by dots or crosses around their symbols. These figures are often called dot/cross diagrams. The overall electron structures of the atoms and ions are shown below the symbols.

The sodium atom loses the one electron in its outer shell to form an Na⁺ ion with an electron structure like neon. The electron given up by the sodium atom is taken by a chlorine atom to form a Cl⁻ ion. The Cl⁻ ion has an electron structure like argon. So, the formation of sodium chloride (Na⁺Cl⁻) involves the *transfer* of electrons from sodium atoms to chlorine atoms. Ions of opposite charge are formed, Na⁺ and Cl⁻. These two ions attract each other.

The bond between the oppositely charged ions is called an ionic or electrovalent bond.

Compounds containing these bonds are known as **ionic** or **electrovalent compounds**. Solid ionic compounds have giant structures containing millions and millions of ions. The structure and properties of ionic compounds were discussed on pages 34–5.

Figure 16.9 shows the electron transfers that take place during the formation of magnesium oxide and potassium sulphide.

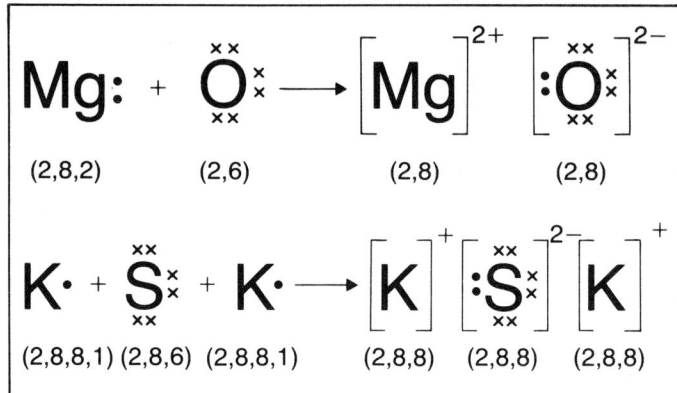

Figure 16.9 *Electron transfers during the formation of magnesium oxide and potassium sulphide.*

Notice the following points:
- all the ions have stable electron structures.
- both compounds contain oppositely charged ions, which attract one another.

Covalent bonds – sharing electrons

Covalent bonds are formed between atoms of non-metals. On their own, chlorine atoms are very unstable. They contain only seven electrons in their outer shell. But if two chlorine atoms come close together, forming a chlorine molecule (Cl₂), the electrons in their outer shells can overlap so that one pair of electrons is shared by both atoms. This is shown as a dot/cross diagram in figure 16.10.

The shared pair of electrons is attracted by the nucleus of each atom. This holds the atoms together with a covalent bond.

The shared pair helps to complete the outer shell of both the chlorine atoms. In dot/cross diagrams with covalent bonds, circles are used to enclose the electrons which belong to each atom.

A covalent bond is formed by sharing a pair of electrons between two atoms. Each atom contributes one electron to the bond.

The atoms in simple molecules and giant molecules are joined by covalent bonds. The structure and properties of

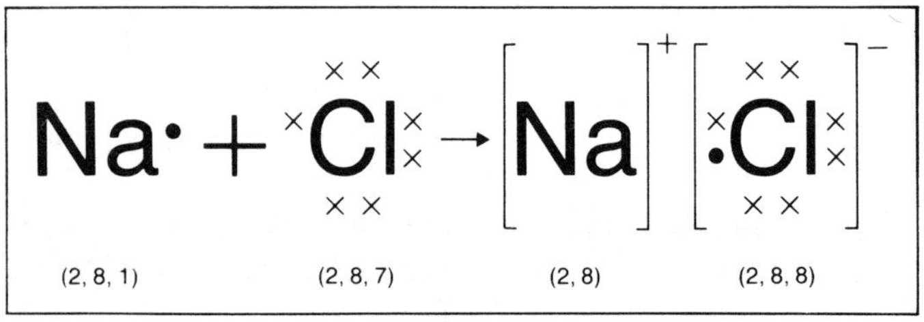

Figure 16.8 *The transfer of electrons when sodium and chlorine react to form sodium chloride.*

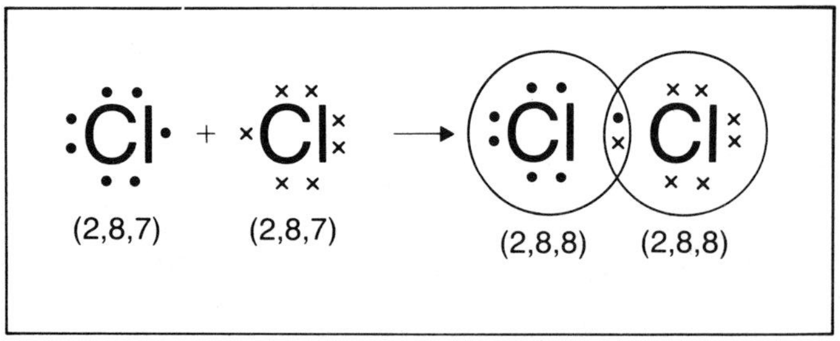

Figure 16.10 *Electron sharing in a chloride molecule (Cl₂).*

simple molecular substances (e.g. water and carbon dioxide) are discussed on page 35. The structure and properties of giant molecular substances (e.g. diamond and graphite) are discussed on pages 62–3.

The dot/cross diagrams and the structural formulae of some common molecular substances are shown in figure 16.11. Notice the following points:
- All the atoms have an electron structure like a noble gas;
- The electron structures are closely related to the structural formulae. Each line in the structural formulae represents one bond. So each line represents one shared pair of electrons.
- Double covalent bonds involve the sharing of four electrons. In oxygen molecules, two oxygen atoms are joined by a double bond. In carbon dioxide, there is a double bond between each oxygen atom and the carbon atom.
- Triple covalent bonds involve the sharing of six electrons, as in nitrogen.

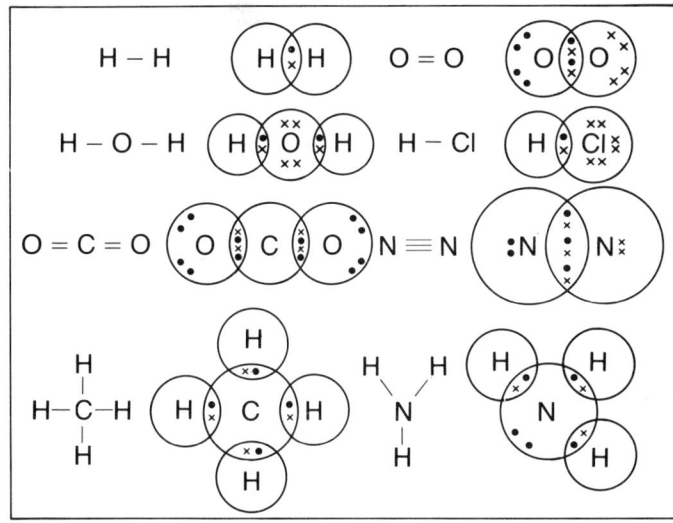

Figure 16.11 *The structural formulas and dot/cross diagrams of some common molecular substances.*

Self test

Questions 1–5

From the list **A** to **E** below
- **A** electron
- **B** ion
- **C** molecule
- **D** neutron
- **E** proton

choose the particle that:
1. results when atoms are joined by covalent bonds.
2. has the smallest mass.
3. has no electric charge and occupies the nucleus.
4. may be positive or negative.
5. is the same as an H^+ ion.

Questions 6–9

The complete electron dot/cross structures for two compounds are shown below.

Choose from **A** to **D** the atom of the element which
6. has an atomic number of 9.
7. forms one covalent bond.
8. transfers two electrons when it reacts.
9. is in group VI of the periodic table.

Questions 10–14

The electron structures of the atoms of five different elements are:

A 2, 8, 1 **B** 2, 8, 6 **C** 2, 4 **D** 2, 2 **E** 2, 8

Choose from **A** to **E** the electron structure of the element that
10. forms ions with a charge of $+1$.
11. forms only covalently bonded compounds.
12. forms no compounds.
13. has an atomic number of 4.
14. forms ions with a charge of -2.

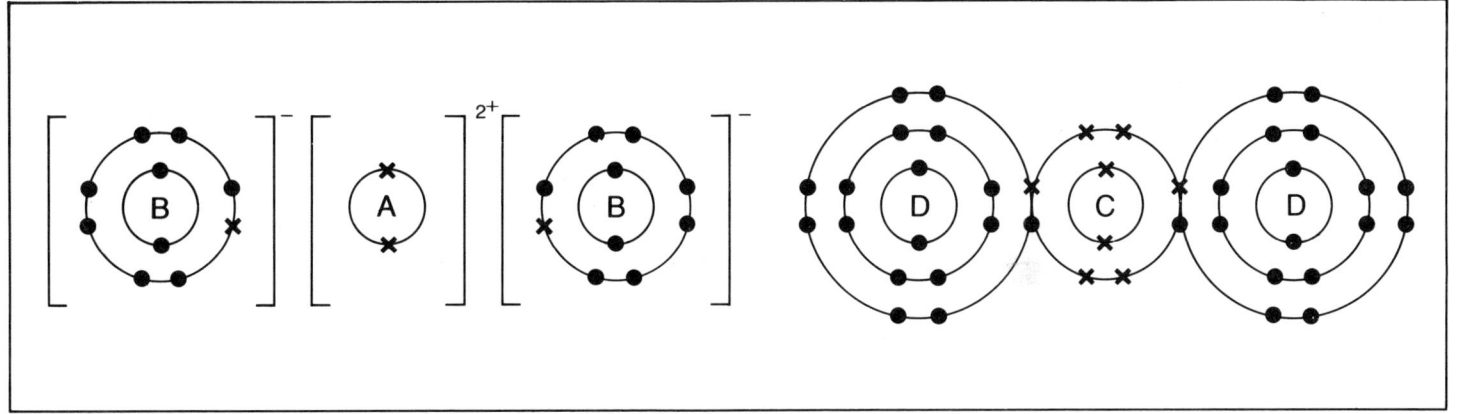

15 An atom of fluorine has an atomic number of 9 and a mass number of 19. How many neutrons does it contain?
A 9 **B** 10 **C** 19 **D** 28

16 How many electrons are present in one ion of $^{31}_{15}Y^{3-}$?
A 12 **B** 15 **C** 16 **D** 18

17 Isotopes have the same
A electron structures.
B mass numbers.
C number of neutrons.
D physical properties.

18 Two particles with almost the same mass are
A an electron and a neutron.
B an electron and a proton.
C a neutron and a proton.
D a neutron and an α-particle.

19 A sample of element X contains two-thirds of $^{30}_{16}X$ and one-third of $^{33}_{16}X$. What is the relative atomic mass of X?
A $30\frac{2}{3}$ **B** 31 **C** 32 **D** $32\frac{2}{3}$

17 Radioactivity

What is radioactivity?

Hardly a week goes by without radioactivity being mentioned in the papers or on television. 'What causes radioactivity?', 'Why is it important?' and 'How is it related to nuclear energy?': these are some of the questions to be considered in this section.

One of the earliest uses of radioactivity was in luminous paints on the hands and numbers of clocks and watches. The luminous paint contains a radium compound. All the time, radium atoms are splitting apart (disintegrating) of their own accord. This spontaneous break-up of atoms is called **radioactivity** or **radioactive decay**. Atoms such as radium that break up (decay) in this way are described as radioactive or unstable.

As the radium atoms break up, they give out **alpha particles** (α-**particles**) at great speed. Alpha particles are ions of helium ($^4_2He^{2+}$). The glow in luminous paints is caused by alpha-particles hitting other particles in the paint. The alpha particles lose kinetic energy and convert it to light energy.

Types of radioactivity

Radioactive decay involving the loss of an alpha particle happens with many large isotopes with a relative atomic mass greater than 210. These include uranium-238, radium-226 and plutonium-238. They try to become stable by giving out alpha particles and forming smaller atoms.

Radioactive isotopes with a relative atomic mass less than 210 often give out **beta particles** (β-**particles**) rather than alpha particles when they decay. Beta particles are electrons ($^{\,\,\,0}_{-1}e^-$). Beta particles are deflected by electric and magnetic fields, they can travel a few metres in air and will pass through thin sheets of paper.

Alpha particles are also deflected by electric and magnetic fields, but they are not as penetrating as beta particles. Alpha particles travel only a few centimetres in air and they do not even pass through thin sheets of paper.

When unstable radioactive atoms emit alpha particles and beta particles, they often emit **gamma rays** (γ-**rays**) at the same time. Gamma rays are electromagnetic waves like light. They are unaffected by electric and magnetic fields, but are much more penetrating than alpha or beta particles. Gamma rays can travel several kilometres in air and they can pass through thin metal sheets. When a radioactive atom gives out gamma rays, it becomes more stable because it loses energy.

The properties and penetrating powers of the three types of radiation emitted by radioactive atoms are summarised in table 17.1.

Half-life

Radioactive decay is completely random. No one knows why a particular atom splits up at a given moment. Experiments show that each radioactive isotope decays at its own rate.

It makes no difference to the rate of decay whether the radioactive isotope used is an element or combined in a compound. Temperature does not affect the rate of decay either. These are important differences between ordinary chemical reactions and nuclear reactions such as radioactive decay.

The rate of decay of a radioactive isotope is shown by its half-life.

The half-life is the time it takes for half of the atoms to decay.

Half-lives vary from fractions of a millisecond to millions of years. For example, polonium-214 has a half-life of 0.15 milliseconds, whereas uranium-238 has a half-life of 4500 million years. The shorter the half-life, the faster the isotope decays and the more unstable it is.

One of the most useful radioactive isotopes is iodine-131, which has a half-life of 8 days. The thyroid gland in our bodies needs iodine to work properly. Doctors use iodine-131 to measure how much iodine is taken up by the thyroid gland. Table 17.2 shows how 1 g of iodine-131 decays. The doctor injects a tiny quantity of iodine-131 into the patient's blood. By measuring the amount of radioactivity in the thyroid gland, doctors can tell how much iodine-131 it has taken up and whether the gland is working properly.

Table 17.1 *The properties and penetrating powers of alpha particles, beta particles and gamma rays.*

Radiation	Nature	Effect of electric and magnetic fields	Penetration of		
			A sheet of paper	Thin aluminium	Thick lead
α	Helium ions ($^4_2He^{2+}$)	Small deflection	✗	✗	✗
β	Electrons ($^{\,\,\,0}_{-1}e^-$)	Large deflection	✓	✗	✗
γ	Electromagnetic waves	No deflection	✓	✓	✗

Table 17.2 *The decay of 1 g of iodine-131 which has a half-life of 8 days.*

Time /days	Amount left/g	Total amount decayed/g
0	1	0
8	$\frac{1}{2}$	$\frac{1}{2}$
16	$\frac{1}{4}$	$\frac{3}{4}$
24	$\frac{1}{8}$	$\frac{7}{8}$
32	$\frac{1}{16}$	$\frac{15}{16}$
.	.	.
.	.	.
.	.	.

Dangers and precautions

The particles and rays emitted by radioactive materials can be dangerous. The most dangerous radiations are the very penetrating gamma rays. Radiation can change the chemicals in our bodies. Sometimes these changes (mutations) kill the cells or cause them to reproduce wrongly. The mutations may result in diseases like cancer or in deformed babies. Very large amounts of radiation can kill, or cause a disease called radiation sickness.

Every day we are all exposed to small amounts of **background radiation**, which comes from radioactive substances in the Earth's crust and from particles and rays entering the Earth's atmosphere. Background radiation is normally very low and harmless.

However, strict safety precautions must be taken in nuclear power stations and in hospitals where high levels of radiation are used. These precautions involve:
- wearing radiation level badges to record the radiation to which someone has been exposed;
- checking the health of workers at frequent intervals;
- checking the radiation level of the working environment at frequent intervals;
- manipulating radioactive materials by remote-control equipment from behind thick walls of glass, lead or concrete;
- transporting radioactive substances inside thick lead or concrete containers.

Using radioactive isotopes

Medical uses

Treatment of cancers. When a dividing cell is exposed to radiation, the genes in the nucleus may be damaged, causing the cell to die. Cancer cells divide more often than healthy cells so they are killed more easily by radiation. Because of this, gamma rays are used in treating cancers. Penetrating gamma rays from cobalt-60 are used to treat growths inside the body. Skin cancers can be treated with less penetrating beta radiation from phosphorus-32 or strontium-90. Although cancer is serious and often fatal, doctors have achieved a high success rate in curing less serious cases, particularly if they are treated early.

Sterilization of medical articles. Dressings and syringes are often sealed in polythene bags and then exposed to intense gamma rays. This sterilizes the articles by killing any microorganisms on them.

Industrial uses

Tracer studies. Tracer techniques use radioisotopes to track where substances move to. These techniques have been used to investigate the flow of liquids, to detect leaks in pipes and to study the wear in machinery.

Silt movements in the Thames estuary have been traced using radioactive gold-198. The silt at a certain point is mixed ('labelled') with tiny amounts of the radioactive isotope. Radiation detectors are then used to trace the movement of the 'labelled' silt.

Level gauges and thickness gauges. Beta and gamma radiation can be used to detect the level of material inside a container.

For example, the level of liquid in a fire extinguisher can be found by placing a radioactive source at one side and a detector on the other. The source and detector are then moved down the vessel together. When the source and detector reach the level of the liquid, there is a sudden decrease in the amount of radiation reaching the detector (figure 17.1). A similar method is used to check the thickness of sheets of paper, plastic and metal.

Nuclear energy

Enormous amounts of energy can be obtained from some nuclear reactions. This energy is used in atomic bombs and atomic reactors.

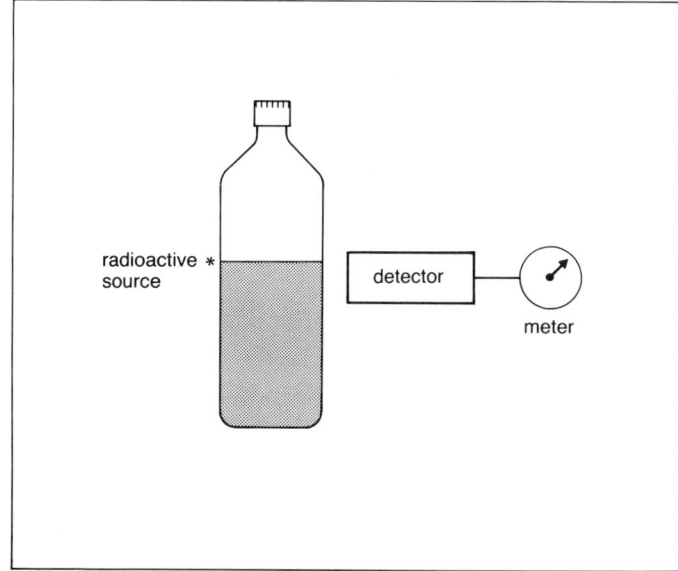

Figure 17.1 *A radiation level gauge.*

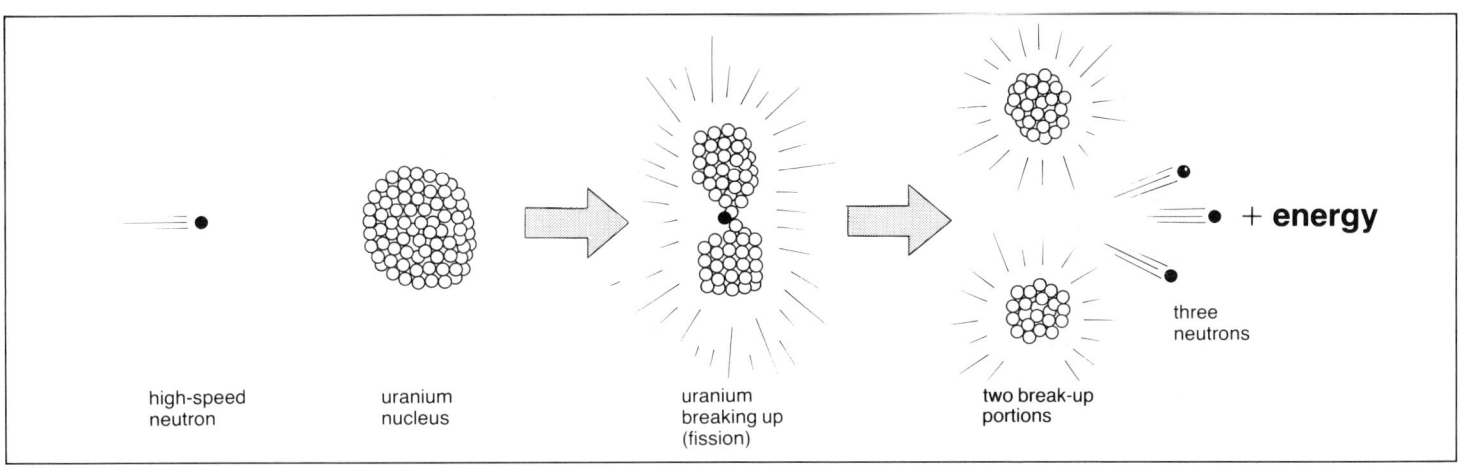

Figure 17.2 *The fission of a nucleus of uranium-235.*

In 1938, the German scientists Hahn and Strassmann were trying to make a new element by bombarding uranium with neutrons. Instead of producing a new element, the neutron caused the uranium nucleus to break up violently into two portions. At the same time, large quantities of energy were given out, together with two or three more neutrons (figure 17.2). This type of nuclear reaction is called **nuclear fission** or **atomic fission**. It is different from radioactive decay in two ways:
- It does not happen of its own accord. It requires bombardment by neutrons.
- The bombarded nucleus breaks up into two fragments of roughly the same size, not one large fragment and one very small fragment.

Atomic bombs and atomic reactors

Natural uranium contains two isotopes: uranium-235 and uranium-238. Only uranium-235 undergoes nuclear fission during neutron bombardment, but only 0.7 per cent of natural uranium is uranium-235. If the concentration of uranium-235 is high enough, sufficient neutrons are released during fission to cause a **chain reaction**. Figure 17.3 shows how an exploding chain reaction can occur in uranium-235. One reaction releases three neutrons. These three neutrons release nine neutrons, then 27, 81, 243, etc. Each time more energy is produced as more uranium-235 undergoes fission. All this happens in a fraction of a second when an atomic bomb explodes.

In an atomic bomb, the fission of enriched uranium-235 happens in an *uncontrolled* manner and enormous amounts of energy are released. In an **atomic reactor** cylinders of uranium are inserted in a large graphite block (pile). A *controlled* chain reaction occurs and the heat released is used to generate electricity. The neutrons released by fission of the uranium are slowed down by collision with carbon atoms in the graphite (figure 17.4).

The temperature of the reactor is controlled by movable rods of boron or cadmium. These rods absorb neutrons. The deeper they are inserted, the more neutrons are absorbed and the slower the reaction becomes. By carefully adjusting the neutron-absorbing rods, a controlled chain reaction can be achieved. Heat is produced and taken away by carbon dioxide, which circulates through the graphite block. The hot gas is then used to make steam, which drives turbines and generates electricity. In the USA, most reactors use water as a coolant in place of carbon dioxide.

More recently, reactors have been developed that use plutonium as the fuel and liquid sodium as the coolant. Unlike uranium, plutonium can use *fast* neutrons so the reactor does not need a graphite pile. These reactors are called **fast reactors**. The first power station to use a fast reactor for generating electricity was the one at Dounreay in Scotland.

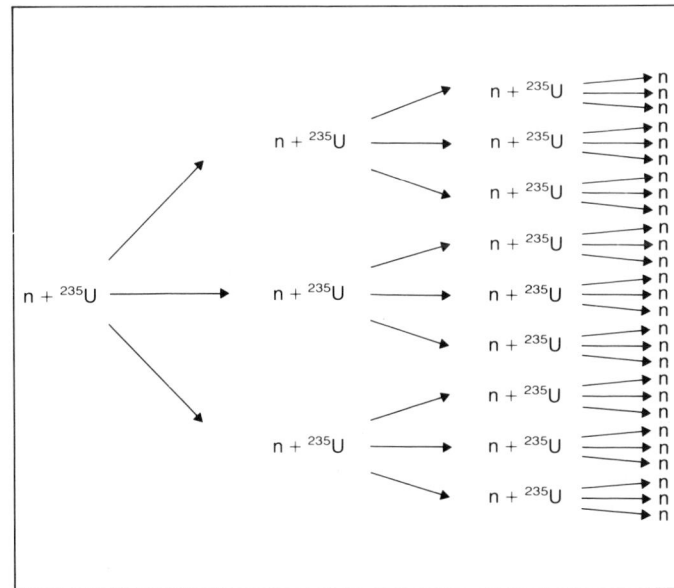

Figure 17.3 *A chain reaction in uranium-235.*

Radioactivity

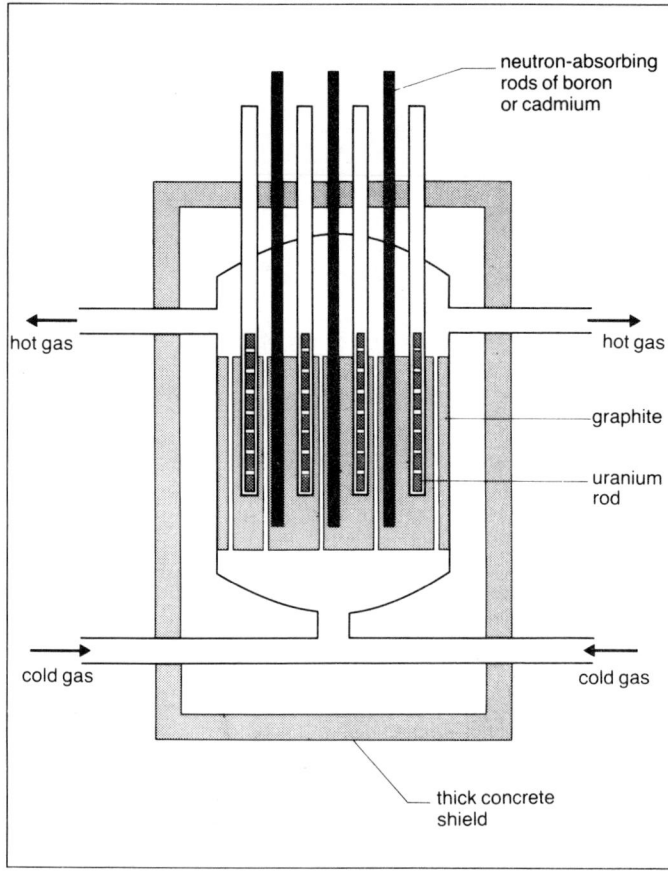

Figure 17.4 *A simplified diagram of a gas-cooled nuclear reactor.*

The nuclear debate

Since the last war, the USA and the USSR have developed increasingly powerful nuclear weapons. The possibility of a nuclear war has created unrest throughout the world. Large numbers of people are now supporters of the Campaign for Nuclear Disarmament (CND) and similar organisations. The increasing use of radioactive isotopes and the growing number of nuclear power stations have also awakened our interest in nuclear technology.

Some people think that nuclear power stations are too dangerous and should not be built. Others think that nuclear power is the only way to guarantee our energy supplies as fossil fuels run out. Table 17.3 summarises the arguments for and against nuclear power.

Table 17.3 *The arguments for and against generating electricity by nuclear power.*

Arguments against	Arguments for
① Radioactive materials may escape from nuclear plants during routine operations or during transport	① Radioactivity is very easy to detect. Any leak could be repaired before it became too dangerous
② There are great dangers of pollution from radioactive waste, which remains active for hundreds of years	② Nuclear energy is essential if we are to meet our energy needs in the future as the reserves of oil and gas run out
③ The disposal of radioactive waste poses great problems. Dumping the waste in deep mines or sealing it in concrete do not guarantee safe disposal	③ By increasing our knowledge of nuclear fission, we shall eventually be able to obtain energy by nuclear fusion. This would solve our energy problems forever
④ There are serious risks of terrorists attacking a nuclear plant	④ The risks and dangers of nuclear technology are no greater than many others that our modern society has to handle
⑤ Nuclear technology helps countries to make nuclear weapons and so increases the chance of a nuclear war	

● Self test

Questions 1–5

From the list **A** to **E** below
- **A** cadmium
- **B** lead
- **C** plutonium
- **D** sodium
- **E** uranium

choose the element that is
1. used to produce nuclear power in fast reactors.
2. used to control the temperature of a nuclear reactor.
3. used as a coolant in some power stations.
4. used as a protection from radiation.
5. used in nuclear reactors after extraction from its ore.

Questions 6–8

Some soil was contaminated by a radioactive isotope. The count rate of a sample of the soil was recorded for 200 days and the results are shown in the graph below.

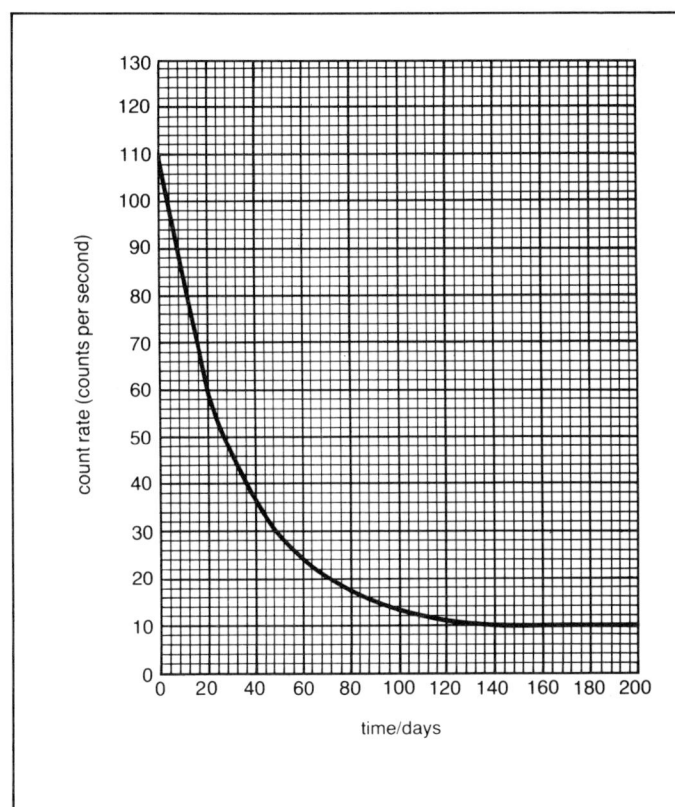

6 What is the background count for the soil in counts per second?
   A 200   B 140   C 110   D 10

7 What is the true count rate from the radioactive isotope in counts per second after 20 days?
   A 72   B 62   C 52   D 6.2

8 What is the half-life of the radioactive isotope?
   A 21 days   B 25 days   C 70 days   D 140 days

Questions 9–14

From the list **A** to **E** below
   A alpha particles
   B beta particles
   C gamma rays
   D neutrons
   E protons

choose the particles or rays that
 9 are deflected most by an electric field.
10 cause nuclear fission in a nuclear power station.
11 consist of positive ions.
12 contain the heaviest particles.
13 form the most penetrating radiation.
14 have a mass of one unit and a charge of one unit.

15 Which one of the following pairs will repel one another most strongly?
   A electron–proton   B electron–neutron
   C proton–proton   D proton–neutron

16 The half-life of a radioactive isotope
   A falls as temperature increases.
   B increases as concentration increases.
   C is half the time that the isotope can exist.
   D stays the same when the isotope forms a compound.

17 Skin cancers can be treated with beta radiation from phosphorus-32. This is because this radiation
   A causes cells to die.
   B does not affect healthy cells.
   C does not penetrate the skin.
   D kills micro-organisms.

18 Both radioactive decay and nuclear fission
   A happen of their own accord.
   B release energy.
   C require bombardment by neutrons.
   D result in a chain reaction.

Sample GCSE Questions

This section includes some sample questions from the GCSE groups. There are two types of questions:

- Structured questions, which are broken down into several parts.
- Free-response questions, where you are expected to write longer, essay-type answers. These questions are less common.

The table below shows the chapters of this book that link most closely with each question.

Structured questions are indicated by a blob (●).
Free-response questions are indicated by an open circle (○).

Outline answers to these questions are suggested at the end. The questions are from the following GCSE examining groups:

- LEAG – London and East Anglian Group
- NEA – Northern Examining Association
- SEG – Southern Examining Group
- WJEC – Welsh Joint Education Committee

Chapter No.	Question No. 1	2	3	4	5	6	7	8	9	10	11	12	13	14	15	16	17	18	19	20	21	22	23	24	25	26	27	28	29	30	31	32	33	34
1 Elements, compounds and mixtures	●																																	
2 The air		●	●	●																											○			
3 Water					●																											○		
4 Particles						●																											○	
5 Chemical calculations							●				●			●	●				●					●	●									
6 Electricity and electrolysis										●	●	●																		○				
7 The periodic table						●				●		●																						
8 Metals													●								●													
9 Acids, bases and salts													●		●	●	●																	
10 Structure of elements and compounds																													○					
11 Energy and fuels																		●	●			●												
12 Simple carbon compounds																				●		●				●	●							
13 Chemicals from crude oil																					●	●	●										○	
14 Reaction rates																								●	●									○
15 Nitrogen and fertilisers																												●	●					
16 Atomic structure														●															●					
17 Radioactivity																													●	●	○			

112

Structured questions

1. Paper chromatography was used by a forensic scientist to find out which one of four ball-point pens (labelled A, B, C and D) was used to write a 'poison-pen' letter.

   A small amount of ink from the note was dissolved in ethanol and the solution made more concentrated.

   A drop of the concentrated solution and a drop of each of the four inks from pens A–D were put on to a piece of filter paper and the experiment carried out.

   The results are shown below.

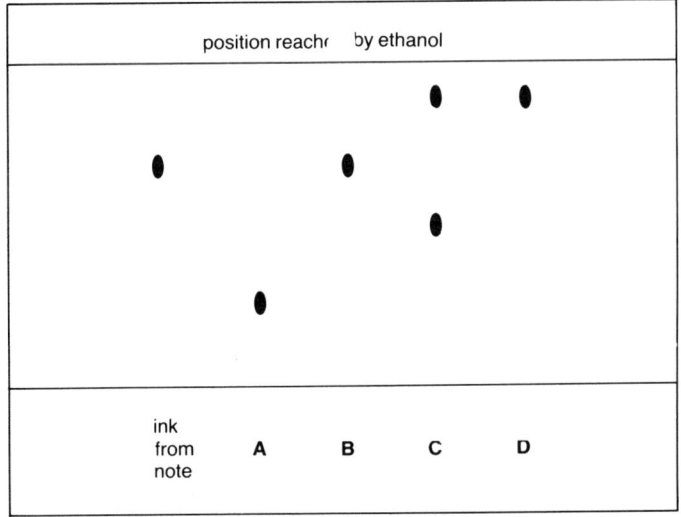

   (a) What is a 'forensic scientist'? **(1 mark)**
   (b) Why is ethanol used rather than water in this experiment? **(1 mark)**
   (c) Explain how the solution of ink in ethanol could *safely* be concentrated. **(2 marks)**
   (d) Which pen (A, B, C or D) was used to write the note? Explain your answer. **(2 marks)**
   (e) Which ink contains a mixture of two dyes? Explain your answer. **(2 marks)**
   (f) Draw a labelled diagram to show how a sample of ethanol could be recovered from a solution of ink in ethanol. **(4 marks)**
   (LEAG Syllabus B Specimen Question)

2. Petrol is a mixture of liquids which are all hydrocarbons.
   (a) (i) What *two* elements are combined in petrol?
       (ii) When petrol vapour is exploded in a car engine these elements are burned to form exhaust gases. Name the *two* major compounds produced in the exhaust. **(3 marks)**
   (b) (i) Name one gas which is also found in exhaust gases and which is extremely poisonous;
       (ii) Explain *why* this gas is formed. **(3 marks)**
   (c) Which gas passes through the car engine almost unaffected? **(1 mark)**
   (d) When a car has reached the end of its useful life it is normally crushed and the steel which it contains is recycled. Explain two reasons why it is important to do this rather than leaving a car to rust away on a scrap heap. **(4 marks)**
   (LEAG Syllabus A Specimen Question)

3. The two most abundant gases in the air are nitrogen (approximately 80%) and oxygen (approximately 20%).
   (a) Shade in and label the pie-chart to show this approximate composition of air. **(2 marks)**

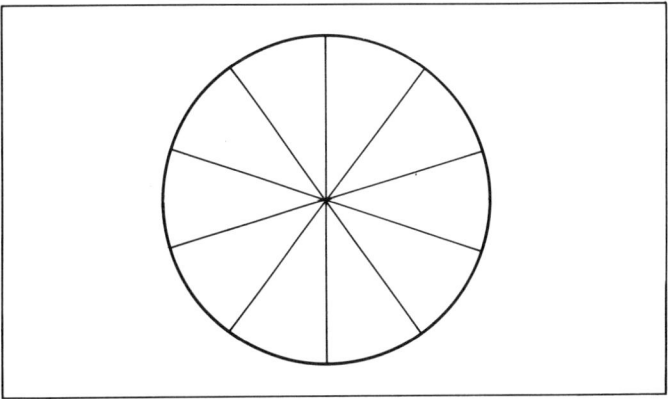

   (b) To separate nitrogen from oxygen, the air is first liquefied. Use a Data Book to find which of these elements is easier to liquefy. Explain your answer. **(2 marks)**
   (c) How is nitrogen separated from liquid air? **(1 mark)**
   (d) Give two large scale uses of nitrogen. **(2 marks)**
   (e) A pupil designed an experiment to measure the amount of oxygen in a sample of air. The diagrams below show the apparatus at the beginning and end of the investigation:

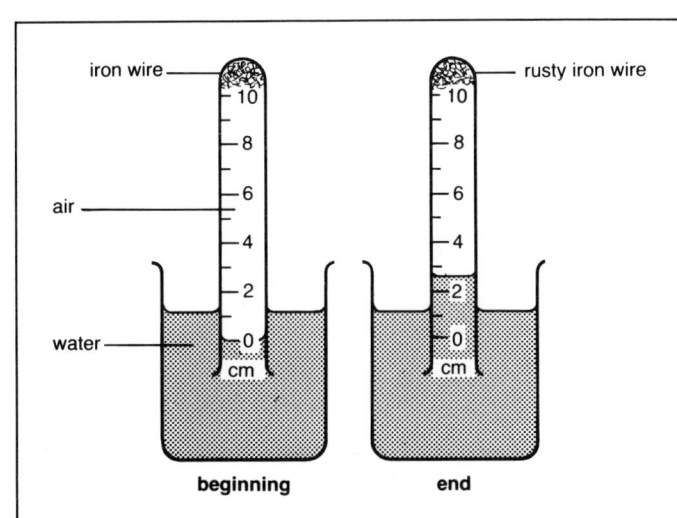

(i) Explain as fully as you can why the water rose up the test tube. **(2 marks)**

The water level rose by 2.5 cm and so the pupil calculated that 25 per cent of the air in this sample was oxygen.

(ii) Explain why the apparatus did not give the known value for the percentage of oxygen of 20 per cent. **(2 marks)**

(NEA Syllabus A Specimen Question)

4 Oxygen gas can be prepared conveniently in the laboratory using the apparatus below. The manganese dioxide is a **catalyst**: a substance which speeds up the reaction but is not used up at all.

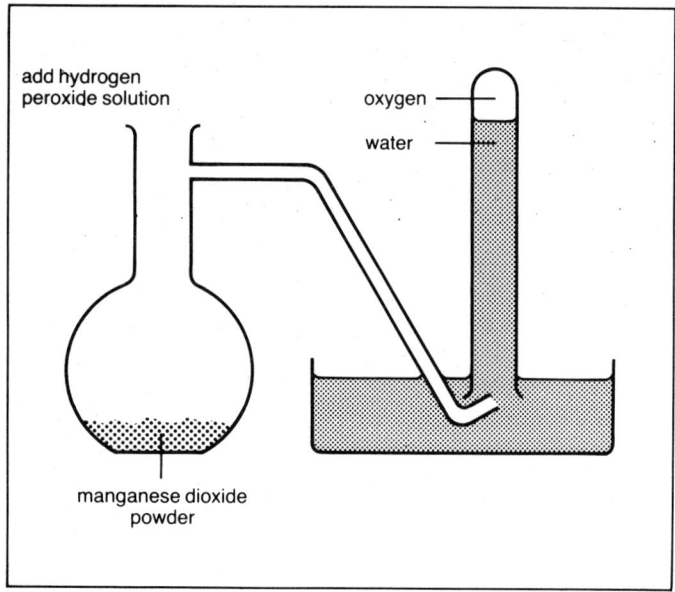

(a) Complete the diagram by drawing the apparatus you would use to add the hydrogen peroxide solution in controlled amounts.

(b) Why is the first test tube of gas not used? **(1 mark)**

(c) (i) Is oxygen very soluble in water? **(1 mark)**
(ii) What evidence have you, from this experiment, to support your answer? **(1 mark)**

(d) How can you prove the gas collected was oxygen?
(i) What would you do? **(1 mark)**
(ii) What would you see? **(1 mark)**

(e) How could a dry sample of manganese dioxide be obtained from the flask after the reaction? (two steps) **(2 marks)**

(f) State and explain one commercial use of oxygen gas.
(i) Use. **(1 mark)**
(ii) Explanation of use. **(1 mark)**

(NEA Syllabus B Specimen Question)

5 (a) (i) How is filtration of reservoir water carried out? **(1 mark)**
(ii) What is the purpose of this filtration? **(1 mark)**

(b) (i) How may a sample of pure water be obtained from seawater? **(1 mark)**
(ii) Explain the process of evaporation in terms of movement of molecules. **(3 marks)**
(iii) Why does the salt in seawater not circulate through the atmosphere in the way the water does? **(2 marks)**

(c) (i) Name one pollutant of river water other than an agricultural fertiliser. **(1 mark)**
(ii) State the source of this pollutant and describe its effect. **(2 marks)**

(d) (i) Why is chlorine added to water supplies? **(1 mark)**
(ii) Tap water usually contains chloride ions rather than chlorine itself. Describe chemical tests that would show:
(I) that tap water does not contain chlorine,
(II) that tap water does contain chloride ions.
(In each case you should name the substances you would use and describe what you would observe.) **(6 marks)**
(iii) Explain in terms of electron transfer what happens when chlorine is converted into chloride ions. **(2 marks)**

(SEG Specimen Question)

6 The table below gives information about four elements, V, W, X and Y, which are in the same group in the periodic table.

Element	Atomic number	Melting point (°C)	Boiling point (°C)
V	9	−220	−188
W	17	−101	−33
X	35	−7	58
Y	53	114	183

(a) Use the melting and boiling points to give the letters of *all* the elements in the table which, at atmospheric pressure and at room temperature, are:
(i) solids
(ii) liquids
(iii) gases. **(3 marks)**

(b) Describe what happens to the particles of a solid when it melts to form a liquid. **(3 marks)**

(c) The next element in this group after Y is Z.
  (i) Would you expect Z to exist under room conditions as a solid, liquid or gas? State your reasons.
  (ii) How many electrons will there be in the outer shell of a Z atom?
  (iii) Using the symbol Z, write down the formula of the ion of Z. **(4 marks)**
  (LEAG Syllabus A Specimen Question)

7 1 cm³ of 3.0 M sodium hydroxide solution was added to 5 cm³ of 1.0 M iron(III) chloride solution in a test tube. After shaking to mix and allowing to stand for 10 minutes, the height of the precipitate was measured. The experiment was repeated using different volumes of the 3.0 M sodium hydroxide solution. The results are shown below.

Volume of 3.0 M sodium hydroxide added (cm³)	1	2	3	4	5	6	7
Height of the precipitate (mm)	4	8	12	16	20	20	20

(a) On the grid below draw a graph of these results;

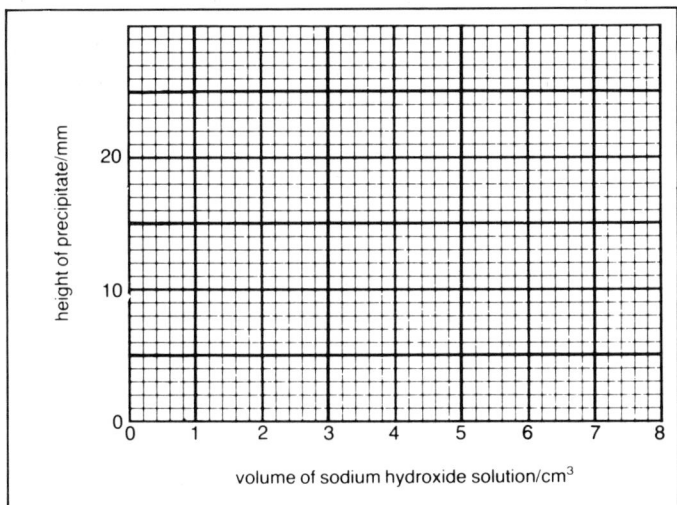

(2 marks)

(b) Explain why the height of the precipitate did not change from the 5th to the 7th cm³. **(1 mark)**

(c) Calculate the number of moles of sodium hydroxide in 5 cm³ of 3.0 M sodium hydroxide solution. **(1 mark)**

(d) The equation for the reaction is:

$3NaOH(aq) + FeCl_3(aq) \rightarrow Fe(OH)_3(s) + 3NaCl(aq)$

state the number of moles of iron(III) chloride required to react exactly with 5 cm³ of 3.0 M sodium hydroxide solution. **(1 mark)**

(e) Show how the answer to (d) compares with the results of the experiment. **(2 marks)**

(f) Describe how you would attempt to obtain a pure dry sample of the precipitate formed in the experiment. **(2 marks)**
(LEAG Syllabus B Sample Question)

8 Food cans are made of mild steel with a layer of tin, about 10^{-7} cm (0.0000001 cm) thick, deposited by electrolysis. This electroplating can be done in the laboratory using the following apparatus.

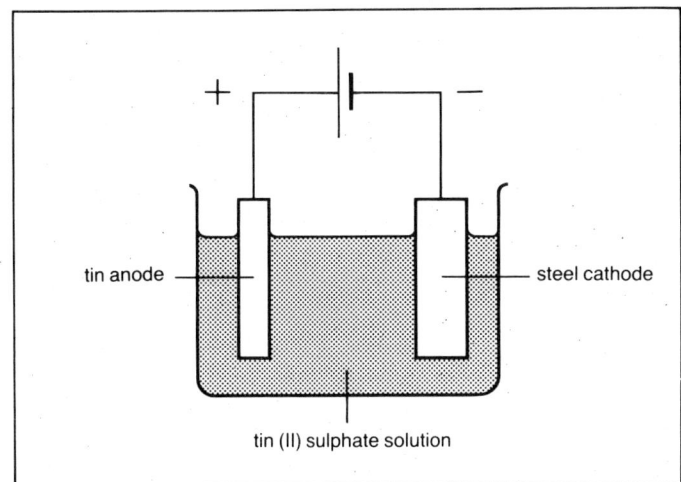

(a) How does the mass of the cathode change during the experiment? **(1 mark)**

(b) Why does the mass of the cathode change? **(1 mark)**

(c) (i) Do the tin ions in tin(II) sulphate solution carry positive or negative charge? **(1 mark)**
   (ii) How did you decide your answer to (c) (i)? **(1 mark)**

(d) Why is the concentration of tin(II) sulphate the same at the end as at the beginning of the experiment? **(1 mark)**

(e) How could you change the apparatus to deposit the tin more slowly so that it would stick better to the steel? **(1 mark)**

(f) (i) What type of chemical would you use to react with and remove the iron oxide coating from the steel before it is electroplated with tin? **(1 mark)**
   (ii) What type of reaction takes place between the iron oxide and the chemical used? Write a word equation for this reaction. **(2 marks)**

(g) (i) Steel used to be plated by dipping it in molten tin forming a layer of tin 0.005 cm thick. Why has this method been replaced by electroplating? **(1 mark)**

(ii) How do the manufacturers know when the right thickness of tin has been deposited on the steel? **(1 mark)**

(h) Suggest reasons why food cans are made from mild steel plated with tin rather than tin or mild steel alone. **(2 marks)**
(NEA Syllabus B Specimen Question)

9 Sodium chloride (NaCl) is a very important raw material in the chemical industry. When sodium chloride solution is electrolysed, hydrogen gas forms at the cathode, chlorine gas at the anode and sodium hydroxide solution remains.

(a) State one important use of the hydrogen gas produced by the electrolysis of the sodium chloride solution. **(1 mark)**
Sodium hypochlorite (bleach) (NaOCl) is formed by reacting together chlorine and sodium hydroxide solution:

$$Cl_2(g) + 2NaOH(aq) \rightarrow NaCl(aq) + NaOCl(aq) + H_2O$$

(b) Why does household bleach (e.g. Domestos) contain sodium chloride? **(1 mark)**

(c) Sodium hypochlorite is used to purify swimming pools. It is labelled:

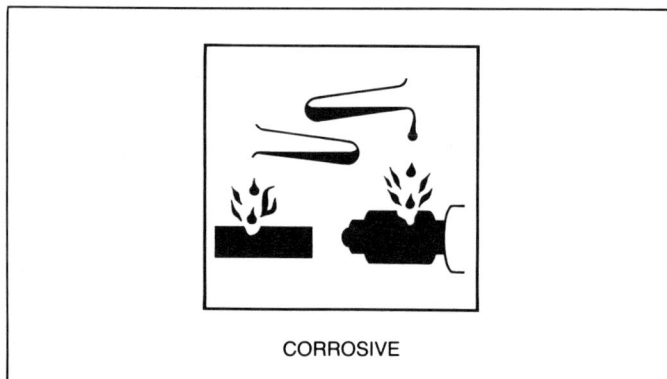

CORROSIVE

It gives toxic gas with acids:

$$NaOCl(aq) + 2HCl(aq) \rightarrow Cl_2(aq) + NaCl(aq) + H_2O(l)$$

(i) What is meant on the label by 'corrosive'? **(1 mark)**
(ii) Name the toxic gas given off with acids. **(1 mark)**
(iii) Why must swimming pool water be kept at a pH of about 7.6? **(1 mark)**

(d) Other substances made from sodium chloride include sodium metal and sodium carbonate.
(i) State the method and conditions needed to make sodium metal. **(2 marks)**
(ii) What other substance would you need to make sodium carbonate (Na_2CO_3) commercially from sodium chloride? **(1 mark)**

(e) Use the information given in this question to help you write a suitable warning to be printed on the label for a container of household bleach. The corrosive label is already on the container. Include in the warning notice precautions for using and storing the bleach. **(4 marks)**
(NEA Syllabus B Specimen Question)

10 The diagram below shows the electrolysis of concentrated sodium chloride solution.

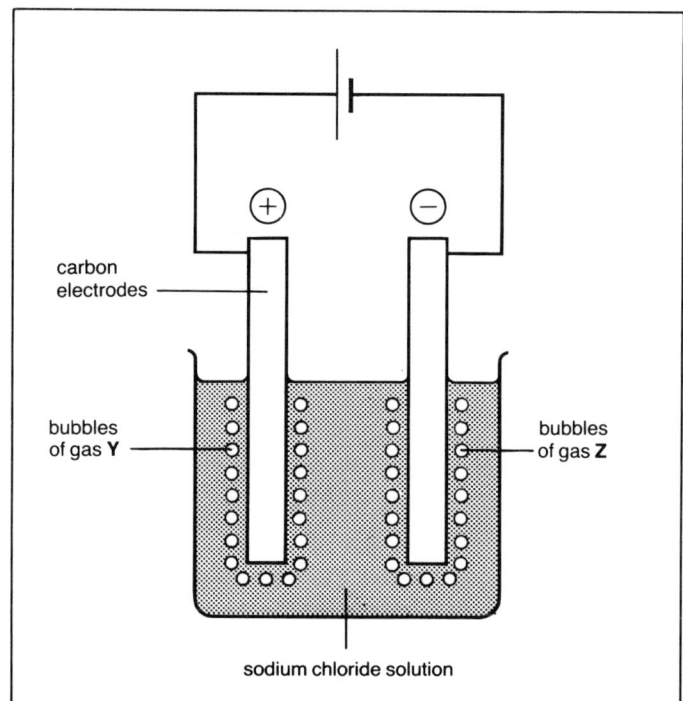

(a) Name the gases Y and Z. **(2 marks)**

(b) If a few drops of universal indicator are added to the solution before electrolysis starts, the indicator is green. As electrolysis happens, the indicator gradually turns blue.
(i) What is the pH of the solution when the indicator is green? **(1 mark)**
(ii) Explain why the electrolysis causes the indicator to go blue; **(3 marks)**
(iii) Name a compound produced on an industrial scale by electrolysis of sodium chloride solution. **(1 mark)**

(c) In the electrolysis of copper(II) chloride solution the electron transfer at the negative electrode is shown by the following equation:

$$Cu^{2+}(aq) + 2e^- \rightarrow Cu(s)$$

(i) What does (aq) stand for? **(1 mark)**
(ii) What would you expect to *see* at the negative electrode during this electrolysis? **(2 marks)**

Substance	Solid substance		Molten substance		
	Appearance of solid	Does the solid conduct electricity?	Does the melt conduct electricity?	Product at + electrode	Product at − electrode
A	White solid	No	Yes	Bromine	Lead metal
B	Yellow solid	No	No	(Does not conduct)	
C	Grey solid	Yes	Yes	None	None

(d) The table above gives information about three substances A, B and C when they are solid and when they are molten.

    (i) Suggest possible identities for substances A and B. **(2 marks)**

    (ii) What type of bonding does solid B have? **(1 mark)**

    (iii) What type of bonding does solid C have? **(1 mark)**

    (iv) When the melted substance A conducts electricity what particles are carrying the current? **(1 mark)**

(e) (i) Predict the products of electrolysis of an aqueous solution of aluminium sulphate using inert electrodes. Explain how you arrive at your answer. **(4 marks)**

    (ii) Why is cryolite added to aluminium oxide during the electrolytic manufacture of aluminium? **(1 mark)**

(SEG Specimen Question)

11 (a) Cadmium (Cd) is an element in the same group of the periodic table as zinc. Cadmium carbonate is insoluble in water and reacts in the same way as zinc carbonate with dilute acids. Cadmium sulphate is soluble in water and crystallizes as a salt hydrate.

    (i) Give the formulae of cadmium carbonate and cadmium sulphate. **(1 mark)**

    (ii) Describe the preparation of a dry, crystalline sample of hydrated cadmium sulphate from cadmium carbonate. **(5 marks)**

(b) Beryllium is in the same group of the periodic table as magnesium and forms a hydrated sulphate of formula $BeSO_4 \cdot xH_2O$.

In an experiment to determine the formula of the hydrate, it was found that 3.54 g of the hydrate gave 2.10 g of the anhydrous salt.

Determine the formula of the hydrated sulphate by the following steps ($A_r(H) = 1$; $A_r(Be) = 9$; $A_r(O) = 16$; $A_r(S) = 32$).

    (i) Calculate the mass of water in the hydrate.

    (ii) Calculate the relative molecular masses of anhydrous beryllium sulphate and water.

    (iii) Determine the ratio of the number of moles of beryllium sulphate to water and hence deduce the formula of the hydrate. **(4 marks)**

(WJEC Specimen Question)

12 Titanium is the seventh most abundant element in the earth's crust. One form in which it occurs is rutile (TiO_2). In extracting titanium from its ore, rutile is first converted to titanium(IV) chloride ($TiCl_4$) and this is then reduced to the metal by heating it with sodium or magnesium in an atmosphere of argon. Titanium(IV) chloride is a simple molecular covalently bonded substance.

(a) Given that the titanium atom has four outer electrons used for bonding, draw a diagram to show the bonding in titanium(IV) chloride (only the outer electrons of the chlorine atoms should be shown). **(2 marks)**

(b) Write a balanced equation for the reaction of titanium(IV) chloride with sodium. **(1 mark)**

(c) (i) In which physical state would you expect to find titanium(IV) chloride at room temperature?

    (ii) Explain why the physical state of titanium(IV) chloride differs from that of sodium chloride at room temperature. **(3 marks)**

(d) Suggest a reason why it is necessary to carry out the reaction of titanium(IV) chloride with sodium in an atmosphere of argon. **(1 mark)**

(e) Titanium is expensive in spite of the fact that it is relatively abundant in the earth's crust. Suggest a reason for this. **(1 mark)**

(f) Titanium is used in the structures of supersonic aircraft and space vehicles. Suggest *two* properties it might have that make it more suitable than other metals for this purpose. **(2 marks)**

(LEAG Syllabus A Specimen Question)

Sample GCSE Questions

13 The table below shows how four metals (W, X, Y and Z) react with dilute hydrochloric acid: (W, X, Y and Z are *not* the chemical symbols):

Metal	Reaction with dilute hydrochloric acid
W	Slow production of hydrogen
X	Rapid production of hydrogen Solution gets warm
Y	No reaction
Z	Very fast production of hydrogen Solution gets hot

(a) (i) Describe a suitable test for hydrogen.
(ii) Say what result you would expect the test to give if hydrogen was present. **(2 marks)**

(b) Arrange the four metals in order of reactivity with the most reactive metal first. **(2 marks)**

(c) When a piece of W is added to copper(II) sulphate solution, a reaction takes place very slowly. A brown deposit forms on the metal and the solution turns colourless.
(i) What is the brown deposit formed?
(ii) What type of reaction is taking place?
(iii) What difference would you expect if an equal mass of powdered metal W was used in place of the single piece of metal? Explain your answer. **(4 marks)**
(LEAG Syllabus B Specimen Question)

14 The following diagram is a simple outline of a blast furnace.

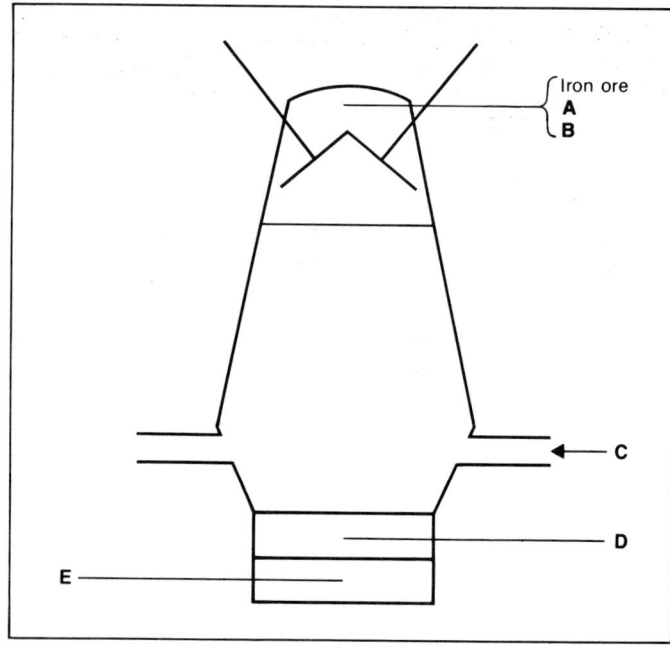

(a) Complete the labelling of the diagram by writing the names of the raw materials A, B and C, and the names of the products D and E. **(5 marks)**

(b) Name the type of chemical reaction involved when iron ore is converted to iron. **(1 mark)**

(c) Complete the equation for the conversion of iron ore to iron. **(2 marks)**

$$Fe_2O_3 + 3CO \rightarrow \_\_\_\_\_ + \_\_\_\_\_$$

(d) Explain why aluminium is not extracted from its ore by a similar process to that used for iron. **(2 marks)**

(e) Iron reacts with chlorine according to the equation:

$$2Fe + 3Cl_2 \rightarrow 2FeCl_3$$

What is the relative molecular mass of iron(III) chloride ($FeCl_3$)? (Fe = 56, Cl = 35.5) **(1 mark)**

(f) How many grams of iron would be required to make 16.25 g of iron(III) chloride? **(2 marks)**

(g) 'Iron' tablets are sold at chemists' shops. Barium chloride solution can be used to show whether the iron is present as iron(II) chloride or iron(II) sulphate.
(i) What is the observation if iron(II) chloride is present? **(1 mark)**
(ii) What is the observation if iron(II) sulphate is present? **(1 mark)**
(NEA Syllabus A)

15 Magnesium sulphate crystals ($MgSO_4.7H_2O$) can be made by adding excess magnesium oxide (MgO), which is insoluble in water, to dilute sulphuric acid.
(a) Why is the magnesium oxide added in excess? **(1 mark)**

(b) The following apparatus could be used to separate the excess magnesium oxide from the solution. Label the diagram by giving the correct words for A, B, C and D. **(4 marks)**

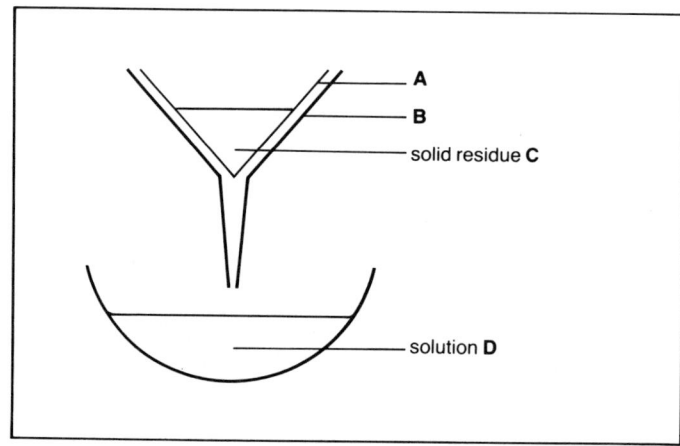

(c) Given the relative atomic masses: H = 1, Mg = 24, O = 16, S = 32, calculate the relative formula mass of:
  (i) magnesium oxide (MgO);
  (ii) agnesium sulphate crystals ($MgSO_4.7H_2O$).
  (3 marks)

(d) Use your answers in (c) to calculate the maximum mass of magnesium sulphate crystals that could be obtained from 2.0 g of magnesium oxide.
  (2 marks)

(e) Describe how you would obtain pure, dry crystals of magnesium sulphate from magnesium sulphate solution. **(4 marks)**
  (LEAG Syllabus A Specimen Question)

16 Many acidic substances are found in nature or in the home. These substances can be detected by the use of indicators.

(a) (i) Name a suitable indicator to detect acids;
  (ii) What is observed when this indicator is placed in an acidic solution? **(2 marks)**

(b) The pH scale is used to indicate how acid or alkaline a substance is.
  (i) Give the name of a household substance that might have a pH of 5.
  (ii) A colourless liquid has a pH of 7. What does this indicate about the solution? **(2 marks)**

(c) The battery in a car contains fairly concentrated sulphuric acid. Explain why it is important not to spill any of the acid and how it could be neutralised using ordinary household substances.
  (3 marks)
  (LEAG Syllabus A Specimen Question)

17 Glucose ($C_6H_{12}O_6$) is a white crystalline solid and is an example of a carbohydrate. By the process of fermentation, an aqueous solution of glucose can be converted into a mixture of ethanol (C_2H_5OH) and water. Ethanol is a colourless liquid which boils at 78°C. It may be converted into the unsaturated hydrocarbon, ethene (C_2H_4) by passing ethanol vapour over heated aluminium oxide. Ethene is a gas at room temperature and is not soluble in water.

(a) Explain what is meant by the following:
  (i) carbohydrate;
  (ii) hydrocarbon;
  (iii) unsaturated. **(3 marks)**

(b) Complete and label the diagram below of the apparatus you would use for preparing and collecting a sample of **ethene** free from ethanol vapour. **(2 marks)**

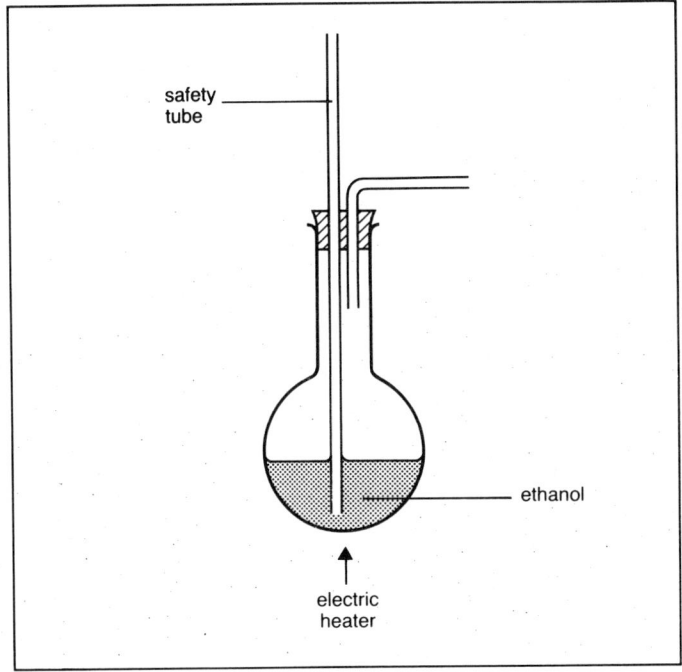

(c) The heat given out when 1 mole of ethanol is burned is 1380 kJ mol^{-1}. Calculate the fuel value of ethanol in kJ per gram. (Relative molecular mass of ethanol = 46) **(2 marks)**

(d) When a mole of propanol (C_3H_7OH) is burnt 2017 kJ of heat energy are given out. Explain why this is different from the value for ethanol.
  (1 mark)

(e) Give one example of an important compound formed by addition polymerisation and the monomer from which it is formed. **(1 mark)**
  (LEAG Syllabus B Specimen Question)

18 The label on a bottle containing a brand of 'health drink' reads as follows:
  Ingredients: Glucose, vitamin C, flavouring essence (including caffeine), fruit acid, lactic acid, preservative, carbon dioxide.
  Carbohydrate content (as monosaccharide) 19.3 g per 100 cm^3.
  Energy content 340 kJ per 100 cm^3.

(a) What colour would a piece of universal paper become when dipped into the drink? **(1 mark)**

To check the 'energy content', 10 cm^3 of the health drink were heated on a water bath to evaporate all the water in the drink.

(b) Why was the health drink sample heated on a water bath instead of directly over a bunsen burner? **(1 mark)**

The solid residue from the evaporation was placed in a crucible and the apparatus shown below was set up.

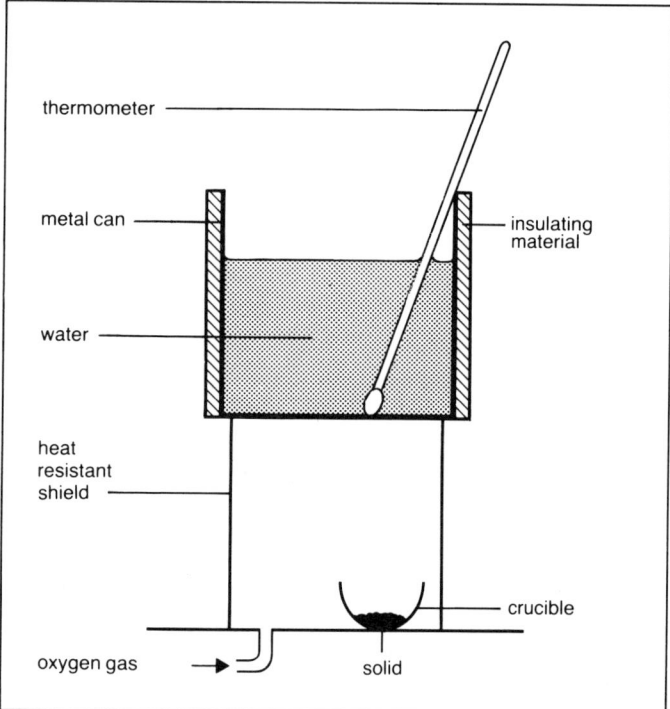

500 cm³ of water were placed in the metal can and its initial temperature recorded. The supply of oxygen was turned on and the solid ignited. The temperature of the water was recorded again once all the solid had burned.

Readings Initial temperature of water = 19.6 °C
Final temperature of water = 34.6 °C

(c) Why was a metal can used to hold the water rather than a glass beaker? **(1 mark)**

(d) Calculate the amount of heat (in kJ) absorbed by the water in the can. (4.2 J of heat is needed to raise the temperature of 1 g of water by 1°C) **(3 marks)**

(e) (i) Use your answer from (d) to estimate the 'energy content' of 100 cm³ of the health drink. **(1 mark)**
    (ii) Give *one* reason, other than heat losses to the air, why the 'energy content' measured by the experiment is different from that quoted on the label. **(1 mark)**

(f) The heat of combustion of glucose ($C_6H_{12}O_6$) is -3200 kJ/mol.
    (i) Write a balanced equation for the complete combustion of glucose. **(2 marks)**

(ii) Draw an enthalpy level diagram to show the change in heat energy when glucose burns. **(2 marks)**

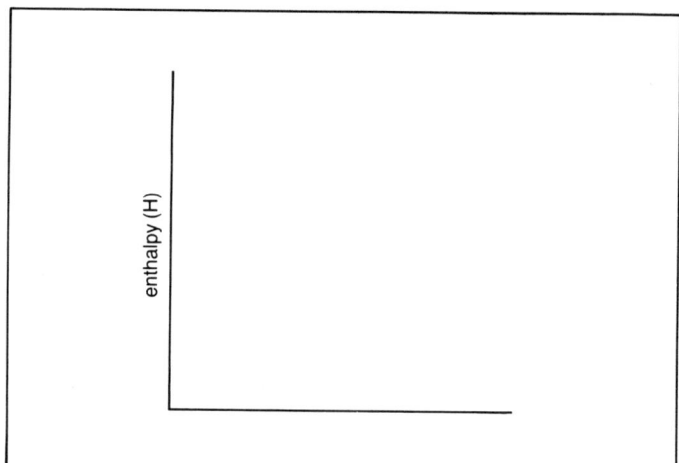

(g) Why is it useful for energy content values to be printed on many foods? **(3 marks)**
(SEG Alternative Syllabus Specimen Question)

19 Carbon dioxide can be prepared by adding hydrochloric acid to calcium carbonate.
(a) (i) Name the salt produced by the reaction;
    (ii) What else is produced by the reaction, besides the salt and carbon dioxide? **(2 marks)**

(b) When a gas jar containing carbon dioxide is upturned over a burning splint, the flame goes out.

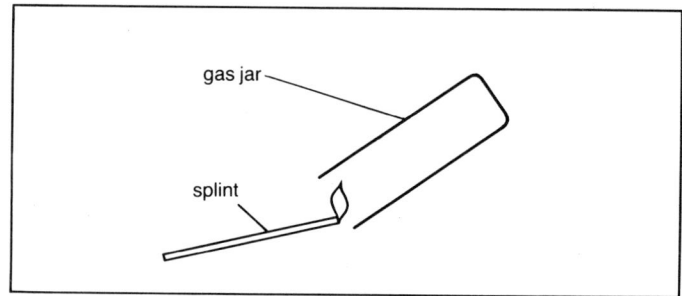

What *two* properties of carbon dioxide does this illustrate? What piece of equipment used widely in everyday life makes use of these properties? **(3 marks)**

(c) If a piece of magnesium is burned in a gas jar of carbon dioxide, a white powder and particles of a black solid are formed.
    (i) What is the black solid?
    (ii) What is the white powder?
    (iii) Write a word equation for the reaction in (c). **(3 marks)**
(LEAG Syllabus A Specimen Question)

20 (a) Ethane and ethene are both hydrocarbons. Explain what is meant by the term **hydrocarbons**. **(2 marks)**

(b) Write the structural formulae of ethane (C_2H_6) and ethene (C_2H_4), showing *all* the covalent bonds by lines. **(2 marks)**

(c) Ethane is the second member of the homologous series of alkanes. Give the names and formulas of the first and third members of this series. **(2 marks)**

(d) Petrol, the fuel used in car engines, is a mixture of hydrocarbons. One of the hydrocarbons present in petrol is octane (C_8H_{18}), which burns completely in oxygen according to the equation:

$$2C_8H_{18} + 25O_2 \rightarrow 16CO_2 + 18H_2O$$

(i) Calculate the volume of oxygen that must be available if 100 cm^3 of octane vapour are burned completely, all volumes being measured at the same temperature and pressure.

(ii) This process is **exothermic**. Explain the meaning of this term in terms of the energy conversion taking place.

(iii) What mass of water vapour is produced when 114 g of octane are completely burned? (Relative molecular masses: water = 18, octane = 114) **(6 marks)**

(e) Suggest reasons why:
(i) a black solid collects in the exhaust pipe which leads the fumes away from a car engine;
(ii) it is dangerous to run a car engine in a closed garage. **(4 marks)**
(LEAG Syllabus A Specimen Question)

21 (a) In oil refineries, petroleum, which is a mixture of an homologous series of alkanes, is distilled in a fractionating column to give various fractions. Some of these are used directly as fuels, some are subjected to catalytic cracking to give chemical feedstocks, and others are used to make plastics and other polymers.
(i) Why are oil refineries usually found close to ports? **(1 mark)**
(ii) State what is meant by an homologous series of alkanes. **(2 marks)**
(iii) State what is meant by a fuel, giving an example of a fuel produced directly in an oil refinery. **(2 marks)**
(iv) State two properties necessary for a good fuel. **(2 marks)**
(v) Explain what is meant by **catalytic cracking** and give an example. **(2 marks)**

(b) Polypropene is an example of a thermoplastic and bakelite is an example of a thermoset. State the difference between a thermoplastic and thermoset and explain the differences in properties in terms of molecular structure. **(3 marks)**

(c) Why do plastics represent an environmental problem? **(3 marks)**
(WJEC Specimen Question)

22 The following is a list of the typical contents of a dustbin for a family of four in one week.

Aluminium	0.55 kg
Polythene/plastic	0.25 kg
Waste food	4.50 kg
Iron	1.30 kg
Glass	1.75 kg
Paper	4.15 kg

Much of the waste in this dustbin can be changed back into useful metal, plastic, glass or paper products if it is processed correctly. First, some of the parts of the rubbish must be separated from the rest.

(a) (i) Give *one* method which could be used to separate objects made of iron from domestic rubbish. **(1 mark)**
(ii) Most scrap iron is converted into steel. What must be added to pure iron to change it into steel? **(1 mark)**
(iii) Give one important use of steel and state a property of steel that makes it particularly suitable for this purpose. **(2 marks)**

(b) (i) Waste glass can be re-melted and used again. Give one problem which might be found when using empty bottles in this way. **(1 mark)**
(ii) Outline one *other* way in which the waste of glass containers can be avoided. **(1 mark)**

(c) (i) What percentage of the family's total waste is plastic? **(1 mark)**
(ii) Give *one* reason why plastic causes a serious pollution problem. **(1 mark)**
(iii) Plastic waste can be disposed of by burning it. Give one advantage and one drawback of this method. **(2 marks)**

(d) Explain why so many manufacturers use plastic packaging in spite of the pollution problems. **(3 marks)**
(SEG Alternative Syllabus Specimen Question)

23 This question is about the formation of alcohol (ethanol) from sugars and its possible use as an alternative to petrol as a fuel for car engines.

One source of sugars is sugar cane which is crushed and the juices mixed with yeast. The mixture is allowed to stand for 2 or 3 days at around 30°C.

The liquid product is then fractionally distilled, most of the ethanol being in the middle of three fractions.

(a) Name *one* other crop that is a useful source of sugars. **(1 mark)**

(b) The equation for the reaction that changes the sugar glucose into ethanol in the presence of yeast is given below:

$$C_6H_{12}O_6(aq) \rightarrow 2C_2H_5OH(aq) + 2CO_2(g)$$

  (i) What does the symbol (aq) indicate about the glucose? **(1 mark)**
  (ii) What is the purpose of the yeast in the reaction? **(1 mark)**
  (iii) Why is this reaction *not* speeded up if the mixture is boiled? **(1 mark)**
  (iv) Give the name of the process that converts glucose into ethanol in this way. **(1 mark)**
  (v) Why is the same reaction important in bread-making? **(1 mark)**

(c) One of the advantages of ethanol over petrol is that, unlike petrol, ethanol is a **renewable energy source**.
Explain the meaning of the term **renewable energy source**. **(1 mark)**

(d) What other possible advantages might ethanol have over petrol as a fuel for car engines? **(2 marks)**

(e) Methylated spirits is a mixture of ethanol (about 90 per cent) and methanol (about 10 per cent) together with a small quantity of purple dye.
Explain why the ethanol is treated in this way before being sold as 'meths'. **(3 marks)**
(SEG Alternative Syllabus Specimen Question)

24 A portion of 0.1 M hydrochloric acid was added to an excess of small pieces of magnesium ribbon. 120 cm^3 of hydrogen were collected at room temperature and pressure. The equation for the reaction is:

$$Mg(s) + 2HCl(aq) \rightarrow MgCl_2(aq) + H_2(g)$$

(a) How many moles of hydrogen were collected? (Molar volume = 24 litres at room temperature and pressure.) **(1 mark)**

(b) What volume of 0.1 M hydrochloric acid was used? **(2 marks)**

(c) What mass of magnesium is needed to produce this volume of hydrogen? **(2 marks)**

(d) Sketch a graph to show the change in the volume of hydrogen collected during the course of the experiment. Label this graph A. **(2 marks)**

(e) On the same axes, sketch a graph showing the change in volume of hydrogen collected during the course of the experiment if the same volume of 0.1 M hydrochloric acid had been added to an excess of *powdered* magnesium. Label this graph B. **(2 marks)**
(NEA Syllabus A Specimen Question)

25 (a) An architect was commissioned to supervise some restoration work that was being carried out on a cathedral. The cathedral stood in the centre of a heavily industrialised city and parts of its limestone walls were badly corroded by the effect of 'acid rain'.
  (i) Give the chemical name and formula of limestone. **(2 marks)**
  (ii) Give the name of *one* other form of this compound. **(1 mark)**
  (iii) What is acid rain? Explain how it is formed in the atmosphere. **(3 marks)**

(b) The architect wanted to know if the rate of corrosion of the limestone was significantly different in winter when average temperatures are about 5°C and in summer when average temperatures are about 18°C.
  (i) Draw a diagram of the apparatus suitable for carrying out an experiment the architect could do to measure the rate of the reaction at two different temperatures. **(4 marks)**
  (ii) Explain briefly how you could use the apparatus to measure the rate of reaction. **(5 marks)**
  (iii) Sketch a graph showing the type of result the architect could obtain from each experiment. Indicate clearly which result refers to which temperature. **(4 marks)**

(c) Calcium carbonate reacts with hydrochloric acid according to the equation

$$CaCO_3 + 2HCl \rightarrow CaCl_2 + H_2O + CO_2$$

What volume of carbon dioxide would be obtained if 25 grams of calcium carbonate were completely dissolved in dilute hydrochloric acid? (Ca = 40, C = 12, O = 16, Molar Volume = 24 litres at room temperature and pressure.)
(3 marks)
(NEA Syllabus B Specimen Question)

26 Excess of calcium carbonate was added to a known volume of dilute hydrochloric acid and a gas was produced. The volume of gas produced was recorded every ten seconds and the results are shown below.

Time (seconds)	10	20	30	40	50	60	70	80	90	100
Total volume (cm^3)	130	225	300	360	410	440	470	490	500	500

(a) Draw a graph of the *volume of gas produced* against *time*. Use suitable scales and plot the volume on the vertical axis and the time on the horizontal axis. **(3 marks)**

(b) Estimate the volume of gas produced after 65 seconds. **(1 mark)**

(c) What would be the time taken to produce 400 cm^3 of gas? **(1 mark)**

(d) After what time did the reaction stop? **(1 mark)**

(e) Why did the reaction stop? **(1 mark)**

(f) Suppose the experiment were repeated with the same quantities of materials but with the hydrochloric acid (of the same concentration) at a higher temperature. On the same graph sketch a second curve to show the results you would expect. Label this curve 'experiment 2'. **(2 marks)**

(g) Draw and label the apparatus you would use to do the experiment and measure the volume of gas produced. **(2 marks)**

(h) The gas produced turned lime water milky. Name the gas. **(1 mark)**
(WJEC Specimen Question)

27 Most of the people in the world do not have enough to eat, so we must think of ways of growing more food. Sometimes chemicals are spread on the ground to provide food for plants.
(a) What is the general name given to chemicals used by farmers to help plants grow? **(1 mark)**

(b) Ammonia is an important chemical used as a plant food.
 (i) Which *two* elements are combined together to obtain ammonia?
 (ii) From which raw materials are these elements obtained to make ammonia gas? **(4 marks)**

(c) (i) Unfortunately these two elements combine together slowly so chemists use a catalyst. Name the catalyst used in making ammonia and explain its economic importance.
 (ii) Describe *one* other way in which chemists can speed up a reaction. **(3 marks)**

(d) Spreading chemicals on the land can have bad effects as well as good. Mention *two* bad things which might occur when chemicals are spread on the land. **(2 marks)**

(e) (i) Give the chemical name of a polymer which can be used to make a bucket.
 (ii) Describe *one* advantage of the polymer material over steel for making a bucket. **(2 marks)**
(LEAG Syllabus A)

28 Information about some common fertilisers is given in the following table.

Name	Formula	Solubility in water
Ammonium phosphate	$(NH_4)_3PO_4$	Readily soluble
	NH_4NO_3	Readily soluble
Potassium nitrate	KNO_3	Readily soluble
Urea	$CO(NH_2)_2$	Dissolves slowly

(a) Name the compound whose formula is NH_4NO_3. **(1 mark)**

(b) Calculate the mass of 1 mole of urea. (Relative atomic masses: H 1; C 12; N 14; O 16.) **(1 mark)**

(c) Why is urea a slow-acting fertiliser? **(1 mark)**

(d) How can good plant growth be maintained if chemical fertilisers like those in the table are *not* used? **(2 marks)**

(e) Another substance which may be added to soil is hydrated lime $Ca(OH)_2$.
 (i) What is the chemical name for hydrated lime? **(1 mark)**
 (ii) What is the main reason for adding hydrated lime to soil? **(1 mark)**
 (iii) Why should hydrated lime and ammonium phosphate *not* be applied to the soil at the same time? **(2 marks)**
(SEG Alternative Syllabus Specimen Question)

29 The following symbols represent atoms of the elements hydrogen, oxygen and potassium:

^1_1H; $^{16}_8O$; $^{39}_{19}K$; $^{40}_{19}K$

Hydrogen and potassium form compounds with oxygen of formula H_2O and K_2O respectively.
(a) (i) Give the electronic structures of the elements:
 hydrogen; oxygen; potassium. **(1 mark)**
 (ii) By means of diagrams or otherwise, show the electronic changes that take place in the formation of H_2O and K_2O and state the type of bonding involved in each case. **(4 marks)**
 (iii) Why does water (H_2O) have a lower melting point and boiling point than potassium oxide (K_2O)? **(2 marks)**

(b) (i) Why are there two different types of potassium atom? **(1 mark)**
 (ii) $^{40}_{19}K$ is radioactive and gives $^{40}_{20}Ca$ as a product.
 Deduce the type of radioactivity emitted by potassium. **(1 mark)**

(iii) the half-life of $^{40}_{19}$K is 1×10^9 years. If 1 g of the isotope decays, what mass would be left after 2×10^9 years? **(1 mark)**
(WJEC Specimen Question)

30 (a) Nuclear power stations have been producing electricity from radioactive elements for about 30 years.
  (i) Name one radioactive metal that is used in nuclear power stations after extracting it from ores found in the earth's crust. **(1 mark)**
  (ii) Name another metal from which nuclear power can be obtained and which is made in nuclear reactors. **(1 mark)**
  (iii) State one of the dangers that must be avoided in nuclear power stations and describe the precaution that is taken to avoid that danger. **(2 marks)**
(b) The half-life period of carbon-14 (^{14}C) is 5736 years. What does the term 'half-life period' mean? **(1 mark)**
(c) State *two* other sources of energy that do not depend on the burning of fuels or the use of radioisotopes and that can be used to make electricity. **(2 marks)**
(NEA Syllabus A Specimen Question)

Free-response questions

31 Write a brief account of *three* of the following.
(a) The treatment of public water supplies. **(5 marks)**
(b) The experimental demonstration of diffusion in gases and liquids. **(5 marks)**
(c) The principles involved in fire fighting. **(5 marks)**
(d) The economic consequences of corrosion and methods for its prevention. **(5 marks)**

(e) The uses of radioactive isotopes and precautions taken in their use. **(5 marks)**
(WJEC Specimen Question)

32 (a) State *three* differences in the properties of sodium chloride and tetrachloromethane (carbon tetrachloride). **(3 marks)**
(b) Explain in terms of the structures of the compounds why they have these differences in properties. **(6 marks)**
(c) Use your knowledge of chemistry to explain the following facts as fully as you can.
  (i) Aluminium wire carries electricity in power lines. **(2 marks)**
  (ii) Graphite is used as a lubricant. **(2 marks)**
(NEA Syllabus A Specimen Question)

33 The list below shows some processes that are used in industry.

Cracking
Fermentation
Polymerisation

Using *one* example from industry in each case, describe briefly how each process may be used to manufacture a product useful in everyday life. **(10 marks)**
(LEAG Syllabus A Specimen Question)

34 Discuss the manufacture and importance of sulphuric acid. Your answer should include reference to the chemistry of the process, the factors affecting the siting of a plant, problems associated with storage and transport, and the economic importance and uses of sulphuric acid. **(10 marks)**
(LEAG Syllabus A Specimen Question)

Suggested answers to sample GCSE questions

Note. These answers are the authors' own suggestions, not those of the examining groups. They are only suggested answers; other correct versions may be possible.

Structured questions

1. (a) A scientist who helps police with their investigations.
   (b) Ball-point ink dissolves in ethanol, but not in water.
   (c) Put the solution of ink in a dish and stand the dish over a beaker of hot water. (Do *not* heat the solution directly with a bunsen or have naked flames near the ethanol.)
   (d) B. The ink from the note travelled the same distance as the ink from the pen B during the chromatography.
   (e) The ink from pen C. During chromatography it separates into two spots.
   (f) The labelled diagram should show distillation apparatus, for example like figure 1.3 on page 3.

2. (a) (i) Hydrogen and carbon.
       (ii) Water and carbon dioxide.
   (b) (i) Carbon monoxide.
       (ii) Inside the car engine there is not enough oxygen to turn all the carbon in the fuel to carbon dioxide (CO_2). Some carbon is turned to carbon monoxide (CO) instead.
   (c) Nitrogen.
   (d) Possible reasons:
       – recycling the steel solves a waste disposal problem – rusting cars are unsightly;
       – recycling helps save iron ore, which is a limited resource;
       – recycling saves energy, because making new steel needs more energy than recycling scrap.
       (Only two reasons needed)

3. (a)

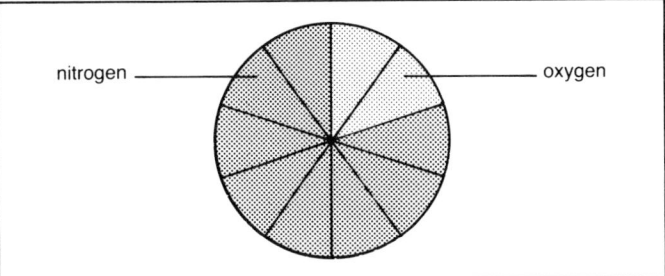

   (b) From a Data Book, the boiling points of the gases are: oxygen, −183°C; nitrogen, −196°C. Oxygen boils at a higher temperature than nitrogen, so it is easier to liquefy.
   (c) By fractional distillation.
   (d) Possible uses:
       – for making ammonia;
       – as an unreactive atmosphere to stop things reacting with air, for example in welding;
       – liquid nitrogen is used to freeze some foods to preserve them.
       (Only two uses needed)
   (e) (i) The iron wire reacted with oxygen in the air to form rust. This removed oxygen from the air in the tube, and the water rose up the tube to replace this oxygen.
       (ii) The value of 25 per cent is calculated assuming that the length of the tube is 10 cm. In fact, the length of the tube is equivalent to about 11 cm, because of the space above the 10 cm line at the top of the tube.
           Also, the pressure of the air at the beginning and end of the experiment was not the same, because the water levels are not the same. This means the volumes cannot be compared directly.
           (Only one of these two reasons is required)

4. (a)

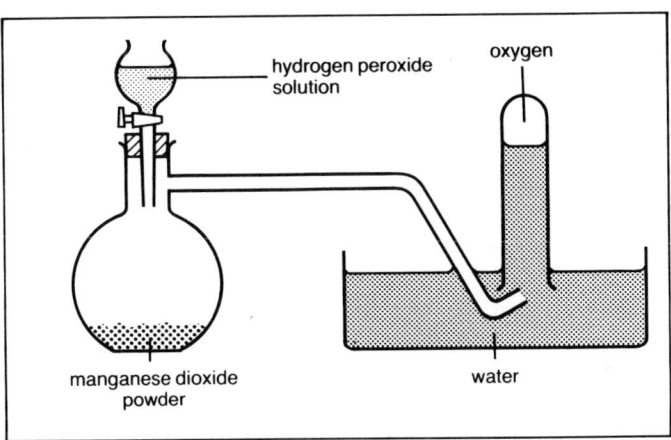

125

(b) It contained air displaced from the apparatus.
(c) (i) No.
   (ii) Oxygen is being collected over water. If it was very soluble, it would dissolve in the water.
(d) (i) Place a glowing splint in the test tube of gas.
   (ii) The splint would relight.
(e) Filter the mixture from the flask. When all the manganese dioxide has been filtered off, dry it in an oven.
(f) Examples:

(i) Use	(ii) Explanation of use
In hospitals – for patients with breathing difficulties For divers and mountaineers	Oxygen is essential to life
For welding, in 'oxy-acetylene' torches	Oxygen is essential for combustion of fuels
In steel making	Oxygen removes impurities from iron by oxidising them

(Only one use and explanation needed)

5 (a) (i) Water is passed through a filter-bed of sand and gravel.
   (ii) To remove solid particles.
(b) (i) Distil the sea water.
   (ii) In a liquid, particles are constantly moving. Occasionally, particles have enough energy to escape from the surface of the liquid into the air. As more and more particles escape, the liquid evaporates into the air.
   (iii) Salt (sodium chloride) is an ionic solid, so it does not vaporise at normal temperatures.
(c) For example:

(i) Pollutant	(ii) Source	Effect
Detergents	Households	Foaming in rivers
Oil	Refineries, factories, etc.	Harms water life
Metal compounds, e.g. lead, mercury	Industry	Poisonous to water life
Sewage	Households	Upsets balance of water life

(d) (i) To kill bacteria and other microorganisms.
   (ii) (I) Test with indicator paper. Paper will *not* be bleached. Chlorine bleaches indicator paper.
   (II) Add silver nitrate solution. Chloride ions will give a white precipitate.
   (iii) Chlorine molecules gain electrons to form chloride ions:
   $$Cl_2 + 2e^- \rightarrow 2Cl^-$$
   (Answer in words *or* give the equation. You don't need both)

6 (a) (i) Y. (ii) X. (iii) V and W.
(b) When the solid is heated, the particles vibrate faster. Eventually, the particles have enough energy to move away from their original positions and they move around each other as a liquid.
(c) (i) Solid, because the trend on moving down the group is from gas to solid.
   (ii) Seven.
   (iii) Z^-.

7 (a)

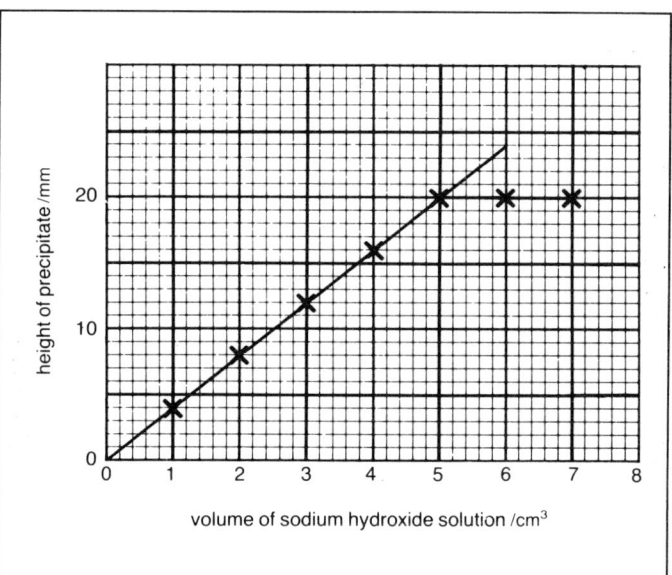

(b) After 5 cm³, enough sodium hydroxide solution had been added to react with all the iron(III) chloride.
(c) Number of moles = concentration of solution in mole/dm³ × volume of solution in dm³
   = 3.0 × 0.005
   = 0.015 mole
(d) 3 moles NaOH react with 1 mole $FeCl_3$
   ⇒ 0.015 moles react with **0.005 mole $FeCl_3$**.
(e) In the experiment, the graph shows the reaction was complete after 5 cm³ of sodium hydroxide had been added. This means:
   5 dm³ of 3.0 M sodium hydroxide reacts with 5 dm³ of 1.0 M iron(III) chloride
   or 0.015 moles sodium hydroxide react with 0.005 moles iron(III) chloride.
   These are the same as the calculated amounts in (d).
(f) Pour the mixture from the test tube into a filter. Wash the precipitate with water. Allow the precipitate to dry in air.

Structured Questions 127

8 (a) It increases.

(b) Because it is being deposited on it.

(c) (i) Positive.
(ii) Tin is deposited on the negatively charged cathode, so tin ions must carry a positive charge, in order to be attracted to the cathode.

(d) Because at the anode tin is dissolving and forming tin ions at the same rate as tin ions are being deposited on the cathode.

(e) Move the anode and cathode further apart.
or Put a resistor in the circuit to reduce the current.
or Reduce the concentration of tin(II) sulphate.

(f) (i) An acid.
(ii) Neutralisation.
For example:
iron oxide + hydrochloric acid → iron chloride + water

(g) (i) Electroplating gives a thinner layer, which uses less tin. Electroplating also gives a more even layer of tin. (You only need to give one reason).
(ii) By measuring the increase in mass of the steel.
or By timing it.

(h) Tin alone would be too soft.
or Tin alone would be too expensive.
Mild steel alone would rust.

9 (a) – As a fuel.
– In some lighter-than-air balloons, but only where there is no risk of explosion.
– For making margarine.
– For making ammonia.
(only one needed)

(b) Bleach is made by reacting chlorine with sodium hydroxide. This forms sodium chloride as well as sodium hypochlorite.

(c) (i) Attacks and dissolves away certain materials, such as metals and human tissue.
(ii) Chlorine.
(iii) pH 7.6 is slightly alkaline. If the swimming pool water becomes acidic, chlorine will be given off by the reaction of acid with sodium hypochlorite.

(d) (i) Electrolysis of molten sodium chloride.
(ii) Calcium carbonate.

(e) Do not allow to come into contact with skin, eyes and clothing.
Washing off any accidental splashes immediately.
Store in a safe place away from children and animals.
Do not mix with acid.

10 (a) Y is chlorine, Z is hydrogen.

(b) (i) 7.
(ii) At the cathode, H^+ ions from water are being turned to hydrogen, leaving OH^- ions behind. The OH^- ions make the solution alkaline, which makes the indicator turn blue.
(iii) Sodium hydroxide or bleach (sodium hypochlorite).

(c) (i) Aqueous (dissolved in water).
(ii) A brown coating of copper would be formed on the electrode.

(d) (i) Substance A could be lead bromide.
Substance B could be sulphur.
(ii) Covalent.
(iii) Metallic.
(iv) Ions.

(e) (i) At the cathode: hydrogen – because aluminium is too reactive to be formed, so hydrogen (from the water) is formed instead.
At the anode: oxygen – from OH^- ions in the water.
(ii) So the aluminium oxide can dissolve in the molten cryolite, which melts at a lower temperature.

11 (a) (i) Cadmium carbonate: $CdCO_3$.
Cadmium sulphate: $CdSO_4$.
(ii) Take a portion of dilute sulphuric acid. Add cadmium carbonate in small portions until there is no more reaction. (You can tell this because there is no more fizzing when the cadmium carbonate is added.)
Filter the mixture to remove any excess cadmium carbonate.
The filtrate is a solution of cadmium sulphate. Heat it to evaporate off the water, until crystals just begin to form.
Cool and allow the crystals to grow. Pour the remaining solution off the crystals. Dry the crystals using filter paper.

(b) (i) Mass of water = 3.54 g − 2.10 g = 1.44 g.

(ii) $BeSO_4 = 9 + 32 + (4 \times 16) = 105$
$H_2O = (2 \times 1) + 16 = 18$.

(iii) Moles of beryllium sulphate $= \dfrac{2.10}{105} = 0.02$

Moles of water $= \dfrac{1.44}{18} = 0.08$

Ratio = 0.02 : 0.08
= 1 : 4
So formula of the hydrate is $BeSO_4 \cdot 4H_2O$.

12 (a)

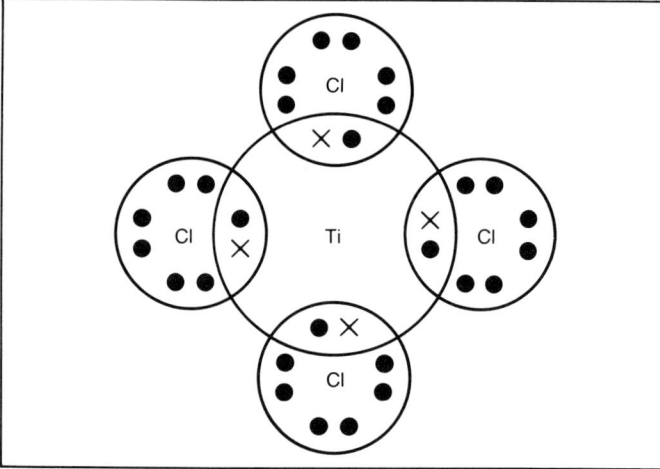

(b) $TiCl_4 + 4Na \rightarrow Ti + 4NaCl$.

(c) (i) Liquid.
(ii) Titanium chloride is simple molecular. $TiCl_4$ molecules are only held to each other by weak forces, so $TiCl_4$ is more volatile. Sodium chloride has a giant structure of ions, strongly held together, so it is a solid.

(d) If you carried out the reaction in an ordinary atmosphere, the sodium would react with oxygen in the air instead of the titanium chloride. And once the titanium had formed, it too would react with oxygen in the air.

(e) Because of the high cost of extracting it from its ore using sodium.

(f) Strong, light, high melting point.
(Only *two* properties needed)

13 (a) (i) Put a lighted splint into a tube of the gas.
(ii) A squeaky pop.

(b) Z, X, W, Y.

(c) (i) Copper.
(ii) A displacement reaction (W displaces copper from copper sulphate).
(iii) The brown deposit would form faster. This is because powdered metal has a higher surface area, so it reacts faster.

14 (a) A and B – coke and limestone.
C – air.
D – slag (molten calcium silicate).
E – iron (molten).

(b) Reduction.

(c) $Fe_2O_3 + 3CO \rightarrow 2Fe + 3CO_2$

(d) Aluminium is more reactive than iron, so aluminium oxide is more difficult to reduce than iron oxide. To reduce aluminium oxide with coke would require an extremely high temperature.

(e) $56 + (3 \times 35.5) = 162.5$

(f) 162.5 g $FeCl_3$ is formed from 56 g Fe
$\Rightarrow$ 16.25 g $FeCl_3$ is formed from **5.6 g** Fe.

(g) (i) No reaction.
(ii) White precipitate is formed.

15 (a) To make sure all the sulphuric acid is neutralised.

(b) A – filter paper.
B – filter funnel.
C – magnesium oxide.
D – magnesium sulphate solution.

(c) (i) $24 + 16 = 40$.
(ii) $24 + 32 + (4 \times 16) + [7 \times (2 + 16)] = 246$.

(d) 40 g magnesium oxide gives 246 g magnesium sulphate crystals

so 1 g gives $\frac{246}{40}$ g

so 2.0 g gives $\frac{246}{40} \times 2.0$ g $= 12.3$ g.

(e) Heat the solution gently in an evaporating basin until crystals begin to form around the edge of the basin. Stop heating and leave to crystallise. When crystals have formed, pour off the remaining solution and dry the crystals using filter paper.

16 (a) For example:

(i) Indicator	(ii) Colour change in acid
Litmus	Turns red
Universal indicator	Turns red
Methyl orange	Turns red
Phenolphthalein	Turns colourless

(Only one indicator needed)

(b) (i) Any weak household acid – for example lemon juice or orange juice.
(ii) It is neutral.

(c) The acid is corrosive. It will attack materials such as metals, clothing and skin.
You could neutralise it using an alkaline household substance such as sodium bicarbonate or washing soda (sodium carbonate).

17 (a) (i) Carbohydrate – a compound containing the elements carbon, hydrogen and oxygen, with the hydrogen and oxygen in the proportions 2 : 1.
(ii) Hydrocarbon – a compound containing the elements hydrogen and carbon only.
(iii) Unsaturated – a compound containing a double or triple carbon–carbon bond.

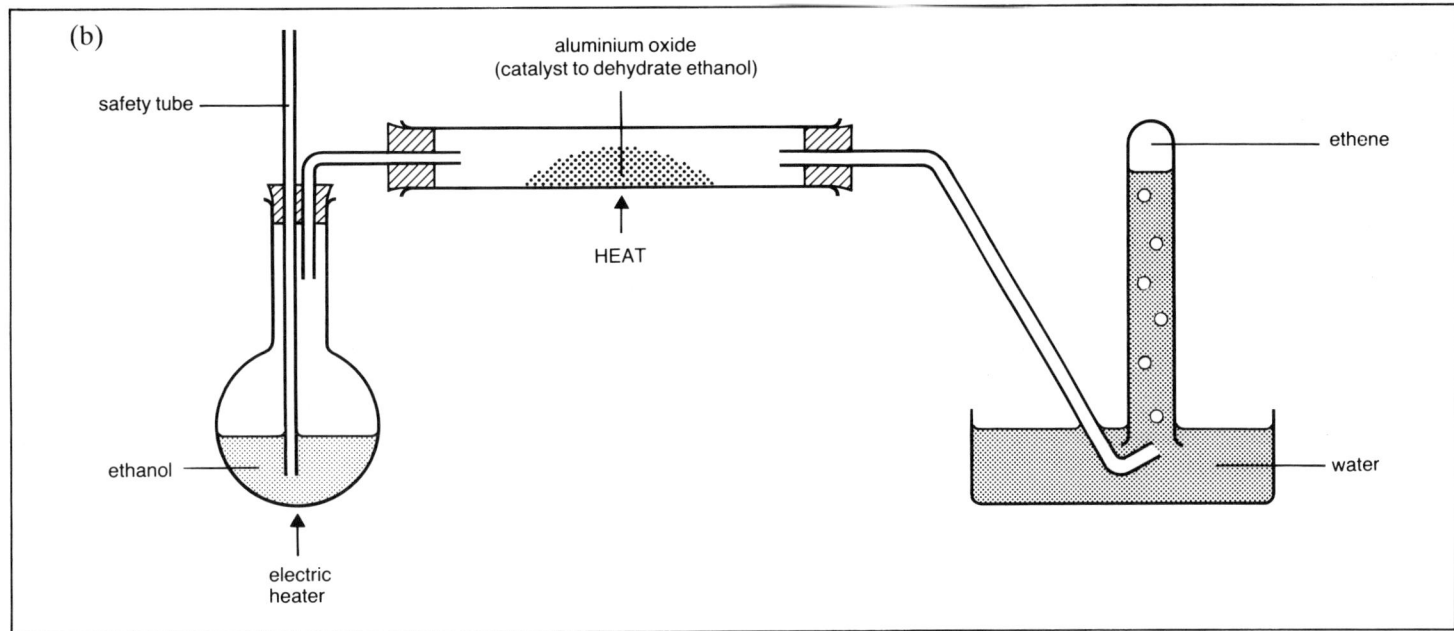

Suggested apparatus is shown above. (Other arrangements are possible. The apparatus should include some way of passing ethanol vapour over the heated catalyst, and collecting the ethene over water.)

(c) 1 mole of ethanol = 46 g
so 46 g ethanol give out 1380 kJ when burned

$\Rightarrow$ 1 g ethanol gives out $\dfrac{1380 \text{ kJ}}{46 \text{ g}} = 30$ kJ/g.

(d) Each molecule of propanol has an extra C atom and two extra H atoms compared with ethanol.

(e) For example:

Addition polymer	Monomer
Polythene (polyethene)	Ethene
Polyvinylchloride	Vinyl chloride
Polystyrene	Styrene
Polypropene	Propene

(Only one example required.)

18 (a) Orange or red.

(b) Direct heating would have been too strong and would have broken down some of the substances in the drink.

(c) Metal conducts heat better than glass.

(d) Temperature rise = 34.6 − 19.6 = 15°C
Mass of water = 500 g
Heat absorbed = mass of water × temperature rise × 4.2 J
= 500 × 15 × 4.2 J
= 31500 J
= 31.5 kJ.

(e) (i) 10 cm³ of the drink were used in the experiment
so 10 cm³ of the drink has 'energy content' of 31.5 kJ
$\Rightarrow$ 100 cm³ of the drink has 'energy content' of 315 kJ.

(ii) Possible reasons:
− some of the heat was absorbed by the can, shield and thermometer;
− the solid was not completely burnt.
(Only one reason needed)

(f) (i) $C_6H_{12}O_6 + 6O_2 \rightarrow 6CO_2 + 6H_2O$.
(ii)

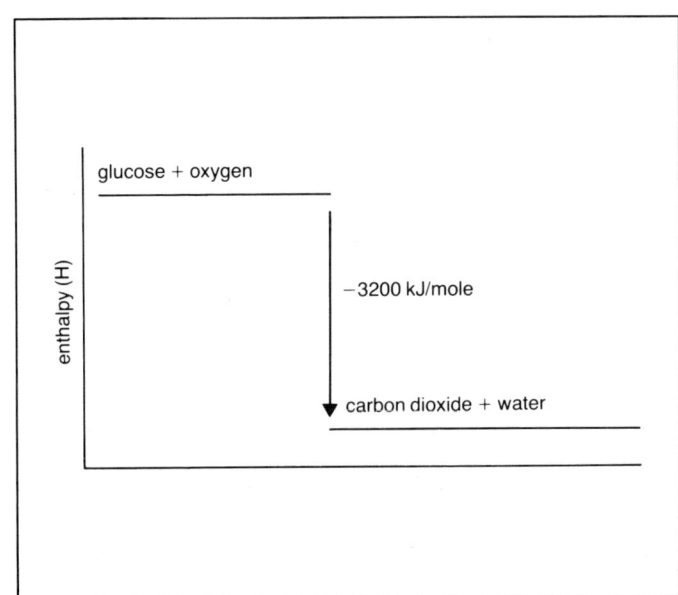

(g) For example:
- weightwatchers need to know how much energy they take in from food, because high-energy foods are fattening;
- knowing your energy intake helps you follow a healthy diet;
- dietitians and nutritionists find the food values useful in planning menus and meals.

(Two reasons needed)

19 (a) (i) Calcium chloride.
        (ii) Water.
    (b) (i) Carbon dioxide is denser than air.
        (ii) Carbon dioxide does not support combustion (it does not allow things to burn in it).
        (iii) Fire extinguisher.
    (c) (i) Carbon.
        (ii) Magnesium oxide.
        (iii) magnesium + carbon dioxide
              → magnesium oxide + carbon.

20 (a) Compounds containing hydrogen and carbon only.
    (b) Ethane   Ethene

    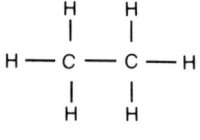   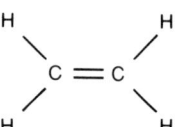

    (c) First member: methane, formula CH_4.
        Third member: propane, formula C_3H_8.
    (d) (i) Octane and oxygen are both gases. When they react, 2 moles of octane react with 25 moles of oxygen.
        So, their reacting volumes will be in the proportions 2 : 25.
        so, 2 cm³ octane react with 25 cm³ oxygen
        ⇒ 1 cm³ octane reacts with 12.5 cm³ oxygen
        ⇒ 1000 cm³ octane reacts with 12 500 cm³ oxygen.
        (ii) An exothermic reaction gives out heat. Chemical energy in the petrol–oxygen mixture is converted to heat when the petrol burns.
        (iii) 114 g octane is 1 mole.
        From the equation:

        $$2C_8H_{18} + 25O_2 \rightarrow 16CO_2 + 18H_2O$$

        we can see that 2 moles octane produce 18 moles H_2O
        ⇒ 1 mole octane produces 9 moles H_2O
        = 9 × 18 g H_2O
        = 162 g water.

(e) (i) The black solid is carbon. Carbon is formed when hydrocarbon fuel (petrol) burns in a limited supply of air.
    (ii) Car exhaust contains some carbon monoxide, formed when petrol burns in a limited supply of air. Carbon monoxide is poisonous, and in a closed garage it cannot easily escape into the air.

21 (a) (i) Because much of our petroleum comes from overseas in ships.
        (ii) A series of compounds with similar chemical properties and formulas that differ by units of CH_2 from one to the next.
        (iii) A fuel is a substance that can be burned in air to produce heat.
        Fuels produced in an oil refinery include refinery gases, petrol, kerosine (paraffin), diesel fuel and fuel oil.
        (Only one required)
        (iv) Necessary properties for a good fuel:
        – easily stored;
        – easily transported;
        – cheap;
        – burns steadily;
        – easy to ignite;
        – does not leave a lot of ash;
        – does not make a lot of smoke.
        (Only two required)
        (v) In catalytic cracking, a catalyst is used to break down a large molecule into several smaller ones.
        For example, alkanes with large molecules can be broken down to give smaller alkane molecules, together with ethene.
    (b) Thermoplastics melt when they are heated. Thermosets cannot be melted on heating. Thermoplastics have polymer chains held together by weak bonds between the chains. The chains can be easily separated by heating. Thermosets have cross-links between polymer chains which hold the chains firmly together.
    (c) Plastics are an environmental problem because they are difficult to dispose of. Most plastics are not biodegradable, so they do not break down naturally. Burning plastic waste can cause air pollution.

22 (a) (i) Use a magnet.
        (ii) Carbon.
        (iii) For example:

Use	Property
Making cars	Strong, easily shaped
Reinforcing concrete	Strong
Making bridges	Strong

(Only one required)

(b) (i) For example:
 – different colours of glass need to be separated before melting;
 – melting glass uses a lot of energy.
 (Only one required)
 (ii) They can be reused, by cleaning the container and refilling it (like milk bottles).

(c) (i) Total mass of waste = 12.5 kg
 mass of plastic = 0.25 kg

$$\Rightarrow \text{percentage of plastic} = \frac{0.25}{12.5} \times 100 = 2 \text{ per cent}$$

 (ii) Most plastics are not biodegradable, so they do not break down naturally.
 (iii) For example:

Advantage	Disadvantage
Plastics are easily burned.	Burning plastic may cause air pollution.
Heat from burning plastic can be made use of.	Burning wastes valuable resources.

(Only one of each required)

(d) Advantages of plastic packaging:
 – low cost;
 – unreactive;
 – waterproof;
 – flexible;
 – can be transparent;
 – can be coloured and made to look attractive;
 – can be moulded to different packaging shapes;
 – thin sheets can be used conveniently like paper for wrappings.
 (Give three advantages)

23 (a) Sugar beet.

(b) (i) It is aqueous, or dissolved in water.
 (ii) Yeast is the living organism that converts glucose to ethanol.
 (iii) Boiling kills the yeast.
 (iv) Fermentation.
 (v) Fermentation produces carbon dioxide, which makes the bread rise.

(c) A renewable energy source can be replaced as it is used up. Petrol is non-renewable: once used, it cannot be replaced.

(d) Ethanol causes less pollution than petrol. Ethanol does not need lead additives as petrol often does.

(e) To stop people drinking it. The methanol makes it poisonous, and the purple dye warns people not to drink it.

24 (a) 24 litres of hydrogen = 1 mole
 $\Rightarrow 24000 \text{ cm}^3$ = 1 mole
 $\Rightarrow 1 \text{ cm}^3$ = $\frac{1}{24000}$ mole
 $\Rightarrow 120 \text{ cm}^3$ = $\frac{1}{24000} \times 120 = 0.005$ mole.

(b) From the equation:

$$Mg + 2HCl \rightarrow MgCl_2 + H_2$$

1 mole of hydrogen is formed from 2 moles of hydrochloric acid
$\Rightarrow 0.005$ moles of hydrogen is formed from $2 \times 0.005 = 0.01$ moles of hydrochloric acid
0.1M hydrochloric acid contains 0.1 moles in 1 litre
$\Rightarrow 0.01$ moles are contained in 0.1 litre = 100 cm^3.

(c) From the equation,
1 mole of hydrogen is produced from 1 mole of magnesium
$\Rightarrow 0.005$ mole of hydrogen is produced from 0.005 mole of magnesium
 = 0.005×24 g magnesium
 = 0.12 g magnesium.

(d) and (e)

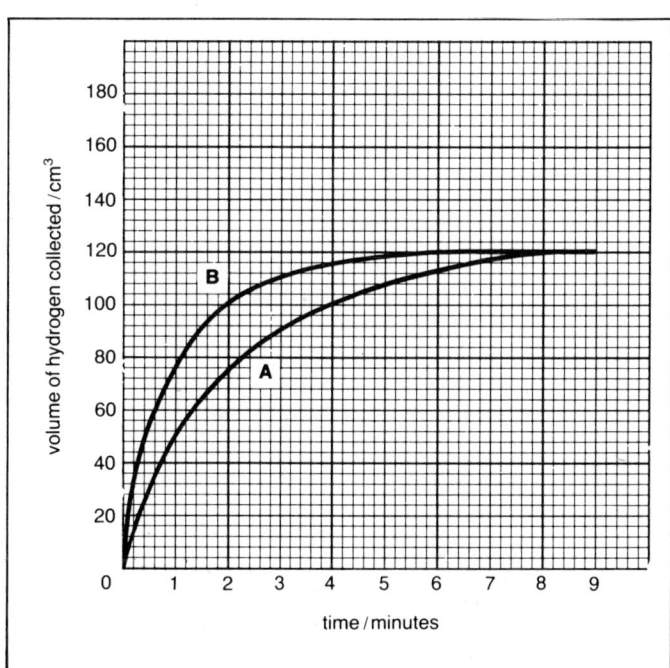

(Graph A has this shape because the reaction starts off quickly, then slows down and stops when 120 cm^3 of hydrogen have been produced.
 Graph B starts off steeper because the magnesium is powdered, and the reaction starts off faster. But graph B levels off at the same value as graph A, because the *mass* of magnesium used is the same.)

25 (a) (i) Calcium carbonate ($CaCO_3$).
  (ii) Chalk or marble.
  (iii) Acid rain is rainfall which has become acidic due to atmospheric pollution.
    It is formed when acidic oxides, particularly sulphur dioxide and nitrogen oxides, are in the atmosphere. These acidic oxides react with rain water, forming acids.

(b) (i) For example:

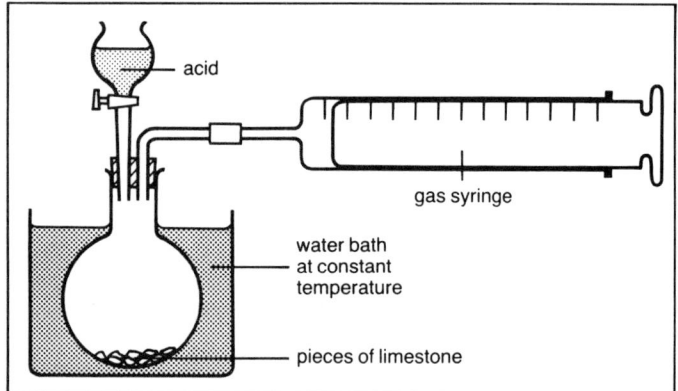

  (ii) Do the experiment first at 5°C.
    Add the acid to the limestone and start timing.
    Measure the volume of carbon dioxide given off at fixed time intervals.
    Plot a graph showing volume of carbon dioxide against time. The steeper the graph, the faster is the rate.
    Repeat the experiment at 18°C, using exactly the same amounts of acid and limestone. Plot the results on a second graph.
    (The apparatus used does not have to be exactly as shown here. The important thing is to have apparatus that will enable you to measure the amount of carbon dioxide given off at different times.)
  (iii)

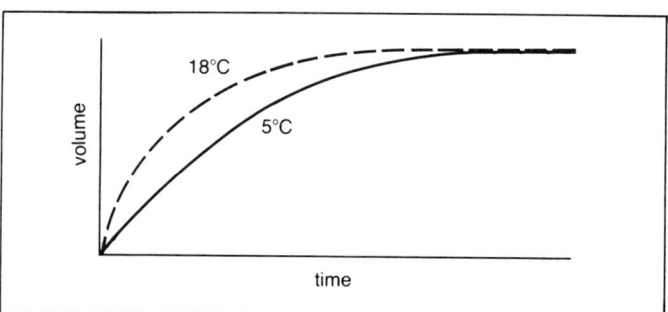

(The graphs should both be steep at first, levelling off later. The graph for 18°C should start off steeper than the one at 5°C. The graphs should level off when the same volume of CO_2 has formed.)

(c) 1 mole of $CaCO_3$ weighs 100 g
⇒ 25g of $CaCO_3$ is 0.25 mole

From the equation:
$$CaCO_3 + 2HCl \rightarrow CaCl_2 + CO_2 + H_2O$$
we can see that:
1 mole $CaCO_3$ gives 1 mole CO_2
⇒ 0.25 mole $CaCO_3$ gives 0.25 mole CO_2
1 mole CO_2 has volume 24 litres
⇒ 0.25 mole has volume 0.25 × 24 = 6 litres.

26 (a)

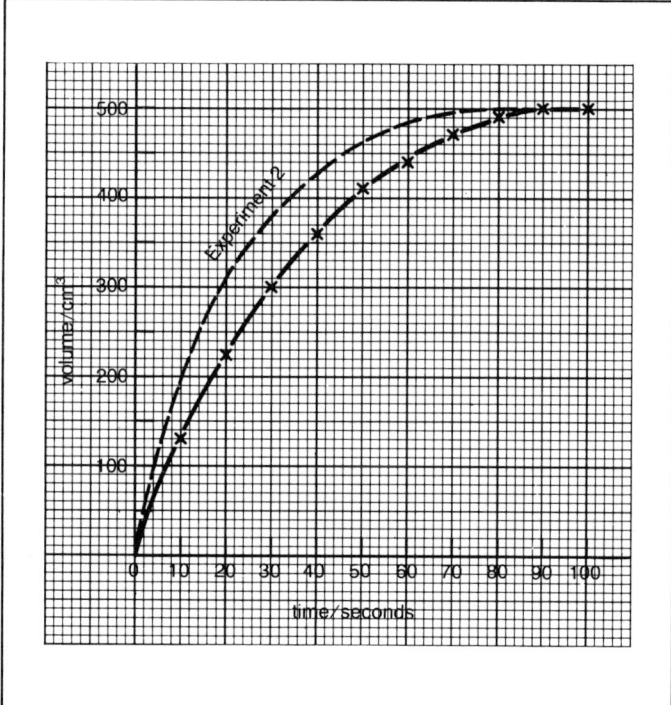

(b) Using the graph above, the volume at 65 seconds is 455 cm^3.
(Your own graph may give a slightly different reading.)

(c) Using the graph above, the time for 400 cm^3 is 48.5 seconds.
(Your own graph may give a slightly different reading.)

(d) The reaction has stopped when the graph first levels off. This is after 90 seconds.

(e) The hydrochloric acid was all used up.

(f) (See graph.) The line for Experiment 2 will start off steeper, but level off at the same value.

(g)

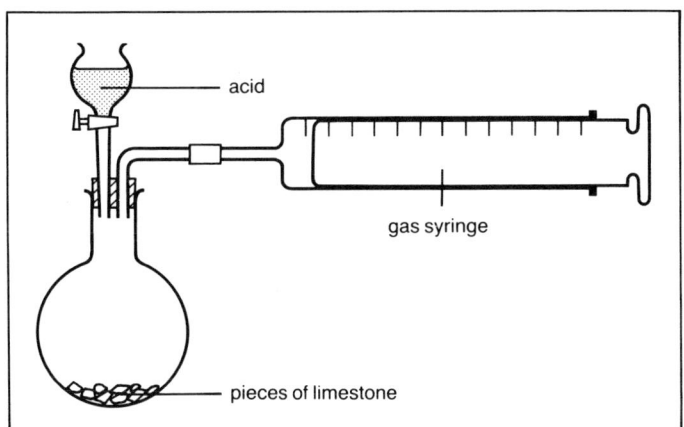

(Your apparatus does not have to be exactly as shown here, though it must include an accurate way of measuring the volume of carbon dioxide.)

(h) Carbon dioxide.

27 (a) Fertilisers.
(b) (i) Nitrogen and hydrogen.
(ii) Nitrogen is obtained from air.
Hydrogen is usually obtained by reacting natural gas or naphtha with steam. It is sometimes obtained by electrolysis of water.
(c) (i) The catalyst is iron. It increases the rate of the reaction so that ammonia can be made more quickly. This makes the process more economical.
(ii) By increasing the temperature.
or By increasing the surface area of any solids.
or By increasing the pressure of gases.
(Only one required)
(d) For example:
 – fertilisers may get washed off the land into rivers and streams, where they upset the natural balance of life;
 – fertilisers may get into the water supply, possibly causing harm to humans;
 – pesticides may kill harmless wildlife as well as pests;
 – pesticides may stay on food crops and cause harm to humans.
(Only two required)
(e) (i) Poly(ethene), commonly called polythene
or poly(propene), commonly called polypropylene.
(ii) – cheaper;
 – lighter;
 – does not rust;
 – the bucket is more easily made.
(Only one required)

28 (a) Ammonium nitrate.
(b) $12 + 16 + (2 \times 16) = 60$ g.
(c) Urea dissolves slowly, so the rain washes it into the soil slowly. This means that it reaches the roots of plants only slowly.
(d) By using natural (organic) fertilisers – for example compost or farmyard manure.
(e) (i) Calcium hydroxide.
(ii) To neutralise acidity in the soil.
(iii) All ammonium compounds react with alkali, giving off ammonia. Hydrated lime is an alkali, so it would react with the ammonium phosphate.

29 (a) (i) Hydrogen 1 (one electron only).
Oxygen 2,6 (two electrons in first shell, six in second shell).
Potassium 2,8,8,1.
(ii)

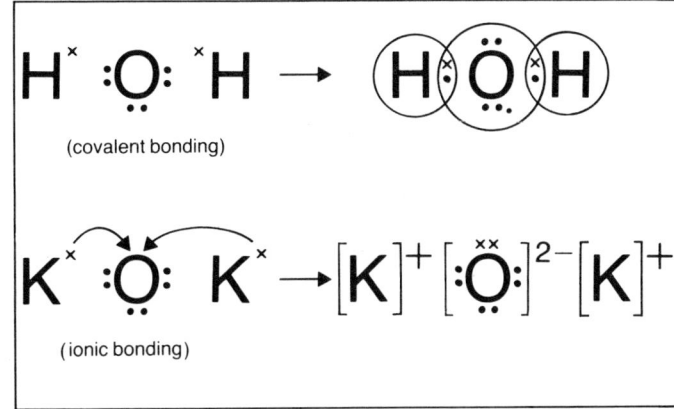

(iii) Water contains simple molecules, with only weak forces holding the molecules together.
The molecules are easily separated, so water is easy to melt and boil.
Potassium oxide has a giant structure of ions. Strong forces hold the ions together, so they are difficult to separate.
(b) (i) The two atoms are isotopes. They have the same number of protons, but different numbers of neutrons.
(ii) $^{40}_{19}K \rightarrow {}^{40}_{20}Ca + ?$

Balancing this equation for mass number and atomic number gives:

$^{40}_{19}K \rightarrow {}^{40}_{20}Ca + {}^{0}_{-1}e$

So the potassium emits electrons, also called beta particles.
(iii) 2×10^9 years is two half-lives. So the amount left will be $\frac{1}{2} \times \frac{1}{2} = \frac{1}{4}$ of original
So $\frac{1}{4}$ g (0.25 g) will be left.

134 Suggested answers to sample GCSE questions

30 (a) (i) Uranium.
    (ii) Plutonium.
    (iii) For example:

Danger	Precaution
Escape of radiation	Thick shielding of reactor with concrete and lead
Exposure of workers to radiation	Workers are regularly checked for radiation dose
Nuclear reactors could get out of control and overheat	Control rods are used to slow down the reactor
Radioactive waste products could escape into the environment	Waste is sealed in concrete or steel containers or buried below the ground

(Only one required)

(b) Half-life is the time for half of the carbon-14 to decay.

(c) For example:
– hydroelectric power;
– solar power;
– wind power;
– wave power;
– tidal power;
– geothermal power.
(Only two required)

Free-response questions

The following suggested answers give only the main points that should be mentioned. For full marks you should link together these points into a complete answer and include diagrams where appropriate.

31 (a) You should describe the *main* stages, and why each is done. Water is passed through screens of metal mesh to remove large objects. Then it is stored in reservoirs to allow particles to settle out. Next it passes through filters (beds of sand and gravel) to remove smaller particles. Finally it is treated with chlorine to kill bacteria.

(b) You need to show you understand what diffusion is – the spreading out of a substance to fill the available space.
You should describe one experiment to show the diffusion of a gas. For example:
– bromine evaporating from a few drops of liquid and diffusing to fill a gas jar;
– a smelly gas or perfume spreading out to fill a room.
You should also describe one experiment to show diffusion in a liquid. For example:
– ink spreading out in water;
– potassium manganate(VII) (potassium permanganate) dissolving and then spreading out when a crystal of it is put in water.

(c) You should show that you understand what makes a fire burn. This is best done by drawing the fire triangle (figure 2.5 on page 9). You should give at least two examples of fire-fighting methods, and use the fire triangle to explain how each works. For example:
Fire blanket   (removes oxygen).
Water   (removes oxygen and removes heat).
Carbon dioxide extinguisher (removes oxygen).
Sand   (removes oxygen and removes heat).

(d) Your answer should concentrate on the corrosion of iron (rusting). You should show that you understand that corrosion costs money because of:
– the cost of painting and protecting against corrosion;
– the cost of replacing things that have corroded away.
Mention at least two methods for preventing rusting, and say how they work (see table 2.4 on page 10 for examples).

(e) You should mention at least two different uses of radioactive isotopes (see page 108 for examples). Try to choose uses that are fairly different from one another – for example a medical use and an industrial use.
You should mention at least three different safety precautions. These precautions are listed on page 108.

32 (a) Sodium chloride is a typical ionic compound, and tetrachloromethane is a typical covalently bonded molecular compound. So the differences in properties would be:
Melting point and boiling point – sodium chloride much higher than tetrachloromethane.
Electrical conductivity – sodium chloride will conduct when molten or in solution. Tetrachloromethane will not conduct at all.
Solubility – sodium chloride will dissolve in water but not in organic solvents. Tetrachloromethane will dissolve in organic solvents but not in water.

(b) Notice that this is the most important part of the question: it carries six marks.
You should first describe the differences in structures.
Sodium chloride has a giant structure of Na^+ and Cl^- ions, formed by transferring an electron from Na to Cl.
Tetrachloromethane has a simple molecular structure, with C and Cl atoms held together by covalent bonds.

The **melting point and boiling point** of sodium chloride are high, owing to the strong attraction between oppositely charged ions. The attraction between molecules of tetrachloromethane is only weak, so it melts and boils easily.

The **electrical conductivity** of molten or aqueous sodium chloride is due to the ions, which act as moving charge carriers. Tetrachloromethane does not conduct because it contains no charged particles.

The **solubility** of sodium chloride in water is due to the attraction of polar water molecules for Na^+ and Cl^- ions. Tetrachloromethane does not dissolve because it has no charges to attract water molecules.

(c) (i) You need to explain why a metal like aluminium conducts electricity.
The free-moving electrons in solid aluminium are able to move along the wire, making an electrical current. A diagram like figure 10.5 on page 60 would be very helpful.

(ii) Describe the layer structure of graphite first. A diagram like figure 10.10 on page 63 would help you do this.
The weak forces between the layers mean that the layers can slip over one another easily. This makes graphite a good lubricant.

33 For each of these processes, you have to:
– choose an example of its use in industry;
– describe how the process is used to manufacture *one* useful product.

For **cracking**, the best example to choose is the cracking of petroleum fractions during the refining of crude oil. This is described on page 000. This reaction can be used to make two useful products: gasoline (petrol) and alkenes. Alkenes are useful for making petrochemicals.

For **fermentation**, you could choose:
– the manufacture of alcoholic drinks;
– the manufacture of alcohol for use as a fuel.

Describe the fermentation process in general (see page 83). Make sure you mention the starting materials (sugar and yeast) and the products (carbon dioxide and ethanol). Then explain how the fermentation process is used to manufacture the particular industrial product you have chosen.

For **polymerisation**, you would do best to choose a simple example. The polymerisation of ethene to form polythene is the simplest (see page 81). Use a diagram like figure 13.10 on page 81 to explain what happens when ethene polymerises. Make sure you explain what polymerisation involves – the joining of several small units (monomers) to form a long chain.

34 Start by describing the chemistry of the process. This is described on page 93. An outline will be enough, because there are several more parts to the question. The most important factors affecting the siting of the plant are:
– closeness to transport facilities for import of raw materials, particularly sulphur, and transport of products;
– closeness to industrial centres where the sulphuric acid will be used.

The problems with storage and transport come from the highly corrosive nature of sulphuric acid. It needs to be stored and transported in containers that will not be attacked by the acid. Glass containers are normally used for storage of the acid.

The major uses of sulphuric acid are shown in figure 14.14, page 92. You must show you realise the importance of sulphuric acid in many different industries.

Answers to self-test questions

Chapter 1
1 B
2 B
3 C
4 C
5 B
6 E
7 D
8 A
9 E
10 B
11 C
12 D
13 B
14 E
15 A
16 C
17 D
18 A
19 C
20 D

Chapter 2
1 C
2 A
3 D
4 B
5 E
6 D
7 A
8 C
9 B
10 E
11 A
12 C
13 D
14 C
15 B
16 C
17 D
18 oxygen
19 carbon dioxide
20 water vapour

Chapter 3
1 C
2 A
3 B
4 A
5 B
6 C
7 D
8 A
9 B
10 C
11 E
12 A
13 A
14 B
15 C
16 D
17 A
18 C
19 D

Chapter 4
1 B
2 D
3 A
4 E
5 A
6 D
7 B
8 C
9 C
10 C
11 D
12 D
13 C
14 zinc oxide
15 } magnesium oxide
16 } and copper
17 (s)
18 (l)
19 (aq)
20 (g)
21 (a) 2
   (b) 3
   (c) 2
   (d) 1
   (e) 5
   (f) 3
   (g) 4

Chapter 5
1 A
2 D
3 B
4 C
5 D
6 A
7 C
8 A
9 B
10 320 g (0.32 kg)
11 880 g
12 48 dm³
13 2 moles
14 160 g
15 0.5 mole
16 1 mole
17 56 g
18 56 tonnes

Chapter 6
1 B
2 C
3 D
4 D
5 B
6 A
7 C
8 E
9 D
10 E
11 A
12 B
13 C
14 zinc
15 negative
16 primary
17 chemical
18 electrical

Chapter 7
1 B
2 E
3 C
4 A
5 A
6 E
7 D
8 D
9 C
10 B
11 B
12 A
13 D
14 sodium oxide
15 } sodium hydroxide
16 } and hydrogen
17 iron(III) chloride
18 } hydrochloric acid and
19 } hypochlorous acid
20 periods
21 alkali metals
22 atomic number

Chapter 8
1 C
2 E
3 B
4 A
5 D
6 A
7 B
8 D
9 A
10 C
11 D
12 E
13 A
14 C
15 D
16 B
17 C
18 } iron
19 } carbon dioxide
20 } calcium oxide
21 } carbon dioxide
22 calcium silicate

Chapter 9
1 C
2 B
3 E
4 D
5 A
6 A
7 B
8 D
9 C
10 D
11 C
12 B
13 A
14 C
15 B
16 A
17 B
18 C
19 white
20 silver chloride

Chapter 10
1 E
2 B
3 D
4 C
5 A
6 C
7 E
8 A
9 D
10 B
11 B
12 C
13 D
14 A
15 B
16 D
17 A
18 B
19 electrons
20 light
21 atoms
22 grains
23 close packing
24 giant

Chapter 11
1 E
2 D
3 C
4 B
5 A
6 B
7 E
8 C
9 A
10 D
11 D
12 E
13 B
14 A
15 B
16 C
17 D
18 USSR
19 Europe
20 200 billion m³/year

Answers to Self-test Questions

Chapter 12

1	C	8	B	15	C	
2	D	9	C	16	D	
3	E	10	C	17	B	
4	A	11	D	18	$CaCO_3$	
5	B	12	B	19	H_2O	
6	A	13	A	20	2HCl	
7	D	14	C	21	CO_2	

Chapter 13

1	C	8	D	15	C
2	B	9	B	16	C
3	A	10	C	17	B
4	A	11	A	18	A
5	B	12	E	19	D
6	A	13	B	20	A
7	C	14	D		

Chapter 14

1	D	13	B
2	C	14	C
3	E	15	B
4	A	16	A
5	B	17	65% (count your answer correct if it is in the range 62–68%)
6	D		
7	A		
8	C		
9	E	18	150 atm. (count your answer correct if it is in the range 130–170 atm.)
10	D		
11	C	19	It rises/increases.
12	D	20	It falls/decreases.

Chapter 15

1	C	7	D	13	A
2	E	8	B	14	A
3	A	9	D	15	B
4	D	10	C	16	B
5	B	11	A	17	A
6	A	12	B	18	C

Chapter 16

1	C	8	A	14	B
2	A	9	C	15	B
3	D	10	A	16	D
4	B	11	C	17	A
5	E	12	E	18	C
6	B	13	D	19	B
7	D				

Chapter 17

1	C	7	C	13	C
2	A	8	A	14	E
3	D	9	B	15	C
4	B	10	D	16	D
5	E	11	A	17	A
6	D	12	A	18	B

Table of Relative Atomic Masses

The tables gives the relative atomic masses of elements.

Element	Symbol	Ar	Element	Symbol	Ar
Aluminium	Al	27	Molybdenum	Mo	96
Antimony	Sb	122	Neodymium	Nd	144
Argon	Ar	40	Neon	Ne	20
Arsenic	As	75	Nickel	Ni	59
Barium	Ba	137	Niobium	Nb	93
Beryllium	Be	9	Nitrogen	N	14
Bismuth	Bi	209	Osmium	Os	190
Boron	B	11	Oxygen	O	16
Bromine	Br	80	Palladium	Pd	106
Cadmium	Cd	112	Phosphorus	P	31
Caesium	Cs	133	Platinum	Pt	195
Calcium	Ca	40	Potassium	K	39
Carbon	C	12	Praseodymium	Pr	141
Cerium	Ce	140	Rhenium	Re	186
Chlorine	Cl	35.5	Rhodium	Rh	103
Chromium	Cr	52	Rubidium	Rb	86
Cobalt	Co	60	Ruthenium	Ru	101
Copper	Cu	63.5	Samarium	Sm	150
Dysprosium	Dy	163	Scandium	Sc	45
Erbium	Er	167	Selenium	Se	79
Europium	Eu	152	Silicon	Si	28
Fluorine	F	19	Silver	Ag	108
Gadolinium	Gd	157	Sodium	Na	23
Gallium	Ga	70	Strontium	Sr	88
Germanium	Ge	73	Sulphur	S	32
Gold	Au	197	Tantalum	Ta	181
Hafnium	Hf	179	Tellurium	Te	128
Helium	He	4	Terbium	Tb	159
Holmium	Ho	165	Thallium	Tl	204
Hydrogen	H	1	Thorium	Th	232
Indium	In	115	Thulium	Tm	170
Iodine	I	127	Tin	Sn	119
Iridium	Ir	192	Titanium	Ti	48
Iron	Fe	56	Tungsten	W	184
Krypton	Kr	84	Uranium	U	238
Lanthanum	La	139	Vanadium	V	51
Lead	Pb	207	Xenon	Xe	131
Lithium	Li	7	Ytterbium	Yb	173
Lutetium	Lu	175	Yttrium	Y	89
Magnesium	Mg	24	Zinc	Zn	65
Manganese	Mn	55	Zirconium	Zr	91
Mercury	Hg	201			

Periodic table

group →	I alkali metals	II											III	IV	V	VI	VII halogens	0 noble gases
period 1	hydrogen H 1 1																	helium He 2 4
2	lithium Li 3 7	beryllium Be 4 9											boron B 5 11	carbon C 6 12	nitrogen N 7 14	oxygen O 8 16	fluorine F 9 19	neon Ne 10 20
3	sodium Na 11 23	magnesium Mg 12 24											aluminium Al 13 27	silicon Si 14 28	phosphorus P 15 31	sulphur S 16 32	chlorine Cl 17 35.5	argon Ar 18 40
4	potassium K 19 39	calcium Ca 20 40	scandium Sc 21 45	titanium Ti 22 48	vanadium V 23 51	chromium Cr 24 52	manganese Mn 25 55	iron Fe 26 56	cobalt Co 27 59	nickel Ni 28 59	copper Cu 29 63.5	zinc Zn 30 65	gallium Ga 31 70	germanium Ge 32 73	arsenic As 33 75	selenium Se 34 79	bromine Br 35 80	krypton Kr 36 84
5	rubidium Rb 37 85	strontium Sr 38 88	yttrium Y 39 89	zirconium Zr 40 91	niobium Nb 41 93	molybdenum Mo 42 96	technetium Tc 43	ruthenium Ru 44 101	rhodium Rh 45 103	palladium Pd 46 106	silver Ag 47 108	cadmium Cd 48 112	indium In 49 115	tin Sn 50 119	antimony Sb 51 122	tellurium Te 52 128	iodine I 53 127	xenon Xe 54 131
6	caesium Cs 55 133	barium Ba 56 137	lanthanum La 57 139	hafnium Hf 72 178	tantalum Ta 73 181	tungsten W 74 184	rhenium Re 75 186	osmium Os 76 190	iridium Ir 77 192	platinum Pt 78 195	gold Au 79 197	mercury Hg 80 201	thallium Tl 81 204	lead Pb 82 207	bismuth Bi 83 209	polonium Po 84	astatine At 85	radon Rn 86
7	francium Fr 87	radium Ra 88 226	actinium Ac 89 227															

58–71 lanthanum series

cerium Ce 58 140	praseodymium Pr 59 141	neodymium Nd 60 144	promethium Pm 61	samarium Sm 62 150	europium Eu 63 152	gadolinium Gd 64 157	terbium Tb 65 159	dysprosium Dy 66 162	holmium Ho 67 165	erbium Er 68 167	thulium Tm 69 169	ytterbium Yb 70 173	lutetium Lu 71 175

90–103 actinium series

thorium Th 90 232	protactinium Pa 91	uranium U 92 238	neptunium Np 93	plutonium Pu 94	americium Am 95	curium Cm 96	berkelium Bk 97	californium Cf 98	einsteinium Es 99	fermium Fm 100	mendelevium Md 101	nobelium No 102	lawrencium Lr 103

key:
lithium — Li — symbol
3 — 7 — relative atomic mass
atomic number

Index

accumulators, 37
acetic acid, 52–3, 83
acidic oxides, 10
acids, 52
    reactions with metals, 46
    strong, 52–3
    weak, 52–3
activation energy, 68
addition reaction, 81
air, 7–11
    composition, 7, 9
    industrial gases from, 7
    normal and exhaled, 9
    pollution, 10–11
alcohol, 82–3
    solubility, 13
alkali metals, 40–1
alkalis, 54
alkanes, 79–80
alkenes, 80–1
alloys, uses, 45
alpha particles, 107
alternative energy sources, 69–70
aluminium, 36, 45, 46
ammonia, 54, 96–7
    Haber process, 91–2
ammonium ion, 97
ammonium salts, 97
amphoteric oxides, 10
anions, 56–7
anode, 32
argon, 42
    uses, 7
atomic bombs, 109
atomic fission, 109
atomic mass, relative, 24
atomic number, 40, 101–2
atomic reactors, 109
atoms, 20
Avogadro constant, 24

bases, 54
basic oxides, 10
batteries, 37
beta particles, 107
biodegradability, 82
biomass, 71
blast furnace, 49
boiling points, 5, 64
breathing, 9
bromine, 42
burning, 8

calcium, 15
calcium carbonate, 74–5, 88
calcium hydroxide, 54
cancer, 108
carbohydrates, 70
carbon, 62
    simple compounds, 73–6
carbon cycle, 71
carbon dioxide, 11, 73–4
    percentage in air, 7
    solubility, 13
carbon monoxide, 11, 73
carbonates, 57, 74
carbonic acid, 52
catalysts, 85
cathode, 32
cations, 56–7
cells, 37
centrifugation, 3
chain reaction, 109
chemical calculations, 24–9
    gas volumes, 28–9
    reacting masses, 28
    reacting volumes of solutions, 29, 34
chemical equations, 21–2
    and moles, 28
chlorides, 57
chlorine, 1, 42
    isotopes, 102
chlorophyll, 70
chromatography, 4–5
chromium plating, 10
combustion, 8
coal, 68
compounds, 1–2
    formation, 103–5
    formulas, 2
    structure, 63–4
conductivity, 31, 32
conductors, electrical, 31
conservation, 69

Contact process, 92–3
cooling curves, 20
copper, 15, 45, 46, 47
    purification, 36
covalent bonding, 35, 104–5
cracking, 80
crude oil
    chemicals from, 78–83
    fractional distillation, 4, 78–9

decanting, 3
decomposition, 2
dehydrating agent, 53
destructive distillation, 68
diamond, 62
diffusion, 19
    explanation, 20
distillate, 3
distillation, 3, 68
    destructive, 68
    fractional, 4, 78–9

electrical conductors, 31
electric currents, 31
electrodes, 32
electrolysis, 32–4
    in industry, 35–6
electrolyte, 32
electron microscope, 59
electrons, 31, 101
    structures, 103
electron sharing, 35
electron transfer, 37
electroplating, 36–7
electrovalent bonding, *see* ionic bonding, 40
elements, 1
    structure, 63
empirical formula, 27
endothermic reactions, 66
energy, 66–71
    changes, 66–7
energy level diagrams, 68
ethanoic acid, *see* acetic acid
ethanol, 82–3
    heat of combustion, 67
evaporation, 3–4
exothermic reactions, 66

Index

Faraday constant, 34
fats, 70
fertilisers
   and food, 95
   manufacture, 98
filtration, 3
fire triangle, 8
firefighting, 8
flame tests, 56
fluorine, 42, 43
food
   and fertilisers, 95
   as fuel, 70
formulas, 20–1
   finding, 27
fossil fuels, 68
fractional distillation, 4, 78–9
fuels, 68–71

galvanising, 10
gamma rays, 107
gases, 19
   mole, 25–6
   volumes, 28–9
giant ionic structures, 34
giant structure, 59
glucose, 70
grains (in metals), 59
graphite, 31, 62
greenhouse effect, 71

Haber process, 91–2
half-life, 107–8
halogens, 42–3
heat of combustion, 67
heat of reaction, 66
helium, 42
homologous series, 79
hydrocarbons, 8, 78
hydrochloric acid, 52
hydrogen, 49–50
   atomic structure, 101
   percentage in air, 7
hydrogen peroxide, 89
hydrogencarbonates, 74
hydrolysis, 70

immiscible liquids, 4
indicators, 52
intermolecular forces, 60, 62

iodine, 42
ion-exchange column, 76
ionic bonding, 34, 104
ionic compounds, 34–5
ions, 20, 32
   charges on, 34
iron, 15, 45, 46
   extraction, 48–9
iron oxide, 9
isomerism, 79–80
isotopes, 102
   radioactive, 108

kinetic theory, 19–20
krypton, 42

limewater, 74
limestone, 75
liquids, 19
   immiscible, 4
   conductivity, 32
   separating, 4
lithium, 40

magnesium, 15, 46, 47
magnesium oxide, 54
margarine, 81
mass number, 101–2
matter, states of, 19
melting point, 54
metalloids, 39
metals, 1
   alkali, 40–1
   displacement reactions, 47–8
   extraction, 48
   properties, 60
   reaction with acids, 46
   reaction with water, 13–14
   reactivity series, 15
   recycling, 49
   structure, 59, 60
   transition, 41
   uses, 45

methane, 8
miscible liquids, 4
mixtures, 2–5
   separating, 3
mole, 24
   chemical equations, 28

   gases, 25–6
   substances in solution, 26
molecular compounds, 35
molecular formula, 27
molecular mass, relative, 24
molecules, 20

natural gas, 68
neon, 42
neutralisation, 54
neutrons, 31, 101
nitrates, 57
nitric acid, 52, 98
nitrogen
   cycle, 95–6
   uses, 7
nitrogen oxides, 11
noble gases, 41–2
   electron structures, 103
non-metals, 1
   structure, 62
nuclear debate, 110
nuclear energy, 108–10
nuclear fission, 109
nucleus, 29, 101

octane, 8
oil, crude, *see* crude oil
organic compounds, 73
oxidation, 8, 10, 37
oxides, classification, 10
oxygen, 7–10
   solubility, 13
   uses, 7

paper chromatography, 5
periodic table, 39–43
pesticides, 99
pH, 52
phosphoric acid, 52
photography, 86
photosynthesis, 70–1
plastics, 81–2
pollution, 69
   air, 10–11
   plastics, 82
   water, 16
polymers, 81–2
potassium, 40
primary cells, 37

proteins, 95–6
protons, 31, 101
pure substances, 2
purity, 5

radioactivity, 107–10
   types, 107
reaction rates, 85–91
   collision theory, 90
reactivity series, 46–7
redox reactions, 10, 37
reduction, 10, 37
relative atomic masses, 24, 102
relative molecular mass, 24
respiration, 9
reversible reactions, 91
rusting, 9–10

salt(s) (*see also* sodium chloride), 1, 36, 54–6
   solubility, 13
saturated solution, 3
secondary cells, 37
semiconductors, 31
shells, atomic, 101
slip (in metals), 60

sodium, 1, 15, 40
sodium chloride (*see also* salt), 1
   electron transfer, 104
sodium hydrogencarbonate, 54
sodium hydroxide, 54
solids, 19
solubility, 3
   and temperature, 13
   salts, 55
solute, 3
solution, 3
solvent, 3
starch, 70
states of matter, 19
   explanation, 20
   symbols, 19
steel, 45, 49
sublimation, 73
sugar, solubility, 13, 14
sulphates, 57
sulphur, 60–1
   allotropes, 61
   properties, 60–1
sulphur dioxide, 11
sulphuric acid, 52, 53
   Contact process, 92–3

sulphurous acid, 52
suspension, 3
synthesis, 1

thermoplastics, 82
thermosets, 82
tin plating, 10
tracer studies, 108
transition metals, 41

universal indicator, 52
unsaturated compounds, 80

water, 13–16
   cycle, 17
   hardness, 76
   pollution, 16
   purification, 16
   reaction with metals, 13–14
   supplies, 15–16

xenon, 42

zinc, 46, 47
   plating, 10